Anthony Van Dyck, *Queen Henrietta Maria*, 1632. Private Collection.
Photograph: Photographic Survey, Courtauld Institute of Art.

Staging the old faith

MANCHESTER
1824
Manchester University Press

Staging the old faith

Queen Henrietta Maria and the theatre of Caroline England, 1625–1642

Rebecca A. Bailey

Manchester University Press
Manchester and New York
distributed in the United States exclusively by Palgrave Macmillan

Copyright © Rebecca A. Bailey 2009

The right of Rebecca A. Bailey to be identified as the author of this work has been asserted by her in accordance with the Copyright, Designs and Patents Act 1988.

Published by Manchester University Press
Oxford Road, Manchester M13 9NR, UK
and Room 400, 175 Fifth Avenue, New York, NY 10010, USA
www.manchesteruniversitypress.co.uk

Distributed in the United States exclusively by
Palgrave Macmillan, 175 Fifth Avenue, New York,
NY 10010, USA

Distributed in Canada exclusively by
UBC Press, University of British Columbia, 2029 West Mall,
Vancouver, BC, Canada V6T 1Z2

British Library Cataloguing-in-Publication Data
A catalogue record for this book is available from the British Library

Library of Congress Cataloging-in-Publication Data applied for

ISBN   978 0 7190 7673 2   *hardback*

First published 2009

18 17 16 15 14 13 12 11 10 09   10 9 8 7 6 5 4 3 2 1

Typeset
by SNP Best-set Typesetter Ltd., Hong Kong
Printed in Great Britain
by the MPG Books Group

For my parents Patricia and Alan Bailey with love

Contents

List of illustrations	*page* ix
Acknowledgements	xiii
Note on the text	xv
List of abbreviations	xvii
Introduction: Counter-Reformation politics and the Caroline stage	1
1 The public discourse of religion in Stuart England	17
2 James Shirley: the early texts, 1625–1629	49
3 'A Case of Conscience': issues of allegiance and identity, 1630–1633	89
4 William Davenant: the chimera of religious reunion, 1634–1637	132
5 'This broken time': the tempering of an international Catholicism, 1637–1640	175
Conclusion	217
Bibliography	226
Index	255

List of illustrations

1 'The Fall of the House in Black-Friers London, 1623', from Samuel Clarke, *Englands Remembrancer* (London: 1657). By permission of the British Library. page 22
2 *Esther Before Ahasuerus*: Photography David Watson, photograph published by kind permission of the National Trust. 38
3 'Jacobus Sherlaeus', frontispiece to James Shirley, *Honoria and Mammon* (London: 1657). By permission of the British Library. 55
4 Frontispiece to Ralphe Mab, *The Character of a Christian as He Is Distinguished From All Hypocrits and Heretickes* (London: 1627). By permission of the British Library. 68
5 Frontispiece to John Cosin, *A Collection of Private Devotions: Or the Houres of Prayer* (London: 1627). By permission of the British Library. 69
6 Hans Holbein the Younger, *Noli Me Tangere*, c.1524, likely devotional image of Queen Henrietta Maria, The Royal Collection © 2007, Her Majesty Queen Elizabeth II. 76
7 Nicholas Hilliard, *Queen Elizabeth I*, c.1575, Tate Britain Gallery, London. © 2007, Tate. By permission of the National Portrait Gallery, London. 107
8 Inigo Jones, *A Temple*, Devonshire Collection, Chatsworth. Reproduced by permission of the Chatsworth Settlement Trustees. Photograph: Photographic Survey, Courtauld Institute of Art. 111

9   'Sir William D'Avenant, Crowned with Bays', frontispiece to William Davenant, *Works* (London: 1673). By permission of the British Library.   133

10 Inigo Jones, *Henrietta Maria as Indamora, Queen of Narsinga*, Devonshire Collection, Chatsworth. Reproduced by permission of the Chatsworth Settlement Trustees. Photograph: Photographic Survey, Courtauld Institute of Art.   146

11 Frontispiece to Ephraim Pagitt, *Christianographie: Or the Description of the Multitude and Sundry Sorts of Christians in the World Not Subject to the Pope* (London: 1635). By permission of the British Library.   152

12 Frontispiece to Thomas Bedford, *A True and Certaine Relation of a Strange-Birth* (London: 1635). By permission of the British Library.   156

13 Frontispiece to Jacques Du Bosc, *L'Honneste Femme* (Paris: 1632). By permission of the British Library.   160

14 'Altar of Repose in George Con's Chapel, 1637', from a pen and ink sketch found among Con's dispatches in the Barberini Library, Vatican. George Albion, *Charles I and the Court of Rome: A Study in Seventeenth Century Diplomacy* (London: Burns, Oates and Co., 1935). By permission of the British Library.   179

15 Inigo Jones, *Henrietta Maria or a Lady Masquer from Luminalia*, Devonshire Collection, Chatsworth. Reproduced by permission of the Chatsworth Settlement Trustees. Photograph: Photographic Survey, Courtauld Institute of Art.   182

16 Frontispiece to John Preston, *The Golden Scepter Held Forth to the Humble. With the Churches Dignitie by Her Marriage and the Churches Dutie in Her Carriage. In Three Treatises* (London: 1638). By permission of the British Library.   187

17 Daniel Mytens, with additions by Anthony Van Dyck, *Charles I and Henrietta Maria*, 1630–1632. The Royal Collection © 2007, Her Majesty Queen Elizabeth II.   188

18 Inigo Jones, *The King*, Devonshire Collection, Chatsworth. Reproduced by permission of the Chatsworth Settlement Trustees. Photograph: Photographic Survey, Courtauld Institute of Art.   198
19 Inigo Jones, *The Queen Descends from a Great Cloud*, Devonshire Collection, Chatsworth. Reproduced by permission of the Chatsworth Settlement Trustees. Photograph: Photographic Survey, Courtauld Institute of Art.   201
20 Inigo Jones, *Henrietta Maria or a Lady Masquer in Amazonian Habit*, Devonshire Collection, Chatsworth. Reproduced by permission of the Chatsworth Settlement Trustees. Photograph: Photographic Survey, Courtauld Institute of Art.   203
21 Inigo Jones, *Design for the Bridge*, Devonshire Collection, Chatsworth. Reproduced by permission of the Chatsworth Settlement Trustees. Photograph: Photographic Survey, Courtauld Institute of Art.   205
22 Inigo Jones, *The Suburbs of a Great City*, Devonshire Collection, Chatsworth. Reproduced by permission of the Chatsworth Settlement Trustees. Photograph: Photographic Survey, Courtauld Institute of Art.   205

Acknowledgements

One of the most satisfying elements in completing this book is the opportunity to thank all those people whose own generosity and support have made my own work possible.

First of all I should like to express my warmest thanks and huge debt of gratitude to Tom Healy, who supervised my doctoral thesis at Birkbeck College, London University with such wisdom, knowledge and infectious enthusiasm. I also wish to thank my PhD examiners Alison Shell and Martin Dzelzainis, whose thought-provoking comments and advice helped to shape my thesis into a book. I am grateful to Sue Wiseman for timely counsel and a continued interest in this project which has greatly benefited from the invaluable suggestions of the once anonymous MUP reader, Julie Sanders.

On a more personal note, I should like to thank John Creaser whose own delight in the curious world of early modern England first stimulated my own fascination for the Caroline court masque during MA studies at Royal Holloway College, London University. Heartfelt thanks are offered to the memory of Avril Bruten, lately of St Hugh's College, Oxford University, whose guidance, integrity and sheer brilliance made her the epitome of a moral tutor and a greatly missed mentor.

I should like to thank the British Academy for granting me a studentship as part of my doctoral studies; the tremendously helpful staff both at the British Library's Rare Books Room and the John Spalding Library; and Fr Ian Dickie and Fr Nicholas Schofield for welcome advice and access to the recusant manuscripts held at Westminster Cathedral Archives. Thanks are also given to Jane Cunningham at the Courtauld Institue of Art, Diane Naylor at Chatsworth House Picture Library and David Watson, photographer for the National Trust, for expert assistance with my illustrations. I am also grateful to the editorial team at Manchester University Press for easing this manuscript through the publication process. Whilst this book has been in production I have benefited enormously from the kind help and scholarly advice both of former colleagues at the University of Bath Spa, and from my new colleagues at the University of Gloucestershire who have welcomed me so warmly into the Department.

Amongst friends not vitally concerned with the actions of Queen Henrietta Maria but who have offered staunch support, understanding and a surprising interest I should like to thank Margaret Beddoes, Alex Corrin, Marie Aimée Dinan de Saldivar, Nicky Dosda, Marie-Alice Hofmaier, Farah Karim-Cooper and Esther Law.

Nor can I forget my friends and researchers extraordinaire at the BBC who over the years have made my escape from the seventeenth century into the reality of the twenty-first so enjoyable – particular thanks are due to Simon Crosthwaite, Caroline Ford, Vanessa Hodgins, Gordon Martin, Lucy McKenna, Melanie Peacock and Garance Worters.

Above all, I wish to thank my family without whose unquestioning support this book would never have been written. Thanks are due to the loving memory of an admirable matriarchy in my own family, my grandmother, Phyllis Maguire, and great-aunt, Eileen Harrison. Especial thanks are owed to Richard and David who happily keep me afloat in innumerable ways and who have cheerfully tolerated the intrusion of Henrietta Maria into family life over too many years. Most of all I wish to thank my parents, whose love, endless encouragement and frequent sacrifices make all things possible. This book is dedicated to them.

Note on the text

In the text, dates are given Old Style according to the Julian calendar but the year is taken to begin on 1 January. I have retained the original spelling in all quotations from early manuscripts and printed works, but i/j and u/v are modernised. Contractions have been expanded and acknowledgement is given where I add my own emphasis within a transcription. For the reader's ease I provide translations of sources in French or Latin.

List of abbreviations

AAW/A	Archives At Westminster Cathedral Series A
AAW/B	Archives At Westminster Cathedral Series B
CSP	*State Papers Collected by Edward, Earl of Clarendon*
CSP Dom	*Calendar of State Papers Domestic*
CSP Ven	*Calendar of State Papers Venetian*
EHR	*English Historical Review*
ELR	*English Literary Renaissance*
HJ	*Historical Journal*
HMC	Historical Manuscript Commission
JEH	*Journal of Ecclesiastical History*
MLR	*Modern Language Review*
MP	*Modern Philology*
N&Q	*Notes and Queries*
PMLA	*Publications of the Modern Language Association of America*
P&P	*Past and Present*
PRO	Public Record Office
RES	*Review of English Studies*
RH	*Recusant History*
SEL	*Studies in English Literature*
TP	*Textual Practice*
YES	*Yearbook of English Studies*

Introduction: Counter-Reformation politics and the Caroline stage

> *Goe tell the Queene, it resteth in her powers*
> *To helpe; the case is hers as well as Ours.*[1]

'The course of the time here is so uneven and uncertaine that we know not our selves in what state we stand, our feares and hopes are in equall balance.'[2] So wrote Fr G. M. Muscott in September 1624, to Fr Thomas More in Rome, in a letter positively crammed with news regarding the imminent conclusion of the marriage treaty between Charles, Prince of Wales, and Henrietta Maria, Princess of France, youngest daughter of Henri IV and sister to Louis XIII. Reporting how 'the match with France is in great forwardnes, some say concluded', Muscott repeatedly returned to the crux of his anxiety, the impact on the English recusant community of this impending union between Prince Charles, England's Protestant heir apparent, and Henrietta Maria, a princess deeply imbued with the spirit of Counter-Reformation Catholicism.[3] Negotiations were swift moving. Muscott's narrative vividly highlights the flux of activity in a fleeting cameo of the Duke of Buckingham, with 'his trunckes... already at the customs house', hastily prepared to dash to France to conclude the alliance. More critically, Muscott rapidly reappraises the situation from an English Catholic perspective even within the letter itself: 'since the writing of this I understand... that the King [James I] is pleased at the insistence of the French ambassador to compassionate the poore afflicted state of catholikes'. Yet Muscott's uncertainty regarding the successful implementation of such a pledge is suggested by his frustrated observation: 'this mitigation will be some present comfort *yet I see not any solide foundations*'.[4] This book seeks to tease out these same 'feares and hopes' of English Catholics, from Henrietta

Maria's arrival in 1625 to the start of the English Civil War in 1642. By re-mapping contemporary understanding of Catholicism in the culture and drama of the period, Caroline theatre is revealed both as a space where the concerns of the English Catholic community are staged and as a shaping force in the survival of the tenaciously adaptable old faith.

Even before Henrietta Maria had set foot on *The Admiral*, the pride of the English fleet, to endure a notoriously stormy Channel crossing, her advent had been widely heralded by the Roman Catholic powers of Europe as a singular opportunity for England's return to the Catholic fold. Repeatedly Henrietta Maria was likened to the Esther of Old Testament history, that biblical figure who successfully pleaded with her non-Jewish husband King Ahasuerus to show clemency to her Jewish compatriots.[5] In a personal behest to his goddaughter Pope Urban VIII had urged Henrietta Maria to act as a 'parent' to the English Catholics and to be like 'Esther illa ellecti populi liberatrix' [Esther the liberator of the chosen people].[6] Similarly, Marie de Médicis, earnestly encouraged the figure of Esther upon her fifteen-year-old daughter: 'qui eut cette grace de Dieu d'estre la déffense et la deliverance de son peuple' [who had the grace of God to be the defender and deliverer of His people].[7] The ultimate Counter-Reformation hope was that once crowned, through Henrietta Maria's influence, Charles I would give succour to the similarly benighted Catholic community, leading to the reconversion of the nation to England's 'old faith'.

This book probes Henrietta Maria's advancement of her papal mission through an examination both of the Queen's self-presentation and of the drama emanating from her household. In a series of striking performances throughout her reign as Queen Consort, Henrietta Maria returned to, and reworked, her own vision of her responsibilities as a Counter-Reformation champion. As early as 1626, in an astonishing departure for English theatre history, Henrietta Maria audaciously enacted this ideal through her elite performance in the title role of Honorat Racan's *L'Artenice*. By 1635 her determination to follow her spiritual adviser Fr Bérulle's advice to engrave this mission 'en votre coeur, imprimez-le en votre esprit' [on your heart, to imprint it on your spirit] is suggested by the incredible spectacle which surrounded the inaugural Mass at her Capuchin chapel, the first purpose-built Catholic church in London since the Reformation.[8] Whilst, as late as 1640,

Henrietta Maria, suggestively sheathed in military armour, provocatively danced a bellicose variant of this role in *Salmacida Spolia*, the final court masque of Caroline rule. From a performance studies perspective, such queenly display is remarkable for its influence on the later, widespread emergence of women on the English stage.[9] But equally integral is the insight which such royal stagings allow into the anxieties and hopes of the English recusant community. The response of those Catholics, like Fr Muscott, to Henrietta Maria's blatantly public manifestation as their visible figurehead energises the texts of the focal dramatists of this book, James Shirley and William Davenant. Deftly picking up the gauntlet thrown down by the Queen in her own flamboyant performances, a fascinating staged dialogue becomes apparent between Henrietta Maria and her professed playwright 'servants': one which transcends and moves between playing spaces from the elite to the commercial theatres.

However, any examination of early modern Catholicism provides the salutary reminder that the outlook of this Roman Catholic body was by no means uniform.[10] As Hillaire Belloc once remarked, in addition to the staunch recusant body there was a 'contemporary wide penumbra of Catholicism'.[11] In this book every effort has been made to consider the complexity of each grouping within this wider community: the aims of Queen Henrietta Maria are examined alongside the concerns of the laity and the clergy; the recusant's anxiety with the church-papist's unease.[12] Opinions documented range from a militant recusancy to a negotiated accommodation with the dominant Protestant state. Notably, this raft of Catholic mindsets is refigured in the texts and outlooks of James Shirley and William Davenant, both of whom were converts to Rome. Shirley's 1620s apostasy was independent from court Catholicism and displays both a militant recusant conviction and this faction's expectations of their Queen. Strikingly, in plays from *The Witty Fair One* (1628) to *The Bird in a Cage* (1633), Shirley consistently creates a heroine whose transforming virtue powerfully negates all impinging danger. In contrast to such ardour, Davenant's gradual conversion is shown to be fostered from within Henrietta Maria's court. Having eclipsed Shirley by 1634, at first Davenant celebrated the Queen's Counter-Reformation triumphs. Yet, by the late 1630s, Davenant's model of religious accommodation, proffered in *Love and Honour* (1634), conflicted with Henrietta Maria's growing inclination towards an aggressive, international style of Catholicism, which Inigo Jones so spectacularly showcased in *Salmacida Spolia* (1640).

This powerful staging of the difficulties confronting English Roman Catholicism, in both the elite and the commercial theatres, deepens our understanding of Caroline drama as a vehicle which allows insight into wider social and political issues. As Martin Butler contends in his pioneering work *Theatre and Crisis: 1632–1642*, Caroline drama has been greatly misunderstood.[13] Once neglected and dismissed by the literary establishment as self-indulgent, through the revisionist forays of scholars such as Julie Sanders, current thinking rightly perceives Caroline theatre as directly engaging with problems of state, society and religion.[14] This book aims to further repatriate Caroline drama as an agent of change at a crucial moment in the history of early modern England by realerting readers to Shirley's and Davenant's challenging response to contemporary religio-political concerns.

Central to this undertaking is my development of Butler's recognition of drama which he terms as 'puritan' or in 'opposition' to the court of Charles I.[15] Puritanism was by no means the only religious force to articulate unease through drama, nor was Charles I the sole monarch addressed. Erica Veevers first established the substantial influence of Queen Henrietta Maria's court in her beautifully crafted *Images of Love and Religion*.[16] The translation of this feminocentric court culture on to the Caroline stage has recently been underscored by the fascinating researches of scholars such as Sophie Tomlinson and Karen Britland.[17] As this book confirms, the powerful staging of an 'oppositional' Catholicism, heightened by the unquestionable authority of the court of Queen Henrietta Maria, progressively widens Caroline theatre's sphere of engagement. Early modern Catholics themselves readily perceived the stage as a space where the religious and political concerns of the day could be scrutinised. In September 1636 Fr George Leyburn reported how the King, Queen and the Palatinate Princes were 'most gloriousely received' during a visit to Christ Church College, Oxford. In remarkable detail, Leyburn recounted how after supper the royal couple were 'intertayned with a new comedy called, the Passions Calm'd or the Floating Iseland'.[18] Strikingly, Fr Leyburn specifically interpreted this staging from within the religio-political perspective of the play's conformist author, William Strode:

represented [was] a king whos name was Prudentius (you may imagine our most prudent prince) and an Intellectus Agens, a person active and wise (you may imagine his Grace of Canterbury); by the passions you may understand the puritans, and all such as are opposit to the courses which our king doth run in his goverment.[19]

With a typically convoluted plot and bereft of its original context, *The Passions Calm'd* is a prime example of what the literary establishment would once have denigrated as escapist and alarmingly sycophantic in 1630s drama. Yet, as Fr Leyburn's review spotlights, Caroline theatregoers (or curious priests thirsty for second-hand theatrical titbits) perceived even the rarefied atmosphere of a university performance as a potentially serious arena for political debate.

Such archival contextualisation is at the heart of this project which rests on the cusp of three areas of revisionist scholarship – those of early modern drama, history and religious history. Although my emphasis is on the drama of the period, the provocative historical insight of Christopher Haigh has been of especial influence; in particular his wise reminder that 'the Reformation was not an inexorable process, carried forward by an irresistible ideological force; it was a succession of contingent events'.[20] As Haigh stresses, the English Roman Catholic community was never completely destroyed: 'it fought back, reorganised itself, and survived'.[21] For those who remained loyal to the old faith, 1625 was a key moment in this process of endurance, a year stamped with all the hallmarks of a possible watershed. Henrietta Maria was not just a devout Roman Catholic but an agent for reform bringing with her, as Roger Lockyer comments, 'the self-confident and assertive attitudes of the Catholic Reformation' together with 'the richness of traditional Catholic worship, with all its musical and visual splendour'.[22] By contrast, for the godly Protestants, Henrietta Maria's arrival was deeply unsettling and her popish presence further fuelled the wider polemical debates which racked the established Church, in particular the contentious rise of Laudianism.[23] As John Bossy shrewdly observed, no account of post-Reformation England can 'make much sense if it does not take notice of the baffling fertility of the religious imagination of Englishmen'.[24] This particularly resonates in the fractured landscape of the turbulent years leading to Civil War. By no means supposing religion to be the sole cause on the highway to Civil War, unquestionably, the deeply engrained threat of 'Popery' within the Protestant consciousness played a vital role in the war which was to rupture the English nation.[25] Religious belief in early modern England was not just about the trappings of doctrine or liturgy. Rather, as Kevin Sharpe observes in *Remapping Early Modern England*, religion should more properly be seen as 'a language, an aesthetic, a structure of meaning, an identity, a politics'.[26] In the stimulating atmosphere of Caroline theatre, Shirley's and Davenant's texts explore, and boldly represent, a 'politics' of English Catholicism.

This renewed interdisciplinary understanding of the integral importance of religious belief, which Fredric Jameson terms 'the master-code' of pre-capitalist society, has led literary scholars to re-evaluate the role which religion played in early modern culture.[27] Such critical sensitivity has stimulated an invigorating exploration of England's old faith, embodied by Alison Shell's masterful *Catholicism, Controversy and the English Literary Imagination, 1558–1660*.[28] Despite Shell's urge for other scholars 'to join in the task of reclamation', in examining the Caroline stage at least, few have answered her call.[29] Perhaps, inevitably, the question of Shakespeare's religion has engulfed most critics' attention.[30] Similar concern has been bestowed on canonical figures such as Ben Jonson.[31] More elusively, Lisa Hopkins has investigated the possible links between John Ford and the old faith, seeing in the text's employment of food and blood a 'yearning' for the 'old Catholicism'.[32] Yet continued Catholic unease at this 'piecemeal Reformation' was a powerfully shaping discourse on the Caroline stage. By teasing out a Catholic 'identity' (expressed in contemporary letters, sermons, histories and even needlework) this book opens out Caroline theatre as a space which deftly explores the anxieties of English Catholics, a crucible which gives voice to an oppositional community's concerns.

Chapter 1 examines the public discourse of religion in Stuart England. Through key events such as the fall of the Blackfriars Room in 1623 and the notorious performances of Middleton's *A Game at Chesse* (1624), care is taken to delineate the spectrum of passionate religious beliefs within England. Far from being confined to arid polemical debates, these religious disputes spilled over into conflicting understandings of personal, cultural and political belief. Revealed within the core of these fierce debates is a nub of

Protestant unease regarding the persistent existence of the Roman Catholic community, which clung to every level of society. This chapter teases out both the Protestant apprehension and the Catholic expectation stimulated by Henrietta Maria's (troubling) arrival with her self-proclaimed mission of, at the very least, ameliorating the plight of those loyal to the old faith.[33] She was hailed as a second Esther by Catholic powers and the potency of this topos the potency of this topos swiftly percolated throughout society. As early as 1626, Queen Henrietta Maria boldly projected her own Counter-Reformation vision to an elite audience in an audacious performance of Racan's *L'Artenice*. Indeed the inherent power of this suggestively supplicant image was to become so indelibly etched within the wider public imagination that it even manifested itself in a retrospective seventeenth-century stump-work (see Figure 2, p. 38).

Chapters 2 and 3 focus on James Shirley's texts from the period 1625 to 1633. Described by Gerard Langbaine as the 'Chief of the Second-rate Poets', with his works patronised by Ben Lucow as 'serviceable vehicles for theatre', James Shirley's dramatic legacy has been haunted by John Dryden's derisive jibes in *Mac Flecknoe*.[34] Scholarly attention has focused either on Shirley's social comedies, such as *Hyde Park* and *The Ball*, or his later plays.[35] This monograph exposes a more subversive force in Shirley's drama, crystallising the difficulties which recusants continued to face, despite the visible presence of their royal champion, and Shirley's key patroness, Queen Henrietta Maria. From examining contemporary reports a gap becomes apparent between Henrietta Maria's own staged ideal of her position as Queen Consort in *L'Artenice* and the English nation's perception of their Roman Catholic Queen. Perhaps, unsurprisingly, suspicion of the Queen's overt Popery alienated her from the dominant Protestant culture. Even rumours circulating about her first ill-fated pregnancy attributed blame to her 'coming back by water from this town, where she had been about her devotions, by reason of the Ember-week, the Monday before'.[36] Significantly though, nor was the Queen's mix of self-consuming French Roman Catholicism and frivolous contempt for the established Church wholly encouraging to the recusant community. Indeed by 1628 Catholic anticipation for, at the very least, religious toleration had been deflated, embodied by Wentworth's lucrative financial policy of compounding with recusants.[37] As

Christopher Wandesford, an Exchequer official, remarked, the 'Papists . . . hang down their Heads like Bulrushes and think themselves like Water spilt on the Ground'.[38]

Chapter 2 explores the circumstances surrounding Shirley's own apostasy, before mapping his engagement with the concerns of the English recusants in three plays from 1626 to 1629. In *The Witty Fair One* (1628) Shirley exposes how the exclusive language of the recusant community was being debased by society's fascination for all things pertaining to Henrietta Maria. In *The Wedding* (1629), through the powerful image of the Magdalene of Roman Catholic tradition, Shirley engages with the dual assault on the Catholic Church from Laudian and Puritan pamphlet literature.[39] Finally, in *The Grateful Servant* (1629) Shirley reminds Henrietta Maria of the possibilities imbued within the recusant imagination upon her arrival into England. With the death of Buckingham the Queen's own sphere of influence had significantly widened. Through the direct parallels evoked between Leonora and Henrietta Maria in *The Grateful Servant*, Shirley urges his royal patroness to reassume her role as both a reforming agent for the English nation and a potential force of salvation for English Catholics.

Chapter 3 delves into that central issue which beleaguered the recusant community, the problematic conception of a loyal English Roman Catholic. As the conformist commentator George Synge admitted: 'who knoweth not Papists have their kindes? There are Papists in faction, Papists in devotion', yet as he questioned, 'doe we acquit all, because we justifie some?'[40] In a series of plays between 1630 and 1633 Shirley stages this dilemma from within the recusant imagination. *Love in a Maze* (1631) dramatises the predicament of the temporiser caught between law and conscience. The recusant Edward Lechmere highlighted this impasse in his stern warning to the church-papist: 'you thinke you heare some tell you there is another waie but nice and ticklish: wherein those who speak, themselves durst not venture; because if it miscarrie, soul and bodie and heaven and all is lost'.[41] Through the steadfast figure of Yongrave, Shirley promotes the religious constancy which was so integral to contemporary Catholic writings. Within the recusant community at least, a staunch Catholic faith was by no means equated with inevitable treachery against the English nation. Rather, in *The Traitor* (1631), Shirley confutes the popish spectre of Protestant nightmare to suggest that the religious temporiser was a greater threat to the security of the state. Deepening his exploration of this complex debate, *The Young Admiral* (1633) forcefully displays the real pain inflicted by the Oaths of Allegiance and Supremacy upon Catholic subjects. Significantly, on the Caroline stage at least, tensions are dissolved through the salutary, outside force of Rosinda who dispels the troubling issue of allegiance, and propels her future husband towards a life of virtue. Once more, Shirley can be seen to be urging Henrietta Maria to fulfil her own proselytising mission. Far from the sycophantic panegyric traditionally ascribed to Caroline drama, Shirley's texts consistently urge Henrietta Maria to achieve her tantalising potential. As the Queen's own bold performance in Walter Montagu's *The Shepherds' Paradise* suggests, by 1632, Henrietta Maria basked in her Counter-Reformation success, signified by the lavish ceremony for the laying of the foundation stone for her new purpose-built Capuchin chapel, and her growing sphere of influence which conspicuously embraced puritan and recusant alike.[42] Notably, in *The Bird in a Cage* (1633), through the figure of Eugenia who is roused from passive encagement to defiant zeal, Shirley overtly engages with the Queen's own complacency to reveal an undercurrent of disquiet within the recusant community.

Chapters 4 and 5 examine Davenant's plays and masques from the period 1634 to 1640. Shirley himself believed that it was his refusal to flatter which most likely led to his displacement by William Davenant from the coveted position of Henrietta Maria's preferred dramatist. To an even greater extent than James Shirley, the texts of Davenant have been adversely affected by the stigma attached to Caroline drama. Attention has focused either on Davenant's comedies or on his later works.[43] Chapter 4 establishes Davenant's own gradual leaning towards Rome as a product of the highly charged religious atmosphere of the Caroline court, where the rise of a fashionable Roman Catholicism was paralleled by the growth of Laudianism. The recusant polemicist Matthew Wilson observed with much satisfaction, by 1633, 'Calvinism, once a darling in England' was 'at length accounted Heresie: yea a little lesse then Treason, men in word and writing using willingly the once fearful names of Priests and Altars'.[44] By the mid-1630s the possibility of religious reconciliation (however misplaced) had led more moderate Catholics such as the Benedictine leader, Leander Jones, and the celebrated Franciscan, Christopher Davenport, to anticipate the long awaited chimera of a reunion between Rome and the established Church of England. However, as militant recusants continued to caution, the established Church, 'desireth much a Reconciliation with the Church of Rome but in a *particular waye of its owne which will not easily be avoided*'.[45] In 1635 Davenant staged two versions of this politically charged negotiation. In *The Temple of Love*, in collaboration with Inigo Jones, he celebrated the Queen's Counter-Reformation success on the elite Whitehall stage. However in *Love and Honour*, in the charged space of the commercial stage, through a series of striking textual doublings, Davenant suggests an alternative to the Queen's ideal of Protestant capitulation, one of mutual compromise.

Chapter 5 continues to mark the growing creative shift between Henrietta Maria and her playwright servant, William Davenant. The years 1637 to 1640 witnessed the climax of the flourishing revival of Catholicism within Henrietta Maria's court. The arrival of her *devôt* mother, Marie de Médicis, and the strong influence of the Papal agent, George Con, impelled the Queen towards an international, extreme style of Catholicism. Such an adamant Roman Catholic stance disrupted earlier cherished (if rather naive) hopes of possible conciliation, and exacerbated the mounting anxiety in Scotland, regarding the combined threat to the Scottish Kirk of Popery and Laudianism. In *The Fair Favourite* (1638) Davenant boldly counsels against the Queen's confrontational attitude. Performed in the tense cultural moment of the Scottish crisis, notably, the Queen of *The Fair Favourite* is a force who seeks to mediate between the divided parties of a fractured kingdom. With Henrietta Maria openly rallying English Roman Catholics to Charles I's standard, such an assertion from within the Queen's household, by a playwright often dismissed as sycophantic, is surprising. However in a wry reflection of Davenant's own obscuring of James Shirley, this dramatic model of queenly arbitration was itself rapidly overshadowed by the spectacular staging of *Salmacida Spolia* (1640). Through the striking appearance of Henrietta Maria as an Esther in Amazon costume, Inigo Jones brilliantly visualised the Queen's defiantly, militant Roman Catholic fervour. Far from building bridges as Martin Butler once argued, this final masque pushes Charles I towards a more oppositional position, a progression which Davenant commemorates with notable unease.[46]

Ultimately, as this book concludes, the very discussion (outside Whitehall) of the drama of the Queen's household signifies the cultural agency of Shirley's and Davenant's texts. Significantly, in *Messallina the History of the Roman Empresse* (1640), the Nonconformist playwright Nathanael Richards directly attacked what he perceived to be the menace of his own papist Queen through an overt engagement with, and inversion of, tropes closely associated with Henrietta Maria's known theatrical preferences. In the volatile political climate of the early 1640s the spectre of the recusant as one of traitorous intrigue was firmly re-entrenched in the Protestant imagination; an absolute volte-face which returned the English Catholic community to the uncertainty of their situation pre-1625. Yet, as Henrietta Maria's letters and actions during the 1640s confirm, she continued to perceive herself as the defender of English Catholics. Above all, as her almoner, the Bishop of Angoulême, reminded her French compatriots in 1645 – and as this book explores through the energy and vibrant debate of Caroline theatre – Henrietta Maria wished to be remembered as a Roman Catholic Queen who 're-established, and made to flourish again the Catholic religion in England'.[47]

Notes

1 Francis Quarles, *Hadassa: Or the History of Queene Ester* (London: 1621), reprinted in Quarles, *Divine Poems: Containing the History of Jonah. Ester. Job. Sions Sonets. Elegies* (London: 1630), p. 131.
2 AAW/A18, G. M. Muscott to T. More, 23 September 1624, p. 363.
3 *Ibid.*
4 *Ibid.*, my emphasis.
5 Susan Wiseman explores the figure of Esther in Civil War women's petitions: see *Conspiracy and Virtue: Women, Writing, and Politics in Seventeenth-Century England* (Oxford: Oxford University Press, 2006), pp. 45–9.
6 'Bref de Nostre Saint Pere le Pape Urbain VIII a Madame s'en allant en Angleterre l'exortant a remettre la Religion Catholique en ces pays dont elle a esté bannie', December 1624, Kings MSS, 135, sigs 527r–530v, sig. 528v. See also Henrietta Maria's letter to Pope Urban VIII in Mary Anne Everett Green (ed.), *Letters of Queen Henrietta Maria, Including Her Private Correspondence With Charles the First* (London: Richard Bentley, 1857), pp. 7–10.

7 François Albert Duffo, *Henriette-Marie de France, Reine d'Angleterre, 1609–1669*, (Paris: 1935). See also Quentin Bone, *Henrietta Maria, Queen of the Cavaliers* (Urbana: University of Illinois Press, 1972), p. 37.

8 Pierre de Bérulle, 'Élévation sur Sainte Madeleine', in Joseph Beaude, Michel Join-Lambert and Rémi Lescot (eds), *Pierre de Bérulle: Oeuvres Complètes*, 5 vols (Paris, Oratoire de Jésus: Les Editions du Cerf, 1996), vol. 3, pp. 407–94, p. 414. All subsequent references are to this edition and appear in the text.

9 Alison Findlay, Stephanie Hodgson-Wright and Gweno Williams, *Women and Dramatic Productions, 1550–1700* (Harlow: Longman Pearson, 2000); Clare McManus, *Women on the Renaissance Stage: Anna of Denmark and Female Masquing in the Stuart Court 1590–1619* (Manchester: Manchester University Press, 2002); Sophie Tomlinson, *Women on Stage in Stuart Drama* (Cambridge: Cambridge University Press, 2005).

10 John Bossy, *The English Catholic Community, 1570–1850* (London: Darton, Longman and Todd, 1975). See also Anne Dillon, *The Construction of Martyrdom in the English Catholic Community, 1535–1603* (Aldershot: Ashgate Publishing, 2002).

11 Brian Magee, *The English Recusants: A Study of the Post-Reformation Catholic Survival and the Operation of the Recusancy Laws* (London: Burns, Oates and Co., 1938), p. xi.

12 A church-papist was an abusive term for those English Catholics who outwardly conformed to the established Protestant Church yet inwardly remained Roman Catholics. For further discussion see Alexandra Walsham, *Church Papists: Catholicism, Conformity and Confessional Polemic in Early Modern England* (Woodridge: The Royal Historical Society, The Boydell Press, 1993).

13 Martin Butler, *Theatre and Crisis: 1632–1642* (Cambridge: Cambridge University Press, 1984). For a typical dismissal of Caroline drama see Clifford Leech, *Shakespeare's Tragedies, and Other Studies in Seventeenth Century Drama* (London: Chatto and Windus, 1950), pp. 159–81.

14 Julie Sanders, *Caroline Drama: The Plays of Massinger, Ford, Shirley and Brome* (Plymouth: Northcote House Publishers, 1999); Matthew Steggle, *Richard Brome: Place and Politics on the Caroline Stage* (Manchester: Manchester University Press, 2004); Ian Atherton and Julie Sanders (eds), *The 1630s: Interdisciplinary Essays on Culture and Politics in the Caroline Era* (Manchester: Manchester University Press, 2006). See also David Lindley, *The Court Masque* (Manchester: Manchester University Press, 1984); J. R. Mulryne and Margaret Shewring (eds), *Theatre and Government Under the Early Stuarts* (Cambridge:

Cambridge University Press, 1993); Stephen Orgel, *The Illusion of Power: Political Theatre in the English Renaissance* (Berkeley: University of California Press, 1975).
15 Butler, *Theatre and Crisis*, p. 2.
16 Erica Veevers, *Images of Love and Religion: Queen Henrietta Maria and Court Entertainments* (Cambridge: Cambridge University Press, 1989).
17 Karen Britland, *Drama at the Courts of Queen Henrietta Maria* (Cambridge: Cambridge University Press, 2006); Tomlinson, *Women on Stage*.
18 AAW/A28, George Leyburn to Farrington (E. Bennett), 3 September 1636, p. 523.
19 *Ibid.*
20 Christopher Haigh (ed.), *The English Reformation Revised* (Cambridge: Cambridge University Press, 1987), p. 6.
21 *Ibid.*, p. 9.
22 Roger Lockyer, *The Early Stuarts: A Political History of England, 1603–1642* (London: Longman, 1989), p. 297.
23 For scholarly insight into these controversies see Anthony Milton, *Catholic and Reformed: The Roman and Protestant Churches in English Protestant Thought, 1600–1640* (Cambridge: Cambridge University Press, 1995); Michael Questier, *Conversion, Politics and Religion in England, 1580–1625* (Cambridge: Cambridge University Press, 1996); Nicholas Tyacke, *Anti-Calvinists: The Rise of English Arminianism c.1590–1640* (Oxford: Clarendon Press, 1987).
24 Bossy, *Catholic Community*, p. 5.
25 Conrad Russell, *The Causes of the English Civil War* (Oxford: Clarendon Press: 1990). See also Caroline M. Hibbard, *Charles I and the Popish Plot* (Chapel Hill: University of North Carolina Press, 1983); Peter Lake, 'Anti-Popery: the Structure of a Prejudice', in Richard Cust and Anne Hughes (eds), *Conflict in Early Stuart England: Studies in Religion and Politics 1603–1642* (Harlow: Longman Group, 1989), pp. 72–106.
26 Kevin Sharpe, *Remapping Early Modern England: The Culture of Seventeenth-Century England* (Cambridge: Cambridge University Press, 2000), p. 12.
27 Fredric Jameson, 'Religion and Ideology: A Political Reading of *Paradise Lost*', in Francis Barker *et al.* (eds), *Literature, Politics and Theory* (London: New Accents, 1986), pp. 35–56, p. 39. See also Achsah Guibbory, *Ceremony and Community from Herbert to Milton: Literature, Religion and Cultural Conflict in Seventeenth-Century England* (Cambridge: Cambridge University Press, 1998); Donna B. Hamilton and Richard Strier (eds), *Religion, Literature and Politics in*

Post-Reformation England, 1540–1688 (Cambridge: Cambridge University Press, 1996); Margot Heinemann, *Puritanism and Theatre: Thomas Middleton and Opposition Drama Under the Early Stuarts* (Cambridge: Cambridge University Press, 1980); Arthur F. Marotti, *Catholicism and Anti-Catholicism in Early Modern English Texts* (Basingstoke: Macmillan, 1999); Debora K. Shuger, *Habits of Thought in the English Renaissance: Religion, Politics, and the Dominant Culture* (Toronto: University of Toronto Press, 1997).

28 Alison Shell, *Catholicism, Controversy and the English Literary Imagination, 1558–1660* (Cambridge: Cambridge University Press, 1999), p. 20.

29 *Ibid.*

30 Dympna Callaghan, 'Shakespeare and Religion', *TP*, 15 (2001), 1–4; Beatrice Groves, *Texts and Traditions: Religion in Shakespeare, 1592–1604* (Oxford: Clarendon Press, 2007); Velma Richmond, *Shakespeare, Catholicism and Romance* (New York: Continuum, 2000); Richard Wilson, *Secret Shakespeare: Studies in Theatre, Religion and Resistance* (Manchester: Manchester University Press, 2004).

31 T. Wilson Hayes, 'Ben Jonson's Libertine Catholicism', in William P. Shaw (ed.), *Praise Disjoined: Changing Patterns of Salvation in Seventeenth-Century English Literature* (New York: Peter Lang, 1991).

32 Lisa Hopkins, *John Ford's Political Theatre* (Manchester: Manchester University Press, 1994), p. 75.

33 Green, *Queen's Letters*, Henrietta Maria to Urban VIII, 6 April 1625, p. 9.

34 Gerard Langbaine, *An Account of the English Dramatic Poets, 1691* (Menston: Scolar Press, 1971), p. 474; Ben Lucow, *James Shirley* (Boston: Twayne Publishers, 1981), p. 8; James Kinsley (ed.), *The Poems and Fables of John Dryden* (Oxford: Clarendon Press, 1962), pp. 238–43. For a comprehensive Shirley bibliography see Ruth K. Zimmer, *James Shirley: A Reference Guide* (Boston Mass.: G. K. Hall, 1980).

35 Ira Clark, *Professional Playwrights, Massinger, Ford, Shirley and Brome* (Lexington: University Press of Kentucky, 1992); Rosemary Gaby, ' "Of Vagabonds and Commonwealths": *Beggars' Bush, A Jovial Crew* and *The Sisters*', *SEL*, 34 (1994), 401–24; Richard J. Hodson, 'Caroline Town Comedy, 1628–1642' (PhD dissertation, University of York, 2000); Sanders, *Caroline Drama*.

36 Letter from Mr Beaulieu to Sir Thomas Puckering, 20 May 1628, Thomas Birch (ed.), *The Court and Times of Charles the First*, 2 vols (London: Henry Colburn, 1848), 1, p. 355.

37 K. J. Lindley, 'The Lay Catholics of England in the Reign of Charles I', *JEH*, 27 (1971), 199–221.

38 Alan Dures, *English Catholicism, 1558–1642: Continuity and Change* (Harlow: Longman Group, 1983), p. 73.
39 See Robert Butterfield, *Maschil: Or, a Treatise to Give Instruction, Touching the State of the Church of Rome Since the Councell of Trent* (London: 1629), p. 134.
40 George Synge, *A Rejoynder to the Reply Published by the Jesuits Under the Name of William Malone* (Dublin: 1632), pp. 6–7.
41 Edward Lechmere, *A Reflection of Certaine Authors That Are Pretended to Disavow the Churches Infallibilitie in Her Generall Decrees of Faith* (Douai: 1635), sig. *4v.
42 Walter Montagu, *The Shepheard's Paradise: A Comedy Privately Acted Before the Late King Charls by the Queen Consort's Majesty, and Ladies of Honour* (London: 1659).
43 Janet Clare, *Drama of the English Republic 1649–60* (Manchester: Manchester University Press, 2002); Howard S. Collins, *The Comedy of Sir William Davenant* (Paris, The Hague: Mouton, 1967); Robert Shore, ' "Lawrels for the Conquered": The Dilemmas of William Davenant and Abraham Cowley in the Revolutionary Decades of the Seventeenth Century' (PhD Dissertation, University of Cambridge, 1994); Susan Wiseman, *Drama and Politics in the English Civil War* (Cambridge: Cambridge University Press, 1998).
44 Matthew Wilson, *A Direction to be Observed by N. N. If Hee Meane to Proceede in Answering the Book Intituled Mercy and Truth, Or Charity Maintained by Catholiks* (printed secretly in England: 1636), p. 23.
45 AAW/A28, *Short Instructions: Instruction for the Agent at Rome, 1635*, p. 25.
46 Martin Butler, 'Politics and the Masque: *Salmacida Spolia*', in Thomas Healy and Jonathan Sawday (eds), *Literature and the English Civil War* (Cambridge: Cambridge University Press, 1990), pp. 59–74.
47 *A Warning to the Parliament of England, in an Oration Made to the General Assembly of the French Clergy at Paris, by M. Jaques de Perron, Bishop of Angoulême, and Grand Almoner to the Queen of England* (London: 1647), in Green, *Queen's Letters*, pp. 292–5, p. 295.

1

The public discourse of religion in Stuart England

> Our Countrey, which ought to be even and uniforme, is now made like a piece of Arras, full of strange formes and divers colours.[1]

In June 1625 Dr Meddus, rector of St Gabriel, Fenchurch, recorded the entry into London of Henrietta Maria, youngest daughter of Henri IV of France, bride to Charles I, and England's new Queen Consort. Writing to the Reverend Joseph Mead, Dr Meddus reported that 'last night, at five o'clock (there being a very great shower) the king and queen, in the royal barge, with many other barges of honour, and thousands of boats, passed through London bridge to Whitehall'.[2] Intriguingly, within such a description which included time-honoured, frivolous details such as that 'the king and queen were both in green suits', Meddus felt compelled to observe that Henrietta Maria 'hath already given some good signs of hope that she may ere long, by God's blessing, become ours in religion'.[3] Likewise, Sir Simonds D'Ewes noted in his diary for 1625, how 'on Thursday, the 30th and last day of this instant June, I went to Whitehall purposely to see the Queen; which I did fully all the time she sat at dinner, and perceived her to be a most absolute delicate lady... her face, much enlivened by her radiant and sparkling black eye'.[4] D'Ewes, like Meddus, concluded his description with a comment on the religion of the new Queen, or her lack of it, remarking 'I could not abstain from divers deep-fetched sighs to consider that she wanted the knowledge of the true religion'.[5]

These writings expose the immediate concern stimulated within the wider Protestant consciousness regarding Henrietta Maria's allegiance to the Roman Catholic faith. In this chapter, the anxieties outlined by Dr Meddus and Sir Simonds D'Ewes are pursued to reveal the complexity of the religious situation which greeted the young queen. From exploring the vociferous debates in the months prior to Henrietta Maria's arrival, around events such as the fall of the Blackfriars Room (a catastrophe where the room in which a Jesuit priest was secretly preaching collapsed resulting in the deaths of many of his illicit congregation), and Thomas Middleton's *A Game at Chesse*, religious belief can be very much understood as a key to identity in early modern England. Noticeably, this Protestant sense of self, as the lurid pamphlets and vivid dramas of the mid-1620s illuminate, seemed peculiarly vulnerable to the continued, insidious threat of the old faith. By 1625 the nation's public, and inherently political, discourse of religious division was at a defining moment. Where the English recusant community heralded Henrietta Maria's arrival as an 'occasion chosen by God', equally the militant hopes of Protestant England were projected on to the newly crowned King Charles, who was 'cryed up by all the Godly party in the kingdome'.[6] Emerging from this juxtaposition of extremes is a glimpse of a religious culture stamped by unease and suspicion. From a letter to her brother, Louis XIII, Henrietta Maria's own position seemed unequivocal. As she stated, her 'sincere intentions' were to do 'what may be useful and advantageous to the religion and to the Catholics of Great Britain'.[7] This aspiration is explored as a possible stimulus behind the Queen's own startling court performance in the title role of *L'Artenice* (1626). Suggestively, this powerful image of Henrietta Maria as a protective force for English Catholics is seen to percolate rapidly throughout popular culture, as we examine by means of a beautifully preserved tapestry from the mid-seventeenth century.

1625: a shifting of religio-political alliances

Henrietta Maria's entrance into England as a visibly practising Roman Catholic, sustained spiritually by a train of twenty-eight priests and the right to have a 'Chapel in all the Kings Royall Houses and any wher else, wher she shall reside' cannot be over-emphasised. The impact of this penetrating Counter-Reformation force on England's shifting religio-political 'Arras' was sharpened as the Queen's '*Officers, and all her houshold*' were also granted the '*free exercise of the* Roman *Religion*', whilst the Queen herself enjoyed the wider political support of the Roman Catholic powers in Europe.[8] Henrietta Maria's arrival was particularly significant as she entered a nation at a moment of some flux, and inflamed religious fervour. James I had died barely three months previously. The transition of power to his son, Prince Charles, had been enviably seamless. However religious tensions were heightened by the recent anxiety, particularly within militant Protestant circles, regarding the religious quietism of James I's foreign policy. For godly Protestants, the fearful implication of James I's dynastic ambitions to unite England with the fiercely militant Roman Catholic Spain remained indelibly etched on the public imagination.[9] Indeed, a sense of national crisis had arisen in February 1623, when Prince Charles, in true knight errant fashion, had boldly galloped off on the arduous journey to Spain to personally woo the Infanta Isabella, the devout daughter of a nation widely perceived as encouraging Papal domination.[10] Charles's abrupt return home, with 'not so much as the least infected dust cleaving to his feete, much lesse any corrupted Popish ayre infect[ing] his royall bloud', had been a matter for widespread celebrations.[11] Some two years later, Thomas Brewer vividly recalled the 'Dulcet sounds' of the city bells whose 'shrill voyces, did proclaime the Gaine / of *Englands* Heart, out of the Hate of *Spaine*'.[12] Such apprehension had been tangibly intensified by the continued plight of James I's eldest daughter, Elizabeth of Bohemia. This popular princess, second-in-line to the English throne, was enduring humiliating exile in The Hague, having been forced to flee Roman Catholic Imperial troops in 1619 with her husband, Frederic. To English Protestants, and the reformed European churches, this had seemed the perfect opportunity to embark on a Holy War against Spain but James I had been reluctant to act, preferring peaceful and dynastic measures.[13] With persistent rumours that his own wife, Queen Anna of Denmark, had secretly converted to Roman Catholicism, there were even embarrassing tales of James I's own imminent apostasy to Rome, a fabrication which the King angrily denied in his poem 'The Wiper'.[14]

Reflecting these political concerns, by 1625, the quicksand of religious alliances within England had started to shift. Dr Meddus's misleadingly naive hope that Henrietta Maria would become 'ours' in religion belies the intricate nuances of belief in Caroline England. Such a statement suggests that any division within religion was simply between Roman Catholic and Protestant. This was by no means the case. In 1625 the established Church within England was an umbrella for a breadth of Protestant opinion, ranging in belief from the puritan through to the conformist divine.[15] During the early reign of James I this uneasy alliance had been cemented by a common aim to fight against the mutual enemy of Popery. By the 1620s this bond had begun to crumble. Although still believing Roman Catholicism to be a religion of 'error', ministers such as Walter Curll, William Laud, Richard Montague and Robert Shelford openly questioned the seditious nature of vehemently anti-papal tracts and began to view the puritan as an equally great enemy as the papist. In turn, the puritans, increasingly suspicious of this irenical strain of Protestantism, branded their new advocates 'negative papists'.[16] It was from this group of clerics that the hallmark of what would later be deemed Laudianism was beginning to emerge, with an emphasis on a subtle approach to the challenge of Roman Catholicism, an insistence on the importance of church ceremony and the central idea of the Protestant Church as 'catholic but reformed'.[17]

Returning to Dr Meddus's diary entry for June 1625, equally as misleading was his, at the very least, overly optimistic view that Henrietta Maria would even contemplate changing her religion. The Queen's marriage contract explicitly allowed her to practise her faith, both St James's Palace and Somerset House rapidly becoming known as sites where Roman Catholic ceremonies were conducted.[18] Moreover, Henrietta Maria had become queen of a country with a small but significant number of recusants and church-papists. In the early 1620s increasingly confident in the protection of the impending Spanish match, this community had become alarmingly visible. Sir Ferdinando Gorges reminded the Duke of Buckingham before the Parliament of 1624 how 'within these fewe yeares' the Catholics 'are growne to that hedd in every quarter that they are not onely become insolent and unsufferable to particulars, but most dangerous to the publique peace of this Realme'.[19] Exact figures regarding the size of the English Roman Catholic community are impossible to calculate and in some ways unhelpful. John Bossy estimates a figure of forty thousand in 1603 out of a total population of five million but this does not include the considerable number of church-papists.[20] Despite continuous fiscal penalties, the Roman Catholic body steadily increased during the early seventeenth century; revealing the effectiveness of both the secular priests and the missionary movement spearheaded by the Jesuits and later complemented by Franciscan and Benedictine orders.[21] It was to this group of people that Pope Urban VIII had behested his god-daughter Henrietta Maria to act as a 'parent'. Moreover, as her mother reminded her, although she was now graced with the title Queen of England, the 'highest position' which Marie de Médicis believed Henrietta Maria could 'possibly' hold was that of 'daughter of the Church'.[22] The potential of such a protective role was suggested even before Henrietta Maria set foot in the realm when, in May 1625, Charles observed the agreement of his marriage treaty and instructed the Lord Keeper to suspend all proceedings against recusants.[23] Nor was Henrietta Maria a reluctant novice, propitiously replying to Pope Urban's request: 'nothing in the world . . . is so dear to me as the safety of my conscience and the good of religion'.[24] Indeed Henrietta Maria's arrival, rather than providing expectations for the Queen's conversion to the established Church of England, might more properly be seen as an encouragement to hope for England's return to Rome – the informing dynamic of this book.

What comes across most clearly from these diary entries and snippets of letters is the vitality of religious discourse in early modern England – not only in the public negotiations between European powers but on an everyday level in the private correspondence between humdrum individuals. From the perspective of England today with its apologetically Christian and largely secular society, it is perhaps hard to fully understand such passionate belief. But in 1625 the land which Henrietta Maria entered was quite literally as John Gee suggests an 'Arras' of fervent religious convictions. At the heart of Protestant England's godly anxiety was a fear of the persistent attractions of the 'old faith'. This fostered endless debate, which at times of national crisis erupted into unadulterated scaremongering. Indeed, as Peter Lake has argued, in many ways extremist elements within the established Church fed off, and deliberately manipulated, a demonised caricature of English recusants in order to create its own positive, Protestant self-image.[25] This is nowhere more apparent than in the furore surrounding the collapse of the Blackfriars Room in October 1623 (Figure 1). About two hundred people had secretly congregated to hear the Jesuit preacher Fr Drury. Half-way through the meeting the floor of the room buckled, resulting in about eighty deaths. At its most basic level, as the Jesuit missionary John Floyd pointed out, this accident was quite simply 'the standing or falling of an house'.[26] But in a culture

1 'The Fall of the House in Black-Friers London, 1623', from Samuel Clarke, *Englands Remembrancer* (London: 1657).

where the importance of image could not be overestimated this was a vivid spectacle. The first exclamation of one survivor, as Thomas Goad reported, was 'O what advantage will our adversaries take at this?'[27] The answer was quickly found in the rash of pamphlets which sprang up around this calamity. Polemicists greedily attempted to harness such misfortune for the benefit of their own cause. The range of responses from within the established Church alone suggests the religious intricacies of early modern England.

But what ultimately becomes apparent from a disaster such as the Blackfriars Room incident is the sheer impossibility of Protestant England successfully containing the threat of Roman Catholicism. Looking at the list of those who died in the catastrophe one is struck by the broad range of the victims' jobs and social class: Lady Webbe *'in Southwarke'*, John Galloway *'Vintener in Clerkenwell Close'*, Mistress Summers *'wife to Captaine* Summers *in the Kings Bench'*, Richard Fitzgarrat *'of Graies Inne, Gent'*, John Sturges *'the Lord* Peters *man'*, Edward Revell *'servant to Master* Nicholas Stone *the Kings Purveyor'*, Thomas Brisket, *'his wife, and his sonne and maide'*.[28] Indeed, in the very act of writing such an all-encompassing list there is a sense in which this assembly escapes definition. The meeting at Blackfriars did not just comprise recusants. Undoubtedly some were 'obstinate Papists' but others were 'silly novices, some ignorant newters, some went out of curiosity, some under colour of the better confirmation of their opinions, some to bee eare Witnesses of the same of these rarely qualified Priests; some as companions to others, some for novelty and some as temporizers'.[29] This elusive quality increases if we consider how news of the gathering was passed on by word of mouth, with John Gee learning about it when 'lighting upon some Popish company at dinner'.[30] The location itself, Blackfriars, was specifically chosen as a deliberate tactic to help those needing to escape detection: 'by reason of the water, and conveniency of landing people, who otherwise might be watched comming by land, either entangled by the inconvenience of debt, or other difficulties of as great consequence'.[31]

Such disquiet within the dominant Protestant culture at the insidious menace of Roman Catholicism – scattered throughout society and endemic to all classes – was not confined to the pages of vociferous polemical tracts. Rather, the wide brushstrokes of this public discourse were brilliantly translated on to the stage, nowhere more spectacularly than in Thomas Middleton's *A Game at Chesse*. Running from 9 to 14 August 1624, before being forcibly suppressed, *A Game at Chesse* was the talk of London, and reveals the strength of the religious discourse in the land which Henrietta Maria entered some ten months later. To an early modern audience, Middleton's dramatisation of the contemporary fear of Spain's suspected ambition of universal Roman Catholic domination proved electric. This was especially so because in this stage battle between the Black and White Houses, the audience appeared to witness the old enemy Spain (symbolised by the Black House) destroyed by a triumphant England; the monster of Roman Catholicism and Jesuitical cunning defeated by the virtue of the White House, an embodiment of the English Protestant establishment. However, shot through this reincarnation of the victorious spirit found after the Spanish Armada was the more subversive identification of a questionable collusion between the Black and White Kingdoms. Persistently out-manoeuvred, the White King (daringly alluding to James I) shows a lack of perception, action and a credulous naivety, which is far removed from the ideal leader of militant Protestant hopes. As the Venetian ambassador, Alvise Valaresso, commented in his contemporary critique of the play: 'the Spaniards are touched from their tricks being discovered', but King James's 'reputation is affected much more deeply by representing the case [i.e. ease] with which he was deceived'.[32] Middleton's play ostensibly ends in triumph for the White House but, as the Epilogue underlines, this is itself a dramatic ploy. Moments after the Black House had been swept into the ignominious hell mouth of the 'bag', the White Queen's Pawn, still breathless from triumph on stage, openly addresses those English Catholics among the assembly, 'by envy's mark denoted, / To those night glow-worms in the bag devoted' (*Game*, epilogue, 5–8).

Vanquished on stage, Roman Catholicism remained an indefatigable presence in seventeenth-century England. John Chamberlain's comprehensive list of audience members, freely documents the presence of 'papists', whilst the letters of the Spanish ambassador, Don Carlos Coloma, detail how recusants and church-papists 'went secretly to see the play'.[33] Middleton's chief 'discovery' was not the victory of the White Knight's checkmate but his staging of Stuart realpolitik. Damningly Middleton concludes that complete Protestant victory over the amorphous spectre of Roman Catholicism (which even penetrated into the heart of James I's own royal marriage) would continue to elude a House more grey than white. The veracity of such an assumption is underscored by the diplomatic dance which the Spanish ambassador Coloma derogatorily recorded as taking place some forty miles outside London. At the very moment Middleton's play was being staged, fastidiously ignoring Coloma's complaints against the 'shamelessnesse' of 'the actors' known 'as the King's men', James I and his court were busily engaged 'feasting and fawning upon the French Ambassador' in pursuit of a new Catholic bride for England's heir.[34] From this peripheral entrance on to the stage of English public affairs, Henrietta Maria was swiftly to assume a central role in the nation's vigorous discourse on religion. As we shall explore, over the next twenty years and beyond Henrietta Maria's visible, often provocative, position as figurehead of the English recusant community would likewise be openly debated, both in polemical tracts and on the Caroline stage.

The Anglo-French match: 'I should ever have preferred a daughter of *France* to that of *Spaine*'

What must, however, be recognised is that in contrast to the menacing union with Spain 'which all good Protestants feared', the prospect of a French, Roman Catholic bride for Prince Charles was greeted with marginally more approval. Sir Simonds D'Ewes records how 'the English generally so detested the Spanish match, as they were glad of any other which freed them from the fear of that'.[35] Importantly, the broader elements of the established Church of England did not perceive the Roman Catholic Church in France to be as fanatically aggressive as its Spanish counterpart. Traditionally regarding itself as the eldest daughter of Rome, the French Church claimed special privileges, crucially viewing the Pope as supreme in matters spiritual but not necessarily temporal.[36] Most reassuring from an English Protestant prospective was the notorious fact that Henrietta Maria's father had himself been a feared Huguenot leader who had famously converted to Catholicism, in exchange for the crown of France. Hopes that Henrietta Maria might prove as similarly fluid in her religious inclinations had stimulated George Goring to send his future Queen 'divers of our common prayer books in French'.[37] Indeed, Henrietta Maria herself playfully built on the uncertainty surrounding her religion, as Dr Meddus noted: 'those of our nation that know best her disposition are very hopeful his majesty will have power to bring her to his own religion. Being asked, not long since, if she could abide an Huguenot, "Why not?" said she; "was not my father one?"'[38]

Not all English Protestants shared the optimism of Goring and Meddus. With the admitted benefit of hindsight, D'Ewes qualified his own statement with the reservation, 'wiser men feared much danger would ensue to the Gospel and true religion by this marriage, the lady being educated in popery'.[39] Yet, turning to Prince Charles's royal predecessors, comfort could be found in the marriage of Henry V to his French bride, Katherine. Most eloquently, in the militant Protestant tract *Vox Coeli*, Charles's own brother, Prince Henry, the much lamented budding champion of God-fearing English Protestants was heard to give his ghostly blessing, declaring: 'I should ever have preferred a daughter of *France* to that of *Spaine*.'[40] By 1625 genealogical links between the two countries were freely established in tracts such as *Genealogie et Alliance de l'Ancienne et Renommee Maison de la Trimoville* and openly celebrated in Ben Jonson's *The Fortunate Isles and Their Union*, where the Gods sing of 'joyning the bright Lillie and the Rose'.[41] Crucially, in the eyes of Protestant Europe, the combined forces of England and France had the opportunity to conquer the fearsome might of Spain, a point clarified by Sir Thomas Overbury as early as 1609:

> Now the only entire body in Christendome that makes head against the *Spanish* Monarchy, is *France*; and therefore they say in *France*, that the day of the ruin of *France*, is the Eve of the ruine of England: And thereupon *England* hath ever since the *Spanish* greatness, enclined rather to maintaine *France* rather than to ruine it.[42]

Such enhanced cultural currency lies behind the 1625 reprint of Chapman's *The Conspiracie and Tragedy of Charles Duke of Byron, Marshall of France*. Set in France's recent past, the tragedy focuses on the effective containment of the Catholic traitor, the Duke of Byron, by Henrietta Maria's own father. Notably, Henri IV is portrayed as a ruler who respects Protestant England, admires Elizabeth and realises the inherent danger of the militantly Catholic 'cunning' Spaniard.[43]

This initial positive gloss on Henrietta Maria's heritage reflects the projection of militant Protestant hopes on to Prince Charles in the months around his accession to the throne. In the early 1620s, as the anonymous tract *The Interpreter* suggests, the reputation of the English Protestant had been diminished. In Europe he was perceived as 'an indifferent man':

> That with all faiths, or none, hold quarter can . . .
> Hee at the Chappell can a Bishop heare;
> And then in Holborne a Religious Frear:
> A Masse nere troubles him, more than a play,
> All's one; he comes all one from both away.[44]

An injection of fresh vigour was necessary. By 1624 the heir apparent, Prince Charles, was freely presented as such an ideal figure, precisely because he had already survived the twin horrors of Spain and aggressive Roman Catholicism. William Bedell deliberately dedicated his 1624 tract, *The Copies of Certaine Letters Which Have Passed Between Spaine and England in Matter of Religion*, to 'the most high and excellent Prince, Prince Charles' because, where others such as James Waddsworth (recipient of Bedell's letters and chaplain to England's ambassador for Spain) had surrendered to Rome, Prince Charles had stood firm.[45] Similarly, Charles's quest to Spain, far from springing from the impetuosity of youthful romance, was transformed into the dogged pursuit by the most godly of Englishmen into the 'business of Christendom'; more precisely, to gauge Habsburg intentions to help restore Elizabeth of Bohemia and her family to the Palatinate.[46] Finding Spain had no design to aid his sister, Prince Charles on his return to England had urged his father to declare war, and had taken an active role in instigating the Parliament of 1624 with the central aim of funding this worthy cause.[47] The swelling ranks of the militant element of the established Church must have believed that they had finally found a champion for their Holy War, a worthy successor to Queen Elizabeth and the blighted promise of Prince Henry. With the decline of James I's health, this focus on Prince Charles intensified so that in 1624 he was very much the 'rising glory of that House of Candour' (*Game*, IV.iv.18). Surely no coincidence that 'upon New-years night, the prince only being there', Prince Charles commanded the King's Players to perform Shakespeare's *Henry IV Part 1*, 'att Whitehall'.[48] This signified that, like this earlier Prince of Wales, he too:

> ... like bright metal on a sullen ground,
> [His] reformation, glitt'ring o'er [his] fault,
> Shall show more goodly and attract more eyes
> Than that which hath no foil to set it off.[49]

Once again, as with Middleton's *A Game at Chesse*, these religio-political concerns become matter for the stage, in this instance explored by Beaumont and Fletcher in *Cupid's Revenge*.[50] Originally written in 1607–8, *Cupid's Revenge* was performed 'upon Innocents night', 28 December 1624, and performed before Prince Charles and the Duke of Brunswick 'att Whitehall' by the Queen of Bohemia's servants.[51] The text examines the growing distrust between the ageing Duke Leontium and his son Leucippus. Problems first erupt between father and son when Leucippus attempts to rid the country of a superstitious religion. Although ostensibly depicting pagan worship of the God Cupid, parallels with Roman Catholicism are quickly established, this false religion being denounced as: 'a vaine and fruitlesse Superstition; / So much more hatefull, that it *beares the shew / Of true Religion*' (I.i.49–51, my emphasis). Importantly, it is the Duke's children who instigate reform. Leucippus' sister Hidaspes urges that these 'obsceane Images / May be pluckt downe and burnt' (I.i.74–5). Despite the support of the common people, Leucippus' attempts to free the land from false worship are ultimately unsuccessful. Moreover, the final instruction to 'let the broken *Image* . . . / Be reedified' (V.iv.216–17) questions the strength of purpose of Leucippus, formerly dignified as the 'white innocent' (IV.iv.53). Like Middleton's 'discovery' in *A Game at Chesse*, Beaumont and Fletcher in the distant land of Lycia signal the gap between Charles's own ideal self-image, suggested in the performance of *Henry IV Part 1*, and the reality of his actions as Prince of Wales.

Yet, although this Anglo-French match compromised militant Protestant expectations, at the very least, the alarming spectre of a Spanish, Roman Catholic bride for Prince Charles had been deflated. In the eyes of the broader established Church, the daughter of Henri IV could not be so dangerous as the Infanta Isabella, as the heartfelt prayer of Lord Haughton praised: 'blessed is the Ariadne that brought us out of the Spanish labirinth into the french Elisian fields'.[52] Any persistent concerns were assuaged by the eagerness of the newly proclaimed King Charles to prove himself in battle against England's spiritual arch-enemy. Such a combination of events, to some extent, explains John Donne's conviction that under the guidance of Charles I, even with the impediment of a Catholic bride, the essential principles of England's established Church would be fundamentally secure. In his *First Sermon Preached to King Charles*, Donne warned his congregation against unnecessary anxiety, reproving those who worried that: 'if there fall a broken tyle from the house, hee thinkes *Foundations are destroyed*; if a crazie woman, or a disobedient childe, or a needie servant fall from our *Religion*, from our *Church*, hee thinkes the whole *Church* must necessarily fall'.[53] Such an admonition in turn gives credence to Thomas Brewer's semi-official celebratory gloss on Henrietta Maria's arrival:

> What musicke made they [the bells], when the pride and prime
> Of all her sex (MARIA) in our Land
> Made Her most wisht Arrivall; Hand in Hand,
> Joyning two royall Sisters, to Advance
> The Glories of them both: Great *Britaine, France*.[54]

Roman Catholic expectations: 'this occasion has been chosen by God'

If the joyful paeans of Protestant welcome to Henrietta Maria were in some way forced, the attitude of English recusants to the arrival of this French princess was rather less equivocal. Perceiving in this youthful bride the new hope of a Roman Catholic figurehead, recusant polemicists freely highlighted and inflated any potential link between French and English Roman Catholicism. Most common was I. B. C.'s suggestion that the Catholics of both nations shared 'scarlet rivers of innocent blood', symbolised by John Copinger's tale of 'a certaine Hugonott' who wore 'a chaine about his necke of the eares of priests'.[55] More intriguing was the layering of associations around, and manipulation of, the key figure who bridged these nations, Mary Queen of Scots. French through marriage, Queen Mary (despite the realities of history) was presented as a queen martyred on English soil for her faith. In 1622 the French Cardinal Perron hoped that not only the tears but 'also the bloud' of this 'happy deceased Queene' would lead to the conversion of James I.[56] Across the Channel, by 1625, William Bishop lauded Mary as a modern-day St Helena whose 'godly example' in enduring 'patientlie so manie yeares imprisonment, and at length martyrdome it selfe for her constancie in the same Catholike Roman religion' suggested a potential Constantine in her son, James I.[57] This topos had failed. However, with the advent of Henrietta Maria, fresh allusions were conceived, manifest in the dedication to Charles I of a manuscript history on Mary Stuart:

> the queen of Scotland your Grandmother was given to France, and France hath rendered you a Princesse according to the hearte of God and yours; a Bloom of our Lillies, a Daughter of a King, a sister of a king, a Wife of a King... great Majesties of Britain... as you make but one heart, so make but one Religion.[58]

Most valuable for the recusant community was Henrietta Maria's vibrant presence as a visible reminder of the Roman Catholic faith. Rumours of Queen Anna's apostasy to Rome had abounded, reinforced by occasions such as her extraordinary refusal to take communion at James I's coronation in 1606. But on the whole Anna, like many English church-papists, had practised her Catholicism in private.[59] Precisely because Queen Anna refused to involve herself directly with the Catholic underground movement, her relationship with the Pope fluctuated. In 1612 the Pope decried Anna's lack of zeal, but in 1616 he issued a papal brief in the Queen's praise.[60] By contrast, Henrietta Maria's religious welfare was a cornerstone in cementing the marriage negotiations between France and England.

Pope Urban VIII would grant a dispensation to allow Henrietta Maria to marry Prince Charles only on gaining Louis XIII's solemn oath that he had: 'received promises from this country [Britain], and having represented at Rome and elsewhere that he had really gained something for the Catholic faith'.[61] Accordingly Prince Charles had been asked to formally pledge 'not to endeavour by any means whatsoever to cause Madame to relinquish the Catholic, Apostolic, Roman Religion'.[62] The wider implications for the Catholic community of such a vow were apparent from Fr Muscott's eager report to Fr Thomas More that 'tomorrow' we expect 'the Extraordinary Ambassador from France, his coming as we heard is to take the King's oath'.[63]

Equally beneficial, as Caroline Hibbard points out, was that Henrietta Maria's religious establishment had been carefully constructed not only to ensure the preservation of the Queen's spiritual well-being but also to encourage the possibility of actively promoting Catholicism in England.[64] Wisely, the Jesuit order, so widely reviled in Protestant England, had been deliberately excluded. Instead, the twenty-eight priests had been drawn mostly from the Society of the Oratory. Familiar to Henrietta Maria from their popular presence at the French Court, the Oratorians' founding Counter-Reformation aim was the conversion of Protestants, which had been proved in their successful efforts with the Huguenots. With such a record, the ripple of concern surrounding such palpable Roman Catholicism at the very centre of English society is evident from Dr Meddus's detailed description of the first celebration of Mass which Henrietta Maria attended:

> On Friday last, the queen was at her first mass in Whitehall, which was mumbled over to her majesty at eleven of the clock, what time she came out of her bedchamber in her petticoat, with a veil upon her head... Whilst they were at mass, the king took order, that no Englishmen or women should come near the place.[65]

This deliberate act of segregation by King Charles patently suggests the perceived inherent danger within the open Popery of the new Queen of England.

However, such a popish presence served not only to remind Protestants of their lost heritage but as a prod to the conscience of English Roman Catholics themselves, especially those not willing to bear the burden of temporal disgrace. Anthony Milton argues that at a practical level Roman Catholic and Protestant lived quite calmly side by side: a 'cross confessionalism' remarkably distant from the stark theoretical models offered within oppositional tracts.[66] Apathy was exactly what Rome feared: an attitude summarised in Nicholas Sander's comments that 'if ever the faith shalbe recovered, it must be don by confessing and [professing] it, and not by dissembling'.[67] As early as 1587 Robert Southwell had thundered 'O how unhappy are they, that for the saving of goods, credite temporall authority', asking:

> did not your feete stumble, your eyes dasele, your hart quake and your body tremble, when you came into the polluted Sinagoge? ... could catholicke eares sustayn without glowing, the blasphemous, reprocheful, & rayling speaches against your true mother the Catholicke Churche?[68]

Notably, simultaneous with Henrietta Maria's arrival into England, there was an eruption of Roman Catholic printing, which reiterated these accusations to form a cumulative sense of real urgency.[69] Sander, in a 1625 reprint of his *Images of Christ*, tells the church-papist that 'going to schismatical Service' may not 'be wincked at'.[70] These warnings against 'spiritual lethargy' hint at two growing concerns within the recusant community: anxiety over the blurring of traditional doctrinal boundaries and, with perhaps more sinister implications, the effects of the anti-papist backlash from the Parliament of 1624. With Prince Charles and the godly Protestants intent upon war against Spain, even before the first Parliamentary session, John Woolley reported how the English Catholics began 'to feare' and 'their heads like to the snaile they begin to pull in already and by reporte many of late goeth to Church which before declared themselves otherwise'.[71]

In the face of such challenges there could not have been a more propitious moment for the arrival of a conspicuous Roman Catholic presence in the very bosom of the Stuart monarchy. From the perspective of many English Catholics, as the handwritten draft of a *Petition to the Pope for the Dispensation for the Marriage of the Prince of Wales with Henrietta Maria of France* makes clear, 'the Catholic people of Great Britain' who for almost 'one hundred years' had suffered 'waves of persecution' believed that 'this occasion has been chosen by God'.[72] Cardinal Richelieu seemed to share in this vision of an 'opportune time'. In a *Letter to the Catholics of*

England written as early as August 1624, he vowed to do everything in his power to ameliorate the difficulties which they continued to face.[73] Nevertheless, whereas English Protestants were relieved to have been saved from the spectre of a Spanish infanta as Queen, it has to be recognised that there was a lingering disappointment amongst some recusants that the Spanish Match had been irrevocably broken.[74] As David Sánchez Cano has deftly illustrated, during Charles's impetuous 1623 sojourn in Spain, to the joy of English Catholics, Philip IV had displayed all the opulence of Counter-Reformation worship to ensure, as one chronicler recorded, that 'God would prepare and soften [Charles's] heart, so that he would yield to the Roman Catholic Church'.[75] Distinct dissatisfaction with the parallel efforts of the French ambassador to negotiate some redress for the Catholic community framed contemporary letters. Fr Muscott in his newsletters to Thomas More in Rome concluded that 'wee ar fed with an empty spoone': 'ther is juggling in the world and that the French are deluded with faire words and false reports for . . . if you did but [see] the complaints and lamentations of catholikes and see the miseries they suffer it would pitty your hart . . . we are scourged and used miserably'.[76] Indeed, with the marriage treaty finally concluded even the French ambassador, the Duc de Chevreuse, was heard to complain that despite his zeal for 'the cause', he greatly mistrusted 'that all' would 'not be well' and found 'things to faule shorte of that they expected'.[77]

'Where the battle is great so is the glory': Henrietta Maria as Counter-Reformation Champion

What is remarkable is that against this shifting background of religious uncertainty, at barely fifteen years of age, and in the face of some recusant disappointment, Henrietta Maria's own intentions scarcely seemed to falter. Rather, within her husband's predominantly Protestant court, Henrietta Maria quickly established and prioritised the rituals of Roman Catholic worship for her own household. Such clarity of purpose is foregrounded on what should have been the happy occasion 'of the *publication of the* [royal] *marriage* and a *feaste at courte*'.[78] Fr William Ward observes how 'our Queene was somewhat indisposed' on this Sunday of royal celebrations. So these key state rituals were abruptly postponed until the following Tuesday. Yet, as Fr Ward continues, despite such infirmities, on this very same day, the Queen came 'about 12 a clocke by water from Whitehall to *Somersette house* to the duke of Cheverous where she heard service performed with great Reverence by monsieur Berule'.[79] Henrietta Maria's visible royal progress to Mass acutely suggests just how aware Henrietta Maria was of the potency of her actions. If, as the performance theorist Barbara Browning argues, 'the body says what cannot be spoken', then by deliberately and very publicly choosing to place herself at Mass, as opposed to a court festival in her honour, Henrietta Maria was clearly underscoring the importance which she placed upon her role as daughter of the Church.[80] Likewise, and with even greater effectiveness, by flagrantly refusing to attend her own coronation service in February 1626 (most probably to avoid being anointed by a Protestant bishop) Henrietta Maria can indeed be seen, as Alison Shell convincingly argues, to be possibly dissociating herself 'from the proceedings of a Protestant nation'.[81] The young Queen's sensitivity to the effective impact of such 'performance' was again, perhaps, behind episodes such as her rigorous retreat during the Holy Week of 1626. To the consternation of some Protestants, the Queen and her ladies were widely reported to be living cloistered together like nuns. Salvetti records how for this Easter the long gallery in Somerset House was specially 'divided and fitted up with cells, and a refectory, and an oratory, in the manner of a Monastery. There they sang the Hours of the Virgin.'[82] The individual devotion which stimulated such queenly conduct should by no means be denigrated. However, such actions also clearly indicate how adroitly Henrietta Maria, together with her priestly advisers, was able to operate in a country where, as we have seen, the slightest exploit with religious implications was pored over in the minutest detail.

At the same time as establishing these blatant Catholic practices both within her household and on the larger public stage, Henrietta Maria was busily engaged upon another project which would display her combined position as daughter of the Church and Queen of England: her first theatrical sponsorship of a play at court. Karen Britland has succinctly argued that *L'Artenice* is very much 'an assertion of the queen's identity, of her position within her own household and of her status as a princess of France'.[83] For Henrietta Maria an integral part of such an 'identity' was her Counter-Reformation mission to champion Catholicism within

England. Yet, by early 1626, in the face of Parliament's repeated demands that the recusancy laws be tightened, the situation for English Catholics, far from improving, was becoming increasingly unsettled. One surviving recusant petition from early 1626 openly urged Pope Urban VIII to insist that Henrietta Maria fulfil her promise to support the Catholic faith within England by 'preserving and strengthening ... the Catholic cause'.[84] Henrietta Maria's own distress for her Catholic subjects, and the worsening relationship between French and English powers, is evident from a letter to her spiritual adviser Fr Bérulle, where she states her hope that 'Dieu apaisera cet orage par vos bonnes prières' [God will appease this storm by your holy prayers].[85] Whilst Bérulle, in turn anxious for the Queen's spiritual welfare, specifically warned Henrietta Maria: 'Madame, ayez en horreur l'heresie, n'ecoutez point l'hérésie; ne prenez point de part a l'heresie, ni a ses mysteres' [Madame, you must have a horror of heresy, do not listen to any point of heresy; do not accept a single point of heresy, nor of her mysteries]. As he bleakly reminded his queenly charge, heresy 'persécute des innocens, elle a tranché la tête d'une Reine, grand'mère du Roi que vous avez pour mari: il la faut donc détester' [persecutes the innocent, heresy cut off the head of a Queen, the grandmother of the King, your husband: it is necessary to detest heresy].[86] Surely it is no coincidence that the groundbreaking play which Henrietta Maria deliberately staged, in which she assumed the title role of Artenice, is one where the heroine dutifully fulfils the gods' wishes regarding her marriage and successfully brings her lover, Alcidor, to a true understanding of faith.

It is important to remember that Henrietta Maria's decision to mount this elite staging of Racan's *L'Artenice* was no theatrical whim. Some two months before the Shrove Tuesday performance, Benjamin Rudyerd writing to Sir Francis Nethersole commented how 'the *demoiselles* mean to present a French pastoral wherein the Queen is a principal actress'.[87] In this interim period Somerset House was a hive of theatrical activity: over £2000 was spent on costumes alone, a theatre was specially erected in the great hall and, according to Salvetti, the twelve ladies who acted with the Queen were specially 'trained'.[88] In terms of English theatrical history alone, Henrietta Maria's startling performance in the title role of *L'Artenice* is of great importance. Clare McManus has explored how, under the auspices of Queen Anna, the female masquer had broken previously sacrosanct theatrical premises by blacking up, cross-dressing and even sporting a beard.[89] In *L'Artenice*, Henrietta Maria continued to push forward the theatrical boundaries against which her mother-in-law, Queen Anna, had transgressed, for this was the first time that a queen of England had spoken on the stage. The progressiveness of such royal behaviour within the English court is evident from Amerigo Salvetti's report to Cosimo de' Medici, the Grand Duke of Florence: 'the performance was conducted as privately as possible, inasmuch as it is an unusual thing in this country to see the Queen upon a stage; the audience consequently was limited to a few of the nobility, expressly invited, no others being admitted'.[90] Even with these restrictions, dismay was voiced. The Venetian ambassador recounts how the play 'did not give complete satisfaction, because the English objected to the first part being declaimed by the Queen'.[91] Within continental Europe however, as Melinda Gough has documented, such theatrical experiences were by no means novel. In 1623, as the Florentine ambassador, Giovanni Battista Gondi, records Henrietta Maria had herself, in equivalent theatrical conditions, 'recited a very beautiful play' together with many 'principal ladies of the court' before Louis XIII and his wife Anne of Austria.[92] As Gough argues, in the French court, far from shocking spectators, such royal performances were perceived as a means of presenting the 'moral virtue' of the Bourbon princesses.[93] So, in this performance of *L'Artenice*, Henrietta Maria can be seen to be drawing on her own theatrical experiences and transferring to the English court her own distinctive culture. Her success is evident from the high praise bestowed by those European ambassadors more familiar with such courtly performances: 'the pastoral succeeded admirably; not only in the decorations and changes of scenery, but also in the acting and recitation of the ladies – Her Majesty surpassing all the others'.[94]

L'Artenice, delivered in the Queen's native language, follows the convoluted suit by Alcidor of the beautiful shepherdess, Artenice. The text hangs on the insistence by 'la bonne Déesse' [the good goddess] that Artenice must marry only someone of her race and lineage. After a catalogue of tribulations, Alcidor is revealed to be Artenice's cousin so with a blood link established the couple are happily united. As we have explored in contemporary pamphlet literature, similarly both French and English, Catholic and Protestant polemicists deftly picked out, and swiftly embedded, links of lineage between King Charles and his new bride. The most potent, as Fr Bérulle's letters suggest, was the bond which Henrietta Maria shared with her royal husband through the figure of Mary Queen of Scots, King Charles's grandmother. Indeed, Fr Bérulle uses this royal lineage to warn the Queen of her vulnerable spiritual position, forcefully reminding Henrietta Maria against the dangers of heresy: 'celui-là même qui la professe en Angleterre, ne peut remonter jusqu'à sa grand-mère, qu'il ne la voie aux pieds d'un crucifix, mourante, et immolée aux fureurs de cet affreux monstre' [He himself who professes this heresy in England, cannot go back as far as his grandmother without seeing her at the foot of the cross, dying and sacrificed to the furies of this horrible monster].[95] In *L'Artenice* such dangers are swiftly transformed. For, on the stage of Somerset House at least, Artenice, in following the wishes of the gods, redeems her lover and restores him to his true heritage.

Strikingly, noticeably close connections are quickly established between Artenice and the gods whom Artenice's mother, Crisante, insists 'il faut pour nous server' [it is necessary that we serve] (*L'Artenice*, p. 94). Even before birth Crisante dedicates Artenice to the particular service of 'la bonne Déesse'. Remembering Henrietta Maria's own vigorous devotion to the Virgin Mary – indeed Fr Bérulle specifically visited the shrine at Loretto to gain celestial assistance during the Anglo-French marriage negotiations – the goddess's heavenly apparitions to Artenice at key moments throughout the play, specifically reminding her of her marital duties, would have been (at the very least) highly suggestive to an elite and partially Catholic audience. This is intensified, as Karen Britland also recognises in her discussion of the play's 'proselytising purpose', when Artenice struggles in her decision to join a religious community.[96] In a key exchange Philotée, the Mother Superior figure of the Temple of Diana, cautions Artenice about the realities of living the monastic life, 'nostre regle est étroitte & mal aisée à suiure' [our rule is strict and not easy to follow] (*L'Artenice*, p. 49). Philotée points out that there are 'plusieurs chemins' [many roads] to eternal life and that to live out a vocation amongst the vanities of daily life is perhaps more rewarding for, as John Milton was to famously argue in *Paradise Lost*, 'où le combat est grand la gloire l'est aussi' [where the battle is great the glory is also great] (*L'Artenice*, p. 48). In a sense this dilemma was exactly the position in which Henrietta Maria found herself. As Caroline Hibbard points out, 'to send so young a princess from a Catholic court to marry and live among heretics was unprecedented'.[97] With the additional papal burden of expectation that Henrietta Maria had undertaken, exacerbated by the renewed demands of the English Parliament against the recusant community, undoubtedly this new queen had a testing time ahead of her. On the very day before her wedding by proxy, Henrietta Maria had retreated (in the hub of international wedding preparations) to the Carmelite convent of the Incarnation in Paris.[98] Yet, like Artenice, the peace which she found there was only temporary. Ultimately, Henrietta Maria's chosen vocation as Queen of England, and protector of English Catholics was very much on the stage of public life. This is the intention which Henrietta Maria displays in *L'Artenice* to her noble audience.[99] In autumn 1625, recognising the difficulties which the young queen faced, Louis XIII and Marie de Médicis encouraged Henrietta Maria to 'avoir un zèle, une constance, un courage dignes de votre naissance, dans l'exercice de la religion at de la piété chrétienne' [to have a zeal, a constancy, a courage worthy of your birth, in the practising of religion and christian piety].[100] Drawing on her cultural heritage, this theatrical moment – with the Queen poised as Artenice on the elite stage at Somerset House – allows the audience a glimpse into Henrietta Maria's projection of a vision which combined her official role as Queen of England with her personal commitment to the Catholic faith. As Mark Franko asserts, for French nobles the elite stage was perceived as the 'most conspicuous arena of self display and transformation'.[101] What could be more natural than for Henrietta Maria to choose to assert her own queenly vocation than through performance? With English Catholics openly appealing to Urban VIII to urge Henrietta Maria to support the Catholic cause, the Queen's answer, and assurance, to both the recusant community and the wider Catholic powers can perhaps be seen in this astonishing court performance. Crucially, as is repeated throughout *L'Artenice*, 'souvent le bon-heur vient lors que moins on l'espere' [often good fortune comes when one has the least hope] (*L'Artenice*, p. 104).

The Roman Catholic appropriation of a biblical heroine: embroidering the Esther topos on the cultural imagination

L'Artenice may have been staged before a deliberately selective audience but the allusions behind this key image of the performance, of Artenice bringing her beloved to a renewed understanding of faith, were by no means confined to the highest echelons of society. Pope Urban VIII had himself proclaimed Henrietta Maria a modern-day Esther. The expectations of English Catholics regarding their new queen are evident from *The Draft of a Petition in Blackloe's Hand Asking the Pope to Apply to the Queen on Behalf of the Catholics*.[102] The common currency which this topos had gained, in recusant circles at least, is suggested by a letter from the beleaguered Richard Smith, Bishop of Chalcedon, when in 1628, he wrote to Henrietta Maria for personal succour in the hope that she would 'prove another Hester in appeasing the king's wrath'.[103] The resonance for English Catholics of such a biblical precedent informs Caroline culture; apparent even from the imaginative design of a seventeenth-century tapestry now hanging in Fenton House, Hampstead. As Figure 2 illustrates, in this overtly contemporary depiction of the Esther story, King Ahasuerus is woven with a striking likeness to Charles I, and the figure pleading at his kingly feet bears a suggestive resemblance to Queen Henrietta Maria.

2 *Esther Before Ahasuerus*, seventeenth-century stump-work hanging in Fenton House, Hampstead.

This style of embroidery, or stump-work as it is more correctly termed, was very much in vogue in Stuart England. John Taylor in *The Needles Excellency* creates a vivid cameo of a country where 'every where is fild / With Ladies, and Gentlewomen skild / In this rare Art'.[104] Perceived as the epitome of a young woman's long training in the skilled art of needlework, these highly crafted panels, beautifully finished with trimmings ranging from spangles to seed pearls, would be used on the side panels of mirrors or to cover caskets.[105] The designs themselves were drawn by professional draughtsmen who borrowed freely from the work of biblical engravers such as Gerard de Jode. The most popular choice of pattern was scenes with strong female heroines, like the Old Testament stories of Rebecca and Eleazar, Solomon and Sheba, and Esther and Ahasuerus.[106] As Rozika Parker persuasively argues, the iconography of women's embroidery 'is rarely given the serious consideration it deserves'.[107] Yet contemporaries of these early modern needlewomen were quick to recognise the stump-work's inherent creativity. Richard Shorelyker stressed in his pattern book *A Schole-House for the Needle* (1632) how his outlines served 'but to helpe and inlarge' the needlewoman's own 'inventions'.[108] Far from being purely frivolous, for some early modern women embroidery was a singular opportunity to engage with the wider world.[109] As Xanthe Brooke, the curator of embroideries at the Lady Lever Art Gallery in Port Sunlight, remarks: 'these seemingly naïve pictures' have 'significant stories to tell . . . they actually reveal much about the activities and expectations of the female population, . . . and occasionally they throw light on developments in the national political, religious, cultural and aesthetic life of English society at grass-roots level'.[110]

This anonymous stump-work of Esther and Ahasuerus, although most likely embroidered in the 1640s–1660s, points to the cultural moment of the mid-1630s. This is suggested by the needlewoman's choice of wide-legged breeches and bucket-topped boots for Ahasuerus, and in Esther's two-tiered sleeve and lace collar which were very much in vogue in the 1630s.[111] Such a dating is reinforced by the incongruously large tulip which appears to levitate behind Esther's lady-in-waiting, a particularly popular motif which points to the 1630s Tulipomania craze. Depicted in the background of the tapestry are key elements of the Esther story: King Ahasuerus on horseback seeking his new bride and wooing Esther who, as Thomas

Heywood glosses in his contemporary version of the biblical story, 'found favour in the eyes of all that beheld her'.[112] In the far right corner, wearing a conspicuous black hat, sits Mordechai, Esther's uncle. This wise counsellor helps Esther to outwit Haman, the King's favourite, who planned to wipe out the Jewish element of the nation, dismissing them to Ahasuerus as a people who 'neither observe they their Kings lawes, nor is it his profit to suffer them' (*Exemplary Lives*, p. 52). The foreground of the stump-work focuses on the decisive moment when Esther, following Mordechai's advice, goes to the King to make 'humble supplication' for the lives of 'her and her people' (*Exemplary Lives*, p. 54). Esther has faced death in going 'uncalled' to the King and it is only after Mordechai points out, 'who knoweth, but thou art come into the Kingdome for such a purpose' (*Exemplary Lives*, p. 55), that she undertakes such an ordeal. Falling prostrate at the King's feet, she begs Ahasuerus 'that he would utterly abolish all those wicked decrees' against her people (*Exemplary Lives*, p. 62). In this principal cameo of the stump-work, the truth behind Mordechai's prophecy is revealed, as the King can be seen to be holding 'his golden Scepter' towards Esther (*Exemplary Lives*, p. 62), a powerful symbol of his vow to grant her wishes, even to bestowing on her half his kingdom.

Examined in such detail it is easy to see why this Esther story was such a potent narrative for the English recusant community, neatly summed up by Thomas Heywood's précis of how Esther's 'beauty so far with the King prevail'd / Joyn'd with her prayer, and fasting she redeemd / All her sad Nation, then, most dis-esteemd' (*Exemplary Lives*, p. 44). Rare examples remain of stump-works which have obvious layers of political meaning: such as Dame Dorothy Selby's infamously anti-papist embroidery of Samuel Ward's engraving of *The Double Deliverance* depicting the defeat of the Spanish Armada and the Gunpowder Plot.[113] In *From Man to Man*, Olive Schreiner contends that within embroidery 'lies all the passion of some woman's soul finding voiceless expression'.[114] So this stump-work from the 1630s can be seen to give 'voiceless expression' to all the possibilities embodied in the recusant community's own Esther figurehead, Henrietta Maria. For the women of the English recusant community this embroidered emblem would have had particular resonance. The recusant matriarchy is credited by historians with playing an integral part in the survival of the old faith, so they would have had a decided interest in the success of Henrietta Maria's mission.[115] With Esther poised at the pivotal moment of triumph, this stump-work is very much wrought as an image of imminent expectation, which, in turn, gives deeper adumbrations to the Water Poet John Taylor's contemporary depiction of a needlewoman as a 'grave Reformer of old Rents decayd'.[116]

With division rife within the established Church, and the oppositional recusant community suspended in a moment of cautious anticipation, what is unquestionable in 1625 is England's deeply entrenched and vibrant religio-political discourse. The arrival of Henrietta Maria and her Roman Catholic train must be examined against these shifting plate tectonics of religious belief. Whilst the expectations of Protestant England focused on Charles I, the hopes of English recusants centred on the advent of Henrietta Maria. Where commentators such as John Gee woefully decried the English religious landscape as 'full of strange formes and colours', Henrietta Maria was surprisingly undaunted; boldly signifying in a groundbreaking performance her avowal to do 'what may be useful and advantageous to the religion and to the Catholics of Great Britain'.[117] For the English recusant community, the magnitude of implications behind Henrietta Maria's stage role of Artenice is eloquently voiced through this painstakingly crafted Esther tapestry. In this stumpwork, as with the Queen's lead role in *L'Artenice*, the usually silenced female voice finds an outlet: this time, the needlewoman, like Ovid's Philomel, uses the 'tedious sampler' to 'sew her mind'.[118] As we will explore in the following chapters, James Shirley and William Davenant engage with this Counter-Reformation ideal to debate on the commercial stage the continuing attractions of the old faith. With the religious landscape of Stuart England very much on the cusp of change, recusants did indeed have reason to hope, as John Floyd prophesied in 1623, that the mists were clearing, to herald the 'surest presage of a fayre Day'.[119]

Notes

1 John Gee, *The Foot Out of the Snare: With a Detection of Sundry Late Practices and Impostures of the Priests and Jesuits in England* (London: 1624), p. 2.
2 Birch, *Court and Times*, vol. 1, Dr Meddus to the Rev. Joseph Mead, London, 17 June 1625, p. 29.

3 *Ibid.*, p. 30.
4 Simonds D'Ewes, *The Autobiography and Correspondence of Sir Simonds D'Ewes, Bart., During the Reigns of James I and Charles I*, ed. James Orchard Halliwell, 2 vols (London: 1845), vol. 1, p. 272.
5 *Ibid.*, p. 273.
6 'Optata occasio a Deo', AAW/A18, 'Draft of a Petition to Pope Urban VIII in Thomas More's hand for the Dispensation for the Marriage of the Prince of Wales with Henrietta Maria of France', p. 549; Thomas Ball, *The Life of the Renowned Doctor Preston* (Oxford: 1885), p. 105.
7 Green, *Queen's Letters*, Henrietta Maria to the King my brother, undated, p. 8.
8 James Howell, *Epistolae Ho-Elianae: Familiar Letters Domestic and Forren; Divided Into Six Sections: Partly Historicall, Politicall, Philosophicall, Upon Emergent Occasions* (London: 1645), section 4, pp. 16–17.
9 For a detailed discussion of this period see Thomas Cogswell, *The Blessed Revolution: English Politics and the Coming of War, 1621–1624* (Cambridge: Cambridge University Press, 1989).
10 Alexander Samson (ed.), *The Spanish Match: Prince Charles's Journey to Madrid, 1623* (Aldershot: Ashgate, 2006).
11 Stephen Jerome, *Irelands Jubilee; Or Joyes Io-Pæan; For Prince Charles His Welcome Home* (Dublin: 1624), p. 212.
12 Thomas Brewer, *The Weeping Lady: Or London Like Ninivie in Sack-Cloth. Describing the Mappe Of Her Own Miserie, in This Time of Her Heavy Visitation; With Her Hearty Prayers, Admonition, and Pious Meditations* (London: 1625), sig. B1v.
13 Peter Lake, 'Constitutional Consensus and Puritan Opposition in the 1620s: Thomas Scott and the Spanish Match', *HJ*, 25 (1982), 805–25.
14 Cogswell, *Blessed Revolution*, p. 34; J. Leeds Barroll, *Anna of Denmark, Queen of England: A Cultural Biography* (Philadelphia: University of Pennsylvania Press, 2001), pp. 162–72.
15 See Katharine R. Firth, *The Apocalyptic Tradition in Reformation Britain, 1530–1645* (Oxford: Oxford University Press, 1979).
16 See the furore over Richard Montague, *A Gagg for the New Gospell? No. A New Gagg for an Old Goose* (London: 1624).
17 This term was first used in a modern critical sense by Florence Higham, *Catholic and Reformed. A Study of the Anglican Church, 1559–1662* (London: SPCK, 1962). Anthony Milton questions Higham's paradigm of the Anglican 'middle way' in *Catholic and Reformed*.
18 John Summerson, *Inigo Jones* (Harmondsworth: Penguin, 1966), especially, p. 76.

19 Gorges to Buckingham, 8 February 1624, SP 14/159/22.
20 Bossy, *Catholic Community*, pp. 182–94.
21 *Ibid.*, pp. 11–74; see also Peter Holmes, *Resistance and Compromise: The Political Thought of the Elizabethan Catholics* (Cambridge: Cambridge University Press, 1982).
22 Bone, *Queen of the Cavaliers*, p. 37.
23 Martin J. Havran, *The Catholics in Caroline England* (Oxford: Oxford University Press, 1962), p. 27.
24 Green, *Queen's Letters*, Henrietta Maria to Pope Urban VIII, Paris, 6 April 1625, p. 9.
25 Lake, 'Anti-Popery', pp. 72–107.
26 I. R. P., aka John Floyd, *A Word of Comfort: Or A Discourse Concerning the Late Lamentable Accident of the Fall of a Roome, At a Catholike Sermon, in the Black-friars At London* (St Omer: 1623), p. 11.
27 Thomas Goad, *The Dolefull Even-Song: Or a True, Particular and Impartiall Narration of That Fearefull and Sudden Calamity, Which Befell the Preacher, Mr. Drury* (London: 1623), sig. E2r.
28 See the lists attached to W. C., *The Fatall Vesper: Or a True and Punctuall Relation of That Lamentable and Fearefull Accident, Hapning on Sunday in the Afternoone, Being the 26. of October Last, by the Fall of a Roome in the Black-Friars . . . With the Names . . . of Such Persons as Perished* (London: 1623), sigs G1v–G3r; Goad, *Dolefull Even-Song*, sigs K1v–K4v.
29 Anon., *Something Written by Occasion of That Fatall and Memorable Accident in the Blacke Frier* (London: 1623), pp. 8–9.
30 Gee, *Foot Out of the Snare*, sig. A4r.
31 Anon., *Memorable Accident*, p. 22.
32 Thomas Middleton, *A Game at Chess*, ed. Thomas Howard-Hill (Manchester: Manchester University Press, 1993), Alvise Valaresso, Venetian ambassador to the Doge and Senate, August 1624, p. 204.
33 John Chamberlain to Sir Dudley Carleton, August 1624; Don Carlos Coloma to the Conde-Duque Olivares, August 1624, quoted in *ibid.*, p. 205, p. 197.
34 Don Carlos Coloma to the Conde-Duque Olivares, August 1624, quoted in *ibid.*, pp. 194–5.
35 D'Ewes, *Autobiography*, vol. 1, p. 257.
36 Peter Heylyn, *A Survey of the Estate of France, and of Some of the Adjoyning Ilands: Taken in the Description of the Principal Cities and Chief Provinces* (London: 1656); William Bouwsma, 'Gallicanism and the Nature of Christendome', in Anthony Molho and John Tedeschi (eds), *Renaissance Studies in Honour of Hans Baron* (Dekalb: University of Illinois Press, 1971), pp. 815–26.

37 Birch, *Court and Times*, vol. 1, Rev. Joseph Mead to Sir Martin Stuteville, 30 April 1625, p. 17.
38 Dr Meddus to the Rev. Joseph Mead, 17 June 1625, *ibid.*, p. 31.
39 D'Ewes, *Autobiography*, vol. 1, p. 257.
40 John Reynolds, *Vox Coeli; Or Newes From Heaven, of a Consultation There Held by the High and Mighty Princes, King Hen. 8 . . . Edw. 6, Prince Henry, Queene Mary, . . . Elizabeth and Anne. Wherein Spaines Ambition and Treacheries . . . Are Unmasked, . . . Particularly Towards England, and Now Especially Under the Pretended Match of the Prince Charles with the Infanta Dona Maria. Whereunto Is Annexed Two Letters Written by Qween Mary From Heaven* (London: 1624), p. 39.
41 Abraham Darcie, *Genealogie et Alliance de l'Ancienne et Renommee Maison de la Trimoville* (London: 1626), especially sigs B2r–B3r; Ben Jonson, *The Fortunate Isles and their Union* (London: 1624), sig. C3r.
42 Thomas Overbury, *Sir Thomas Overbury. His Observations in His Travailes Upon the State of the XVII Provinces as They Stood Anno Dom. 1609. The Treatie of Peace Being Then On Foote* (London: 1626), p. 22.
43 George Chapman, *The Conspiracy and Tragedy of Charles Duke of Byron*, ed. John Margeson (Manchester: Manchester University Press, 1988).
44 Anon., *The Interpreter: Wherin Three Principall Termes of State Much Mistaken by the Vulgar Are Clearly Unfolded* (Edinburgh: 1622), pp. 12–13.
45 William Bedell, *The Copies of Certaine Letters Which Have Passed Between Spaine and England in Matter of Religion, Concerning the Generall Motives to the Romane Obedience. Between J. W. and W. Bedell* (London: 1624), sig. *3v.
46 G. P. V. Akrigg (ed.), *Letters of King James VI and I* (Berkeley: University of California Press, 1984), Letter from James I to Prince Charles and the Duke of Buckingham, 31 July 1623, p. 420.
47 Jerzy Limon perceives a conscious political campaign in the drama of 1623–4 backed by the Prince and Buckingham: see his *Dangerous Matter, English Drama and Politics in 1623–1624* (Cambridge: Cambridge University Press, 1986), especially pp. 1–20.
48 N. W. Bawcutt, *The Control and Censorship of Caroline Drama: The Records of Sir Henry Herbert, Master of the Revels 1623–73* (Oxford: Clarendon Press, 1996), p. 159.
49 William Shakespeare, *Henry IV Part 1*, eds Herbert Weil and Judith Weil (Cambridge: Cambridge University Press, 1997), I.ii.172–5.

50 Francis Beaumont and John Fletcher, *Cupids Revenge* (London: 1615). For ease of reference see Fredson Bowers (ed.), *Beaumont and Fletcher Dramatic Works*, 5 vols (Cambridge: Cambridge University Press, 1970), vol. 2, pp. 317–448.
51 Bawcutt, *Records of Sir Henry Herbert*, p. 159.
52 P. R. Seddon (ed.), *Letters of John Holles, 1587–1637*, 3 vols (Nottingham: 1975), vol. 2, p. 285.
53 John Donne, *The First Sermon Preached to King Charles At St. James*, 3 April 1625 (London: 1625), pp. 13–14; see Evelyn M. Simpson and George R. Potter (eds), *The Sermons of John Donne*, 10 vols (Berkeley and Los Angeles: University of California Press, 1953), vol. 6, pp. 241–61, p. 245.
54 Brewer, *Weeping Lady*, sig. B1v.
55 I. B. C., *A Looking Glasse For New Reformers. Answering Paul Rainalds, Scotishmans Letter Perswading His Brother to Forsake the True Ancient Catholike and Roman Religion* ('Lion', false imprint, probably Bordeaux: not before 1625), p. 355; John Copinger, *The Theatre of Catholique and Protestant Religion* (St Omer: 1620), p. 549.
56 Jacques du Perron, *A Letter Written from Paris by the Lord Cardinal of Peron to Monsr. Casaubon in England*, trans. Thomas Owen (St Omer: 1612), p. 51. See also Copinger, *Theatre of Catholique*, pp. 34, 282.
57 William Bishop, *Maister Perkins Reformed Catholique Together with Maister Robert Abbots Defence Thereof Largly Refuted, and the Same Refutation Newly Reviewed and Augmented* (Douai: 1625), sigs ĕ4r, ī4r.
58 Cited by Alison Shell, *Catholic Imagination*, p. 152.
59 Apparently Anna had a beautiful chapel at Oatlands and Roman Catholic priests always within call at Hampton Court: see Ethel Williams, *Anne of Denmark, Wife of James VI of Scotland, James I of England* (Harlow: Longmans, 1970), p. 200. See also Barroll, *Anna of Denmark*, Epilogue.
60 *Ibid.*, see also W. Bliss, 'The Religious Beliefs of Anne of Denmark', *Historical Review*, 4 (1889), p. 110.
61 Rosso to the Doge and Senate, June 1626. *CSP Ven 1625–1626*, p. 451.
62 HMC Report, Salisbury, XXII, p. 198.
63 AAW/A18, M. G. [Muscott] to Thomas More, December 1624, p. 449.
64 Caroline Hibbard, 'Translating Royalty: Henrietta Maria and the Transition from Princess to Queen', *The Court Historian*, 5 (2000), 15–28, especially pp. 19–20.

65 Birch, *Court and Times*, vol. 1, Dr Meddus to Rev. Joseph Mead, 24 June 1625, p. 33.
66 Anthony Milton, 'A Qualified Intolerance' in Marotti, *Catholicism and Anti-Catholicism*, pp. 85–116.
67 Nicholas Sander, *A Treatise of the Images of Christ and of His Saints: and That It Is Unlawfull to Breake Them, and Lawfull to Honour Them* (St Omer: 1567, reprinted 1625), sig. A6r.
68 Robert Southwell, *An Epistle of Comfort, to the Reverend Priestes & to the Honorable, Worshipful & Other of the Laye Sort Restrained in Durance for the Catholicke Fayth* (Paris: 1588), pp. 167–8.
69 John Gee remarks on this hive of printing activity: 'understand you not, how laborious and vigilant our Adversaries now are, forbearing no time, sparing no paines to captivate and destroy? Witnesse the swarmes of their bookes, which you may heare humming up and downe in every corner both of City and Countrey', *Foot Out of the Snare*, p. 23.
70 Sander, *Images of Christ*, sig. Aiiiir. See also W. B., aka Lawrence Anderton, *One God, One Fayth: Or a Discourse Against Those Luke-Warme Christians, Who Extend Salvation to All Kinds of Fayth and Religion* (St Omer: 1625), p. 98.
71 Cogswell, *Blessed Revolution*, John Woolley to William Trumbull, 28 February 1624, p. 171.
72 'populi Cathci magna Britannia ... qui centum iam annos ... Persecutionum fluctibus agitati ... optata occasio a Deo opportunissimo tempore', from 'Petition to the Pope for the Dispensation for the Marriage of the Prince of Wales with Henrietta Maria of France', AAW/A18, p. 549.
73 AAW/A18, Cardinal Richelieu to the Catholics of England, 15 August 1624, p. 309.
74 AAW/A18, John Colleton to Urban VIII, 1 September 1624, p. 335.
75 Cited by David Sánchez Cano, 'Entertainments in Madrid for the Prince of Wales: Political Functions of Festivals', in Samson (ed.), *The Spanish Match*, pp. 51–74, p. 67.
76 AAW/A18, G. Muscott to T. More, 1 October 1624, p. 371. See also AAW/A18, pp. 375, 385; AAW/A19, p. 9.
77 AAW/A19, William Ward (martyr in 1643) to Rant, June 1625, p. 166.
78 *Ibid.*, p. 166.
79 *Ibid.*, p. 166.
80 Barbara Browning, 'Samba: the Body Articulate', in Ellen Goellner and Jacqueline Murphy (eds), *Bodies of the Text: Dance as Theory, Literature as Dance* (New Brunswick, NJ: Rutgers University Press, 1995), pp. 39–56, p. 43.

81 Shell, *Catholic Imagination*, pp. 152–3.
82 HMC XI (1), p. 57.
83 Britland, *Drama at the Courts*, pp. 35–52, p. 43.
84 'in causa Catholica tuenda et augendam', from 'Draft of the Petition in Blackloe's hand asking the Pope to apply to the Queen on behalf of the Catholics', AAW/A20, p.171.
85 M. Tabaraud, *Histoire de Pierre de Bérulle*, 2 vols (Paris: 1817), vol. 1, pp. 384–5.
86 *Ibid.*, p. 392.
87 Sir Benjamin Rudyerd to Sir Francis Nethersole, December 1625. *CSP Dom 1625–1626*, p. 179.
88 Malone Society, *Collections*, vol. 2 (Oxford: 1931), pp. 328–31; PRO, A. O. I.2424/56.
89 McManus, *Anna of Denmark*, pp. 82–5.
90 HMC XI (1), p. 47.
91 Pesaro to the Doge and Senate, March 1626. *CSP Ven 1625–1626*, pp. 345–6.
92 Giovanni Battista Gondi, Florentine ambassador in Paris, to Grand Duke of Tuscany, 5 October 1623, cited by Melinda Gough, 'Courtly *Comediantes*: Henrietta Maria and Amateur Women's Stage Plays in France and England', in Pamela Allen Brown and Peter Parolin (eds), *Women Players in England, 1500–1660: Beyond the All-Male Stage* (Aldershot: Ashgate, 2005), pp. 193–215, p. 203.
93 Gough, 'Courtly *Comediantes*', p. 201.
94 HMC XI (1), p. 47.
95 Tabaraud, *Pierre de Bérulle*, p. 392. Thanks to M. A. Hofmaier for translation.
96 Britland, *Drama at the Courts*, p. 50.
97 Hibbard, 'Translating Royalty', p. 17.
98 *Ibid.*, p. 19.
99 See also Britland, *Drama at the Courts*, p. 52.
100 Tabaraud, *Pierre de Bérulle*, p. 384
101 Mark Franko, *Dance As Text: Ideologies of the Baroque Body* (Cambridge: Cambridge University Press, 1993), p. 2.
102 AAW/A22, p. 171.
103 AAW/A22, 'A coppy of the Bp of Chalcedon's letter to the Queen in English', December 1628, p. 667.
104 John Taylor, *The Needles Excellency: A New Booke Wherin are Divers Admirable Workes Wrought With the Needle* (London: 12th edition, 1640), sig. A2v.
105 Sidney Hand, *Old English Needlework of the Sixteenth and Seventeenth Centuries* (London: Sidney Hand, 1920), pp. 3–6.

106 Xanthe Brooke, *The Lady Lever Art Gallery Catalogue of Embroideries* (Stroud: Alan Sutton, National Museums and Galleries on Merseyside, 1992), pp. 13–16; see also Margaret Swain, *Figures on Fabric: Embroidery Design Sources and Their Application* (London: A. and C. Black, 1980), pp. 48–9.
107 Rozika Parker, *The Subversive Stitch: Embroidery and the Making of the Feminine* (London: Womens Press Ltd, 1984), p. 12.
108 Richard Shorleyker, *A Schole-House for the Needle* (London: 1632), sig. A2.
109 Susan Frye, 'Sewing Connections: Elizabeth Tudor, Mary Stuart, Elizabeth Talbot, and Seventeenth-Century Anonymous Needleworkers', in Susan Frye and Karen Robertson (eds), *Maids and Mistresses, Cousins and Queens: Women's Alliances in Early Modern England* (Oxford: Oxford University Press, 1998), pp. 165–82, p. 166.
110 Brooke, *Catalogue of Embroideries*, p. viii.
111 Liz Arthur, *Embroidery at the Burrell Collection, 1600–1700* (Glasgow: Glasgow Museums, 1995), pp. 99–100.
112 Thomas Heywood, *The Exemplary Lives and Memorable Acts of Nine the Most Worthy Women of the World, Three Jewes, Three Gentiles, Three Christians* (London: 1640), p. 51. All subsequent references in the text to *Exemplary Lives* are from this edition.
113 Brooke, *Catalogue of Embroideries*, pp. 18–20; Arthur, *Burrell Collection*, pp. 90–1.
114 Cited by Parker, *Subversive Stitch*, p. 15.
115 A. L. Rowse, *The England of Elizabeth* (London: Macmillan, 1951), pp. 488, 491; Bossy, *Catholic Community*, pp. 155–8.
116 Taylor, *Needles Excellency*, sig. A1r.
117 See note 7.
118 William Shakespeare, *Titus Andronicus*, ed. Alan Hughes (Cambridge: Cambridge University Press, 1994), II.iv.39.
119 Floyd, *Word of Comfort*, p. 57.

2

James Shirley: the early texts, 1625–1629

> It is a just complaint amongst the better sort of persons, that the finest witts loose themselves in the vainest follies, spilling much Art in some idle phansie . . . sure it is a thing greatly to be lamented, that men of so high conceit, should so much abase their abilities, that when they have racked them to the uttermost endeavour, all the prayse that they reape of their imployment, consisteth in this, that they have wisely told a foolish tale, and carryed a long lye very smoothly to the end. Yet this inconvenience might find some excuse if the drift of their discourse levelled at any vertous marke. *For in fables are often figured moral truths, & that covertly uttered to a common good, which without a maske would not find so free a passage.*[1]

James Shirley has been described by Arthur H. Nason as 'the preeminent' dramatist of the reign of Charles I: 'the last of the Elizabethans, the prophet of the Restoration . . . friend of the king and champion of the queen'.[2] More grudgingly, Edward Phillips has deemed him 'a just pretender to more than the meanest Place among the *English* Poets . . . by some he is accounted little inferior to *Fletcher* himself'.[3] As Marvin Morillo records, Shirley has been dismissed too often as an 'innocuous craftsman', busily 'rearranging shards from Fletcher, Jonson and Shakespeare into ingeniously wrought but empty pieces for the players at the Cockpit'.[4] Indeed, Algernon Swinburne openly berates Shirley's 'multitudinous works' as having 'absolutely no principle of life, no reason for being, no germ of vitality whatever'.[5] Yet, if we turn to one of the rare contemporary critiques of Caroline drama, Abraham Wright's commonplace book *Excerpta Quaedem per A. W. Adolescentem* compiled in the 1640s, Shirley's plays emerge as this theatregoer's preferred stage experience. Wright favours Shirley's *The Bird in a*

Cage over Shakespeare's *Hamlet* and even provides directions as to the best place to acquire Shirley's texts in London, namely the bookseller Francis Eglesfield's shop in the churchyard of St Paul's Cathedral: 'see for Shirleys plaies at the marigold in the yard'.[6] Armed with such a testimony one has to question the image constructed by critics of Shirley, of a playwright overshadowed by the dramatic brilliance of his Jacobean counterparts, and, in turn, the paradigm of Caroline drama itself, which until the final decades of the last century was indicted for frivolous decadence.

Martin Butler was the first to challenge this archetype in his seminal work *Theatre and Crisis*. By deftly repositioning plays from the 1630s firmly within the political contexts of their staging, Butler has transformed critical understanding of the Caroline theatre. Focusing on texts which repeatedly articulate issues which he describes as in 'opposition' to the King's court or 'puritan', he exposes a drama which in seeking to 'change its world' reveals a society 'seriously at disagreement with itself'.[7] From such a reorientation it can be seen how theatregoers like Abraham Wright actively engaged with stimulating plays, created for an intelligent audience, in a space which encouraged debate. Yet this perception can be fully comprehended only when we recognise that puritanism was not the only sectarian force to voice resistance through drama; nor was the King the only monarch addressed. As is increasingly understood, within the bonds of the royal marriage there were two courts. The Queen's household also had the potential to broker power, dispense patronage and engage with the complex religio-political tensions of the age.[8] Indeed, as we discussed in Chapter 1, barely eight months after arriving in England Henrietta Maria had swiftly showcased her own vision of her role as Catholic Queen Consort in an elite performance of Racan's *L'Artenice*. In the following chapters, as we shall explore, the political possibilities imbued within such a provocative theatrical experience were challenged and redefined on the commercial stage.

Even Shirley's earliest texts are energised by the concerns of the English Roman Catholic community, dynamically shaping and reflecting reaction to this self-imposed figurehead. *The Witty Fair One* (licensed 1628, published 1633) exposes unease at the insistent corrosion of language distinctive to recusant circles by fashionable society's fascination for all things pertaining to the new Queen. The recusant community required a strong (and sympathetic) champion and Shirley engages with this in *The Wedding* (licensed 1626, published 1629) through a wider defence of the institution of the Roman Catholic Church. Finally, in *The Grateful Servant* (licensed 1629, published 1630), through the figure of Leonora, a foreign princess who brings salvation to her adopted homeland, Shirley urges the transforming possibilities of Henrietta Maria's own position as Queen Consort. Crucially all three texts have a feminocentric crux: a layering of images which not only directly engages with the Queen's stage persona of Artenice but is rooted in the matriarchal essence of the English Catholic community. Such a searching focus seriously questions Adolphus Ward's belief that Shirley's 'chosen sphere of fancy was a world of sun and sweetness'.[9] And it is peculiarly fitting, for significantly, this playwright servant of the Queen is himself traditionally believed to have had recusant convictions.

James Shirley's self-positioning within the Roman Catholic community

Anthony Wood in his *Athenae Oxonienses* is the first biographer to mention Shirley's apostasy. Having allegedly gleaned his information from Shirley's son, a 'butler of Furnival's Inn, in Holborn', Wood recounts how

> soon after entring into holy orders, [Shirley] became a minister of God's word in, or near to, St. Albans in Hertfordshire. But being then unsetled in his mind, he changed his religion for that of Rome, left his living and taught a grammar school in the said town of St. Albans; which employment also he finding uneasy to him, he retired to the metropolis, lived in Greys-inn, and set up for a play-maker, and gained not only a considerable livelihood, but also very great respect and encouragement from persons of quality, especially from Henrietta Maria the queen consort, who made him her servant.[10]

From this tale of 'unease', and with varying degrees of enthusiasm, Shirley has been assumed into the English Roman Catholic tradition. Joseph Gillow's proud affirmation of Shirley's Catholic beliefs in his *Bibliographic Dictionary of English Catholics* proves a stark contrast to Barnett-Smith's apologetic condescension in *The Gentleman's Magazine*:

> There was a fine touch of conscientiousness in Shirley; he changed his religion from no interested motives; indeed, it would have been to his worldly interests to have stifled his convictions; so that, however we may regard the faith which he adopted, we must at least do him the justice to admit that he firmly adhered to it through dark and evil days.[11]

Critics such as Ben Lucow and R. K. Zimmer have concurred with Barnett-Smith. Lucow concludes that Shirley's conversion would 'appear to be a matter of personal conviction' for 'the conversion to Catholicism is supposed to have occurred in the early 1620s, before he began writing for the theatre and before Charles and Henrietta Maria came to the throne'.[12] Yet, in this early modern period where religion and politics are so inextricably entwined, Lucow's assertion that Shirley's apostasy had 'no bearings on his political beliefs or on his goals in the theatre' has to be questioned.[13] Shirley's religious outlook directly informs the public discourse of his theatrical texts, and the corpus of evidence surrounding these principles suggests firm recusant convictions.

The documented facts regarding Shirley's life come from a mix of parish and educational records, and court documents. Born on 7 September 1596, Shirley attended the Merchant Taylors' School from October 1608 to June 1612. Briefly working for Thomas Frith, as a scrivener based in London's Royal Exchange, Shirley matriculated at Katherine Hall, Cambridge, in Easter 1615, and received his degree on 4 April 1617.[14] By June 1618 Shirley was living in the parish of St Albans. Having prepared for the ministry of the established Church (apparent in the word 'clerk' after his name upon his marriage on 1 June with Elizabeth Gilmet), Shirley was finally ordained 'deacon and priest' on 19 September 1619. From Wood's account, Shirley then grew 'unsetled in his mind', changed his religion, gave up his living and became the local schoolmaster. Other documents reveal that this series of events was slightly more complex. Evidently, as early as November 1618 Shirley had been attracted to the teaching profession. In this year, when Elizabeth Gilmet's father was mayor of St Albans, Shirley was promised the headmastership of the grammar school, a position which he assumed in January 1621 and continued in until 1624. It is difficult to ascertain Shirley's precise status during these three years. Was he simply a teacher or did he combine teaching and clerical duties?[15]

If documented records remain inconclusive (which is by no means unusual in these uncertain times), internal evidence provides a strong case for Shirley's apostasy. Circumstances surrounding Shirley's time in St Albans are of special concern. Sandra Burner's research into the *Acta of the Archdeaconry of St Albans* reveals that as early as 1620 Shirley demonstrated a strong inclination for the church ceremony traditionally associated with Roman Catholicism and promoted within the established Church by clerics such as Lancelot Andrewes.[16] On 31 July 1620 records from the *Acta* state that one Mistress Middleton of St Albans 'spake words agaynst one Mr. Sherley a minister and preacher sayinge rather and better it were to staye at home than go to church to hear one more fitter to be on a stage playe than in a pulpit and *that he use not bowe in the pulpit* with other wordes'.[17] Noticeably Burner's analysis of this court document misses its overtly religious implications: 'so Shirley was preaching from time to time, probably in the St. Albans Abbey Church; and his congregation was recipient or victim of his dramatic sensibility'.[18] Yet such 'dramatic sensibility' would become the focus of virulent polemical debate, as Peter Smart's godly sermon from 1628 spotlights, in his question, does 'religion consist in Altar-ducking... starting up and squatting downe, nodding of heads, and whirling about, til their noses stand Eastwards'?[19]

Mistress Middleton's concern at such popish ways would have been lightly dismissed by at least one noble family of St Albans parish, that of the Calverts of Hertingfordbury. Lady Calvert was a staunch recusant whose strong beliefs influenced not only her husband's conversion but possibly Shirley's own religious 'unease'. Shirley's acquaintance with the Calvert family is convincingly argued by the editor of Shirley's poems, Ray Armstrong. As Armstrong notes, the Rawlinson version of 'Upon a Gentlewoman that died of a Fever' has the added reference 'Sr. G: Ca: Ladie'.[20] After examining every possibility, Armstrong concludes that the most likely identification is with Lady Anne Mynne, wife of Sir George Calvert. Shirley's association of Lady Anne with the New Testament parable of the holy virgins who faithfully tend their oil lamps is, at the very least, a conventional epitaph on a life well lived. But the time of her death, 1622, together with the presentation of this known Roman Catholic as Calvert's 'Lent-him-heaven-on-earth a vertuous wife', intimates that Lady Calvert impressed Shirley on a more profound level.[21] These suggestive religious implications between the Calvert family and Shirley deepen. The year 1625 witnessed Shirley's final abandonment of his troubled career as minister and teacher at St Albans. However, 1625 was also the moment when Sir Calvert, Lord Baltimore openly declared his own recusant beliefs. Amerigo Salvetti records how all the officers of the Privy Council were sworn into their official positions under the new monarch, Charles I, with the exception

> of Lord Baltimore, Secretary of State, who remarked to His Majesty that, as every one knew him to be a Catholic, he could not now serve him in the same high office without exciting jealousy in others, nor was he willing to take an oath so wounding to his religious feelings. It is said that His Majesty replied 'that it was much better thus to state his opinions, rather than to retain his office by equivocation, as some did', which the King could not approve.[22]

Once established in London, the corpus of evidence surrounding Shirley's own beliefs continues to grow. One curious facet pointing to an allegiance to the old faith is the variant coats of arms in two existing portraits of James Shirley. Anthony Wood questioned this appropriation, remarking how Shirley 'was descended from the Shirleys of Sussex or Warwickshire, as by his arms (if he had a right to them) painted over his picture hanging in the school-gallery at Oxon'.[23] In 1855 Evelyn Shirley supported Wood's query, pondering in an article on Henry Shirley, the possible author of *The Marty'rd Souldier*: 'I wish I could include the more celebrated poet James Shirley – the author of those noble verses, "the glories of our birth and state" – also among the worthies of the family tree: but the genealogy of the Shirleys of Sussex is so well ascertained, that I fear this to be impossible.'[24] Subsequent research on the Warwickshire branch of the family also bears no link to the James Shirley born in 1596 to a London merchant family. One could argue that Shirley's adoption of these shields is merely the playwright's desire to gain respectability – the arms giving a veneer of quality to his portraits. But research into the Shirley family poses the question just how highly regarded would this family have been in the eyes of Protestant England? The Sussex branch of the family was renowned for the exploits of Anthony Shirley, whose sojourn in Persia and conversion to Roman Catholicism had become matter for the stage in *The Travels of Three English Brothers* (1607).[25] Rather less colourfully, but equally as subversive the Warwickshire Shirleys (whose shield is depicted in Figure 3) sported

3 'Jacobus Sherlaeus', frontispiece to James Shirley, *Honoria and Mammon* (London: 1657).

a recusant-cum-church-papist lineage, where the women maintained a strict allegiance to the old faith whilst the male heirs conformed to ensure the family's temporal survival. Thus the daughter of John Shirley (1535–1570), Elizabeth, was renowned as one of the founder members of 'the monastery of St. Monica, of the order of Augustine' in Louvain.[26] In contrast to such staunch recusancy, both John Shirley's heir, George (1559–1622) and his grandson, Henry (1588–1632), outwardly conformed to the established Church, although they died firmly 'in the bosom' of their 'Mother the Roman Catholick Church'.[27] However, Henry's younger brother, Thomas, unshackled by the burden of family estates, was renowned not only as an antiquary but as a recusant who from his own account suffered in consequence, 'losses, dishonours, disgraces pecuniary (which were very great) and imprisonment for the love of God'.[28] Indeed the militant stance of Thomas Shirley's circulated manuscript *The Catholic Armorist* (c.1650), which powerfully urged his fellow Catholic gentlemen to 'fight for our deceaved country men . . . and convert our prince and countrie' has led the historian Richard Cust to suggest that 'the image presented in much of secondary literature – of a Catholic laity which was largely passive and quiescent – is in need of modification'.[29] So, in choosing to adorn his portrait with the Warwickshire escutcheon, James Shirley was by no means airbrushing respectability on to the canvas. Rather, he was openly associating himself with a family whose known recusancy was publicly manifest from the very visible symbols of financial loss and secret burial. Lands were seized on the deaths of both Sir George and Sir Henry Shirley, and Sir Henry requested in his will that he be buried 'without any maner of pomp . . . but with as great privacy and silence as is possible, and therefore do desire that it should be done in the dead time of the night, when all or most are asleep'.[30]

Shirley's connection with families loyal to the old faith was not limited to a questionable adoption of a coat of arms, as becomes apparent from Shirley's patronage network. He dedicated his first play *Love Tricks* (licensed 1625, published 1631) to William Tresham, whose family name would immediately conjure up the horrors of the infamous Gunpowder Plot so firmly etched on the Protestant consciousness.[31] Building from this, as Sandra Burner has explored in a comprehensive study of Shirley's patrons, he dedicated plays to Edward Bushell, to the Earl of Rutland and to Sir

Edward Golding, all members of long-standing Roman Catholic families.[32] Shirley's dedication of *Changes, Or Love in a Maze* (licensed and published in 1632) to Lady Dorothy Shirley combined both his employment of the Shirley ensign with this trend of Roman Catholic dedications to suggest that Shirley's aim was indeed to firmly entrench himself within the English Roman Catholic community. This policy was supported in his manuscript poems which contain verses to a variety of Catholics including the Countess of Ormonde, Lady D. C., Gilbert Markham, Gerald Dalby and Izaac Walton.[33] Notably Shirley's success was illuminated in published commendatory verse from Catholic figures such as William Habington.[34]

One could argue that, with a lack of a proven apostasy in 1624, Shirley, in positioning himself under this umbrella of old-faith patronage, was simply manipulating the courtly revival of Roman Catholicism under the influence of Henrietta Maria. Dedicating plays to prominent figures such as the family of Endymion Porter (a Gentleman of the King's Chamber whose suspected Roman Catholic sympathies were augmented by his actively proselytising wife, Olivia), Shirley could be seen to be treading a calculated way to courtly preferment, perhaps reaching his goal in 1633 when honoured with the office of Valet to the Chamber of Queen Henrietta Maria.[35] Matters are further complicated by Shirley's abrupt departure to Ireland in 1636 and the possible implications surrounding his service as principal dramatist under the Protectorate of the fiercely Protestant Earl of Strafford for the period 1636 to 1640.[36] Yet if Shirley was simply exploiting the benefits which could be plucked from moving amongst Roman Catholic circles, one might imagine that the collapse of the court and the closure of the theatres in 1642 would end any such association. Nevertheless, in January 1644, Shirley was specifically attacked in papist terms when *Mercurius Britannicus* denounced the court as debased and beyond the reviving forces of 'Grandfather Ben Johnson, and his Uncle Shakespeare, and his couzen-Germains Fletcher and Beaumont, and nose-lesse Davenant, and *Frier Sherley* the Poets'.[37] The use of the term 'Frier', with its rabidly popish allusions, implies that Shirley's own faith was assumed common knowledge. This proposition gains further credence from Richard Brome's suggestive play on the word 'reform' in his commendatory verse to Shirley's *Via ad Latinam Linguam Complanata* (1646).[38] Shirley's continued Roman

Catholic sympathies are illustrated in his own commendatory verse to Walter Colman's *La Dance Machabre or Death's Duell*, a work dedicated to Henrietta Maria by Colman, who was himself a Franciscan friar suffering imprisonment for his beliefs.[39]

Perhaps the greatest circumstantial evidence which makes probable the tradition of Shirley's recusancy has been found in a Recusant Roll recording convictions from the General Session of the Gaol-Delivery for the City of Westminster. Burner states how 'one Jacobus Shirley, gent' of

> the parish of St. Giles-in-the-Fields appears in an entry for July 15, 1646 . . . the list appears to be a summary of convictions for the years 1643 to 1646. The Shirley in question evidently had not attended church for the past 30 weeks: he was fined 30s. and the fee was a shilling for each absence. That the man was not a merchant is clear from other entries in the list that note the profession of the recusant.[40]

The likelihood of this figure being our James Shirley seems plausible when the document is read against Shirley's will. One beneficiary was a 'Mr. Vincent Cane, my loveing friend', who received 'the summe of Twenty Pounds to be Disposed by him according to a former agreement betwixt Us'.[41] Aline Taylor persuasively argues that this is in reality Vincent Canes, a learned Franciscan friar, widely known as a Roman Catholic apologist. Shirley's usage of 'Mr.' as a legal safeguard, the fact that the money was not for Canes's personal use and the evasive terms in which the bequest was couched were all common practices for recusants wishing to leave money to the Roman Catholic Church.

Reading Shirley's life backwards, it seems credible to suggest that James Shirley firmly adhered to the old faith. Brome's elusive reference in the 1640s, together with contemporary invective in *Mercurius Britannicus*, the recusant record for 1646, and his will of 1666 cumulatively indicate that, in the absence of the inherent benefits of a heavily influenced Roman Catholic court, Shirley remained constant to the Roman Catholic faith. In turn Shirley's conversion in the 1620s is likely, for it seems that Shirley's genuine religious principles led to his court niche rather than a realisation of the advantages of being 'servant to Henrietta Maria' resulting in a timely apostasy. The evidence examined is certainly compelling and Shirley emerges as a figure who acts on his 'unsetled' mind.

Crucially this is a playwright who thinks deeply about religious matters and, as a former minister and teacher, is one who would have been aware of hotly debated polemical issues. Once settled in his religious convictions, Shirley placed himself firmly within the recognised Roman Catholic community, assuming the coat of arms of the known recusant Shirley family, and dedicating plays and verse to both public Roman Catholic figures and private recusant friends. Surprisingly, Sandra Burner argues that ultimately Shirley's religious outlook is of little importance, believing that 'while the tone of many of Shirley's plays was moral and to that extent reflective of a religious temperament, references to religion are few'.[42] Yet, in this age, where people defined themselves by their deeply held beliefs, Shirley's texts can be seen to engage directly with the hotly debated issues of the time. This dissident force exposed in Shirley's drama negates the typical, faintly damning accusations of his 'uncritical devotion to the world of the court'.[43]

The Witty Fair One: reclaiming the language of recusancy

Returning to Whitehall, we last saw Henrietta Maria on Candlemas Day 1626, poised as Artenice in a ground-breaking performance, transmitted to the wider Western world by the reports of foreign ambassadors. The assertive image of hope promoted by this queenly 'principal actress' positively brimmed with latent religious possibilities.[44] However, the Counter-Reformation ideal heralded within this pastoral belied the uncomfortable effect of Henrietta Maria's French Catholicism upon English Protestants and Catholics alike. In these early months of marriage Henrietta Maria was both zealous and astonishingly conspicuous in her devotions: processing through the streets of London to her chapel in St James's Palace and leaving her carriage to go on foot to pray at Tyburn tree, infamous as a place of Catholic martyrdom.[45] Her spiritual adviser, Fr Bérulle, in charged reports, commented with some pride to Pope Urban VIII how 'qu'en arrivant à Londres, Dieu semble lui avoir donné un nouveau zèle pour la religion, et redoubler sa piété' [since arriving in London, God seems to have given her a new zeal for religion, and redoubled her piety].[46] An inherent theatricality emerges from these devotions, manifest in the reaction of the unwitting audiences: 'Sa Majesté y fit ses dévotions avec toutes ses dames. L'action se passa avec tant de piété et de dignité, que les uns étaient baignés de larmes, les autres saisis de respect et d'étonnement' [her Majesty makes her devotions with all her ladies. This practice happens with such piety and dignity, that some are filled with tears, others seized with respect and wonder].[47] The effect of these royal performances was no doubt intensified by the supporting actions of her Oratorian priests who, as Fr Bérulle recalled, 'marché toujours par les villes et à la campagne avec notre habit long, pour accoutumer les Anglais à voir des prêtres en habit et en qualité de prêtres: ce qui ne s'était pas vu dans ce pays-là depuis quatre-vingts ans' [always walked through the towns and countryside in our long [religious] habits, to accustom the English to see priests in monks' habits and in the quality of priests: which had not been seen in this country for the past eighty years].[48]

Equally as provocative as these jolting visual reminders of the old faith's banished traditions were the Queen's glaring absences from vital state occasions, ranging from the Coronation to the investitures of the Knights of Bath and the Order of the Garter.[49] Insinuating suspicions regarding the Queen's new-found religious ardour emerged from Protestant circles. An outraged John Pory castigated the Oratorian priests for their insufferable 'insolences' towards the Queen:

> Yea, they have made her to go barefoot, to spin, to cut her meat out of dishes, to wait at the table, to serve her servants, with many other ridiculous and absurd penances; and if they dare thus insult over the daughter, sister, and wife of so great kings, what slavery would they not make us, the people, to undergo?[50]

Henrietta Maria showed little sign of following her mother's advice to show compassion to those 'pauvres Anglais' who were not of the Catholic faith: 'Quoiqu'ils soient d'une autre religion que vous, vous êtes leur Reine; vous les devez assister et édifier, et par cette voie, les disposer doucement à sortir de l'erreur' [although they are of another religion from you, you are their Queen; you should assist and enlighten them, and by this means, gently incline them to leave the error [of heresy]].[51] Such gentle persuasion was a far cry from the Queen's action in September 1625, when she rudely interrupted a Protestant service in her court by noisily marching through the congregation with her entourage. The Reverend Joseph Mead reported how 'the preacher was at a stand, and demanded whether he might proceed or no, but they still went on; and they passed through the hall where the sermon was preaching, and went to the court gates, and before the sermon was ended returned the same way back again, with a greater noise and disorder than before'.[52]

If such behaviour suggests Henrietta Maria's alienation from the dominant Protestant culture of Caroline England, nor was the Queens's mix of self-consuming Roman Catholicism and frivolous contempt for the Protestant faith entirely encouraging to the English Catholics. The recusant community needed a strong figurehead to act as their defender and deliverer, rather than a Queen Consort who rapidly swung between intense displays of personal piety and unwarranted, if personally satisfying, interdenominational spats. In 1626 recusant concern deepened when the special French ambassador, Maréchal François de Bassompierre, sent to improve relations between the nations, failed in his attempt to elicit a concrete promise of toleration for English Catholics.[53] The Queen herself wrote to Fr Bérulle, newly returned to France, about the 'pauvres catholiques' [poor Catholics] bewailing how 'la persécution est plus grande que jamais. L'ambassadeur et nous tous en sommes au désespoir' [the persecution is greater than ever. The ambassador and I are in despair].[54] Projecting forward to 1628, these anxieties were far from allayed. During the summer assizes at Lancaster, two Catholics were hanged: a Jesuit priest, Edmund Arrowsmith, and a recusant yeoman of moderate means, Richard Hirst.[55] In 1629, fuelled by the twin fears of Arminianism and Popery, Parliament visibly attempted to tighten the laws against recusancy. As Salvetti illuminated in his report to the Venetian ambassador, the Catholics found 'themselves exposed to peril and with no hope of the peace which they anticipated as a consequence of the marriage'.[56] What had quickly become apparent was that recusant hope for, at the very least, a toleration was not to be easily fulfilled.

The Witty Fair One (1628) exposes this anxiety through Shirley's defence of that most precious currency pertaining to an oppositional community, its language. Shirley's sensitivity towards contemporary trends within language is apparent from his earliest play *The School of Compliment*, when the yeoman Ingeniolo attempts to woo a farmer's daughter in terms prescribed to the court, causing the puzzled Bubulcus, to ask: 'What says he, pray, in English?' (III.v.51).[57] As Juliet McGrath has pointed out, 'from the first of James Shirley's plays to the last, the word "language" occurs with surprising frequency'.[58] Most distinctive to Shirley's own vocabulary is the heavy usage of words rooted in the old faith, which continued to represent specific Roman Catholic concepts, such as purgatory, confession and praying for the dead. Shirley's nineteenth-century editors William Gifford and Anthony Dyce freely disregard these terms as an empty reflection of Shirley's own religious beliefs. Yet such precise employment of a notably Catholic lexicon by a dramatist who, as a former schoolteacher and minister, was deeply aware of both the nuances of the English language and the polemics of religious debate, should not be so easily dismissed.[59] Language, to an oppositional community set apart from the dominant culture, was of paramount importance.[60] In the late 1620s a recusant's language was encroached upon from all sides, threatened by Anglican appropriation and increasingly subsumed by fashionable society's fascination for anything characteristic of the new Queen. By restoring words to their true meanings, Shirley signals the opposition of English recusants towards the Protestant establishment and questions the insidious effects of the Queen's French Catholicism.

Fowler in *The Witty Fair One* trifles most with Roman Catholic phraseology.[61] As a profligate typical of Shirley's early plays, Fowler uses language freely peppered with Catholicisms as a fashionable means to woo the virginal Penelope, leering: 'I fear you are an heretic still, and do not believe / as you should do; come, let me rectify your faith, [and] serve you' (II.ii.170–1). Crucial to this exchange is Penelope's realisation that Fowler's language, like his courtship, is purely superficial: 'As you are a gentleman, I know you can swear any thing, 'tis a fashion you are most constant in' (I.iii.41–2), concluding: 'in time I may be converted, and think your tongue / and heart keep house together, [but], at this time, I / presume they are very far asunder' (I.iii.52–4). On one level Fowler is quite simply using the current 'lovers phrases' where, as Cleona extrapolates in Lodowick Carlell's *The Deserving Favourite* (1629), it is the lover's prerogative to 'call their Mistris St. and their affection / Devotion'.[62] Yet, on another level, *The Witty Fair One* subtly explores faddish London society's trivialisation of the spiritual meaning behind Roman Catholic terms. Sophie Tomlinson suggests that Henrietta Maria 'made her mark as much through her dress sense and her private supper parties as she did through her Catholicism and her cult of Platonic love'.[63] Similarly, in *The Witty Fair*

One, Fowler's adoption of Roman Catholic terms has little more meaning than the foolish knight Sir Nicholas Treedle's attempt to master all things French, when his tutor tells him:

> Pardonnez-moi, it is unneccessary; all the French fashions are here already, or rather your French cuts ... a periwig is your French cut and in fashion with your most courtly gallants ... then there is the new cut of your doublet or slash, the fashion of your apparel ... then sir, there is the cut of your leg ... I mean dancing o' the French cut in the leg is most fashionable. (II.i.82–111)

Yet, for English Catholics, such a conflation of religion and fashion had the congruent implication of diluting the individuality of the recusant community.

As Treedle's tutor intimates, and contemporary tracts make clear, despite the sombre backdrop of the siege of La Rochelle, the English court had eagerly succumbed to the allure of continental France. Robert Lovell in *The High Way to Honor* warned: 'take heed all yee whose *speech* is *English, fashion* is *French*', asking 'why doe you thus fly after and flutter in the *fashion* in apparell which is but the demonstration of your miserie?'[64] George Wither scornfully focused on the female gentry who have become so 'frenchifi'd; / That we have scarce a Gentlewoman now / In clothes, more handsome bodied than a Cow'.[65] Word even spread about the uses of French garlic. Thomas Loate writing to George Falcon reminded him how 'my Lady sent you word how to use garlic, and to take it. She thinks it should be good for you, and she says she would take it herself, and she thinks it can do you no harm.'[66] To the puritan-minded, this adoption of French fashions and customs brought the nation one step closer to ungodliness, William Prynne asking: '*What, did ever any of our English Ancestors; did ever any Christian in former Ages, did ever any Saints of God, that wee can heare, or read of, weare a Locke? or Frizle, Powder, Frounce, Adorne, or Decke their Haire?*'[67] Yet this craze for anything related to the French, Roman Catholic Queen would seem to have been viewed with equal scepticism by militant recusants. There is little substance in a fad, and what the language of recusancy gained in circulation it lost in distinctiveness.

This cultural debate is epitomised in *The Witty Fair One* by Fowler, who liberally spouts Roman Catholic terms divorced from proper meaning. Through the active agency of Penelope, and her maidservant Winnifride, who realise the gap existing between the ideal of Fowler's language and the reality of his intents, the potential suitor is tricked by a chastity test into his own pilgrimage of linguistic and spiritual understanding. To an early modern audience the very name Winnifride would be filled with allusions relevant to Fowler's pilgrimage of enlightenment.[68] From the Middle Ages, St Winnifride had been revered as a virgin who risked death rather than loss of her chastity. For English recusants her shrine near Holywell in North Wales remained a popular place of pilgrimage. In 1624 John Gee complained about the open pilgrimage:

> at *Holiwel* in *Wales*, not many miles off the City of *Chester*: whither once every yeer, about *Mid-Summer*, many superstitious *Papists* of *Lancashire*, *Staffordshire*, and other more remote Countries, go *in pilgrimage*, especially those of the feminine and softer sex . . . Let me adde, that they were so bold about *Mid-summer* the last yeere, 1623 that they intruded themselves divers times into the Church or publick *Chappell of Holiwell*, and there said *Masse* without contradiction.[69]

Letters in the Westminster Diocesan Archive corroborate Gee's complaint. Ed Pennant refers to a Jesuit school which was effective in the Holywell area in 1627 about which 'a great magistrate in the neibourhood, that bearing noe affection to the religion complayned to me of great indiscretion and over boldnes'.[70] Crucially, in *The Witty Fair One*, Winnifride's light illuminates Fowler's tawdry actions. Disgraced as a 'Degenerated man' (IV.iv.154), Penelope tells Fowler to: 'go home, and pray / Thy sin may be forgiven, and with tears / Wash thy polluted soul' (IV.iv.164–6). At this juncture Fowler's trial intensifies. Leaving the Worthys' household he enters a seemingly parallel universe where friends gossip in hushed tones about his death. Openly musing: 'If / I be dead, what place am I in?' (V.i.139–40), Fowler returns to the Worthys' home to find an assortment of friends sitting round a coffin. Realising 'I am come to my own burial' (V.iii.32) and deeming his new existence 'a pitiful purgatory' (V.iii.42), Fowler is brought to acknowledge the truth of Penelope's accusation:

> You're dead to virtue, to all noble thoughts,
> And, till the proof of your conversion
> To piety win my faith, you are to me
> Without all life. (V.iii.153–6)

Thus the profligate Fowler undergoes his own pilgrimage through a purgatorial experience (which remained a specifically Roman Catholic concept) to a true conversion where language and meaning are reconciled. Quite 'o'ercome' (V.iii.180) by such active virtue, Fowler achieves a reformed existence within a Caroline text where Roman Catholic 'meaning' is also no longer perceived as a 'stranger to . . . language' (II.ii.228–9).

Central to Shirley's reclamation of recusant language is the emergence within *The Witty Fair One* of the active, transforming agency of female virtue. As we shall explore in *The Wedding* and *The Grateful Servant*, the women of Shirley's texts persistently convert their wayward suitors. Certainly I am not proposing that a depiction of such womanly integrity is innovative within Caroline drama. With the rise of the female audience in the private theatres, as Andrew Gurr has shown, texts and staging were increasingly directed to appeal to the female spectator.[71] Supporting this argument, Sophie Tomlinson's substantial exploration of women on the Stuart stage testifies 'to a newly awakened perception of women's abilities as actors and artists in the Caroline period, and to a fresh valuation of their intellectual and moral qualities'.[72] Building from this revaluation, in Shirley's texts at least, a further influence can be traced. In dramas where suitors repeatedly state their penitence and conversion to women, who are consistently described as 'saints' and 'shrines', Shirley's heroines garner a peculiarly powerful moral presence. This enabling feminocentric force dynamically engages with Henrietta Maria's own role of Artenice which had so vividly showcased the Queen's Counter-Reformation ideals. Yet, in his repeated staging of women whose integrity leads men to conversion, Shirley also draws upon the living history of the English recusant community. John Bossy remarks how Catholic women 'played an abnormally important part' in recusant 'early history'.[73] The actions of women like Lady Calvert and Frances Shirley which, as we have documented, helped to ensure the survival of the old faith suggest that this matriarchal presence continued into the seventeenth century. In *The Wedding* (1626–1629) we explore how Shirley engages with the inspiring resolve of these sympathetically portrayed early modern women to urge Henrietta Maria to fulfil her own position within this English Catholic matriarchy. Moreover, the possibility of exploring on the Caroline stage a successful synthesis between English and French

Roman Catholicism suggests a positive alternative to the widespread unease amongst the more militant recusants with Queen Henrietta Maria's own promotion of a specifically continental style of Catholicism.

The Wedding: refiguring the Roman Catholic Church – Mary Magdalene as Counter-Reformation role model

Marwood's gradual realisation in James Shirley's *The Wedding* (1629) that 'truth is ever constant, / Remains upon her square, firm and unshaken' (II.ii.51–2), has a profound resonance when considered against the insidious polemical questioning regarding the nature of the true church in Caroline England.[74] As early as 1626 the conformist cleric Henry Sydenham, reflecting upon the simmering divisions within the Church of England, bluntly asked: 'Why so much gall in our Pulpit, such wormewood at the Presse . . . to the great disquiet of our Mother Church?'[75] By 1629 his puritan counterpart Henry Burton argued in *Babel No Bethel*: 'when did the state of Religion in our land cry lowder for a repurgation, then now?'[76] A fundamental manifestation of such dissension within the established Church can be found in an increasingly divergent approach towards the Church of Rome. Whilst puritan members continued to perceive Rome as the embodiment of the Whore of Babylon, a growing number of avant-garde conformists (comprising both Arminians and embryonic Laudians), more ironically, allowed Rome the status of being 'debauched' yet essentially true.[77] Such tension within the Protestant community was exacerbated by the intense visibility of Queen Henrietta Maria, a troubling reminder of an opposing archetype of the true church. James Shirley explores (and counters) this nexus of negotiation in *The Wedding*. Engaging with the dual attack on Rome emanating from within the established Church, Shirley attempts to restore fully the integrity of the Catholic Church through the layering of images surrounding his heroines Gratiana and Lucibel. Fascinatingly, the textual origins of these interlinked protagonists are rooted in contemporary writings on the twinned figures of Roman Catholic tradition: the Blessed Virgin Mary and St Mary Magdalene. This focus on the transforming power of female virtue simultaneously recalls the anticipation within the recusant community, and the wider European Catholic powers, on the arrival of Shirley's patroness Henrietta Maria into England.

George Wither's *Britains Remembrancer* neatly encapsulates the fervent religious debate of the late 1620s:

> The followers of *Arminius* some revile
> As troublers of the Churches of this *Ile*,
> Some think the doubts and questions they have moved
> Shal make the *Truth* more known, & more approved.
> The *Papist* sayes, that we afflicted are,
> Because their superstitions banisht were.
> Some *Protestants* beleeve we fare the worse
> For fav'ring them: and that they bring a curse
> Upon the Land.[78]

Written between 1626 and 1629, Wither piercingly assesses the growing division within the established Church. An examination of two frontispieces, both from 1627, sharply illuminates such a transition (Figures 4 and 5). Ralphe Mab's *The Character of a Christian* employs the traditional juxtaposition of the popish heretic in Spanish armour, complete with a shield engraved with 'Humane tradition and Invention' against an early modern, protestant St George, conveniently labelled 'Christian'.[79] Heavenly beams declare the vanity of such rabidly anti-papist symbols as a friar preaching 'pardons' whilst an all-embracing hell fire is greedily fed with 'dispensations', 'popish pensions' and 'honours'. In contrast the celestial banner directed to the Christian soldier proclaims 'the Truth shall make you free' with appropriate depictions of Protestants busily 'searching' the scriptures for a 'sure foundation'. Yet, in the same year, the frontispiece to John Cosin's *A Collection of Private Devotions* (also a work issuing from the press of the established Church) projects a blazing heart enthroned in the middle of an altar, enshrined with the words 'the sacrifice of a contrite hart', over which are emblazoned the initials IHS, the insignia both of Roman Catholicism and of the much maligned Jesuit order.[80] It seems little wonder that to a Puritan figure such as William Prynne, Cosin's text 'stinkes of *Poperie*' and was symbolic of the rise of avant-garde conformism.[81] By 1627 Henry Valentine was urging the need for peace within the established Church, declaring:

> I feare me our owne acrimonies, and distractions fomented by violent spirits... will let in againe the *Sea* of *Rome* upon us... This is the unhapinesse of the *Church* at this time; *Twins* struggle together in her *wombe*, and like the franticke *Philistines* we beat downe one another, turning our Swords into our *owne* bowels.[82]

4 Frontispiece to Ralphe Mab, *The Character of a Christian as He Is Distinguished From All Hypocrits and Heretickes* (London: 1627).

5 Frontispiece to John Cosin, *A Collection of Private Devotions: Or the Houres of Prayer* (London: 1627).

At the centre of these 'acrimonies' was the hotly debated issue within the Protestant community concerning the nature of the true church. For Nonconformists the matter was clear-cut: Roman Catholicism was the incarnation of the biblical Whore of Babylon. Henry Burton's bold championing of the puritan cause is professed in his tract's very title, *Babel No Bethel: That Is the Church of Rome No True Visible Church of Christ*. His rhetoric gains force from his real concern that far from vilifying papists, fellow members of the established Church were, as George Wither remarks, 'fav'ring them'.[83] Joseph Hall articulates such an advanced position: 'our Church is only Reformed, or Repaired, not made new ... plainely, set aside the corruptions, and the Church is the same'.[84] To the Nonconformist it was a small step for prelates with these convictions to openly reassume those church ceremonies previously discountenanced as papist. Francis Rous argued that even tolerating the 'novellizing' spirits of ministers such as John Cosin was like letting 'little theeves ... into the window of a Church ... [that] they may unlocke the dores ... and let in all *Popery*'.[85] Yet, despite puritan fears, these embryonic Laudians by no means perceived themselves to be ushering in a return to the Roman Catholic ways of pre-Reformation England. As Butterfield stated:

> wee may affirme Rome to bee a true Church, and yet the Romish cause gaine nothing by it: for the Popish Religion is never a whit sooner the true Religion, and though we give this attribute to the Church of Rome, yet the Romish faction is nothing the better for it; for all this while, they are not the Orthodoxe Church of God.[86]

Rather, the avant-garde conformist believed that this more 'charitable' approach, combined with a renewed emphasis on church ceremony, might woo that other figure on Ralphe Mab's frontispiece, the 'hipocrit'. Otherwise described as 'neutrall' or 'indifferent', 'crypto-papist' or 'church-papist', this 'hipocrit' symbolised the amorphous and ultimately silent group targeted by Protestant and recusant polemicists alike. As the recusant community recognised, despite its seeming potential for reconciliation, this new image of Rome was equally as dangerous to the old faith's survival. Indeed, the Roman Catholic Church in England now faced a two-pronged attack: the traditional nonconformist image of Rome and the ameliorated, yet alarmingly insinuating, avant-garde perception of Rome as debauched but true. Such recognition is the informing discourse behind Shirley's *The Wedding*. Engaging with Protestant invective through skilful inter-textual weaving, Shirley presents his heroines, Gratiana and Lucibel, not only as figures of saving virtue but as redeeming types of the Roman Catholic Church itself, which directly confronts the Queen's own staged Counter-Reformation vision.

Published in 1629, *The Wedding*, as '*it was lately acted by her Majesty's Servants at the Phenix in Drury-lane*', gained its licence from Sir Henry Herbert between 1626 and 1629. The play focuses on accusations of whoredom against the virginal Gratiana, whose marriage to Beauford is rudely interrupted by Marwood's claim: 'I have enjoy'd her / . . . Gratiana, sinfully; before your love / Made her and you acquainted' (I.iv.191–4). In the ensuing chaos created by this revelation, the astonished Gratiana takes refuge in the house of Justice Landby and with the help of his manservant Milliscent seeks to prove her innocence. Here things get complicated (in typical Shirley fashion) as Milliscent is in fact disguised and is really Lucibel, the missing daughter of Cardona, Gratiana's maidservant. It was Lucibel, disguised this time as Gratiana whom Marwood 'enjoyed' in a plot conceived by Cardona, for financial gain. All is eventually resolved when Lucibel forces Cardona to admit the scheme. With both women's honour restored, Gratiana is reunited with Beauford; a wedding mirrored in the union between Lucibel and Marwood.

Focusing our discussion first on Gratiana, two clusters of images quickly surround this bridal figure to form a stark dichotomy between the actual Gratiana and the figure Marwood professes to know. Warning Beauford that 'I am come to / Divide your soul' (I.iv.16–17), Marwood declares Gratiana as 'false, sinful; a black soul she has' (I.iv.42). His insistence, even when near to death, that 'Gratiana is a blotted piece of alabaster' (II.ii.131) finally convinces Beauford that Gratiana is 'a False woman!' (II.iii.304). Refusing to allow Gratiana to defend herself, Beauford presumes her guilt, asking 'why did nature / Empty her treasure in thy face, and leave thee / A black, prodigious soul?' (II.iii.277–9). Gratiana's plight, humbled before the community and forsaken by Beauford, closely mirrors that of Hero in Shakespeare's *Much Ado About Nothing*.[87] Like Beauford, Claudio reacts hastily to his betrothed's supposed crime, each lover seeing the female blush as a sign of guilt. But there is a significant difference. Claudio focuses on Hero's alleged physical wantonness, declaring: 'she knows the heat of a luxurious bed / her blush is guiltiness, not modesty' (IV.i.39–40). Beauford more allusively portrays Gratiana as one who has a 'black soul', who is a 'false woman' needing 'darkness to obscure thee' (II.iii.281). Such language in the 1620s is resonant of the debates surrounding issues of the true church: the ultimate 'rotten orange' (*Much Ado About Nothing*, IV.i.30), Rome, the Whore of Babylon, denounced by John Cameron as 'a cunningly contrived outside, adorning an ugly and *prodigious* inside'.[88]

Yet, if Beauford's language associates Gratiana with the biblical Whore of Babylon, perceived by the puritan community to be embodied by the Roman Catholic faith, Gratiana herself inverts such an image. Rather, as Captain Landby states, she is all 'a weeping Niobe' (III.i.88), appearing like:

> A water-nymph placed in the midst of some
> Fair garden, like a fountain, to dispense
> Her chrystal streams upon the flowers; which cannot
> But, so refresh'd, look up, and seem to smile
> Upon the eyes that feed 'em. (III.i.90–4)

This image of purity created from Gratiana's tears, with its references to revitalizing waters, forms a stark contrast to Beauford's depiction of her 'black soul'. Even more suggestive is the allusion within the image to the recusant view of the Roman Catholic mother church and the Blessed Virgin Mary, likened by Henry Hawkins in *Partheneia Sacra* to 'an endles *fountain* of spiritual graces and perfections'.[89] Noticeably Beauford is gradually brought to a real belief in Gratiana's virtue. First moved to remorse by false reports of Gratiana's death, Beauford, like Claudio in *Much Ado*, actively repents on hearing Cardona's revelations. Forced to declare to Beauford her false witness, Cardona admits Gratiana's 'virtue was not / To be corrupted in a thought' (IV.iv.160–1). Horrified by the belief that Gratiana, now reperceived as 'chaste / and innocent' (IV.iv.190–1), has drowned herself, Beauford loses himself in passionate self-reproach before being united with his former lover in a mock resurrection scene. The visual force of the staging of the couple's reunion cannot be overestimated. With Gratiana's integrity fully restored, Beauford resumes his proper station, announcing 'Heaven / Let me dwell here, until my soul exhale' (IV.iv.276–7).

Yet, from the perspective of the English recusant community, equally as dangerous in these Protestant debates raging over the nature of the true Church was the increasingly influential argument that 'the Religion of the reformed Churches' was 'not a contrary religion to that of the Romane obedience, but only different, as pure and corrupt, reformed and deformed'.[90] Such a stance essentially enabled an adoption within the established Church of the appealing ceremonial practices of England's old faith. William Bedell neatly illuminates this encroachment on traditional Roman Catholic ritual:

> Judge lastly, and see what a sinne it is for any Catholick to disswade, or be disswaded from such meetings, wherein the *Catholick Faith* is confessed; ... the remembrance of whose perfect *Sacrifice* is celebrated; his *blessed Body and Blood* distributed according to his institution; where penitent sinners are reconciled; the *Dead* reverently recommended into the hands of God; the *Living* informed according to the teaching of the Apostles, to live *Soberly, Justly* and *Godly*; and above all, (if that be not all) *Charitably*.[91]

In *The Wedding*, through the figure of Lucibel, Shirley explores and reworks this supposedly 'corrupt' model of Rome to reveal a theatrical discourse which, far from being vapid or ephemeral, is one of energetic opposition and dissent.

As a seemingly fallen woman Lucibel is an intriguing figure in the play. More sinned against than sinning, her redeeming actions throughout the text consistently portray her as a force for good. Indeed, Beauford delivers a 'joy-ravish'd' (IV.iv.282) eulogy openly deeming Lucibel an 'angel' (IV.iv.286) when she successfully reunites him with Gratiana. Such commendation questions the stigma of Lucibel's own curiously debauched position. With Lucibel's own chastity sacrificed by her mother to save the honour of Gratiana, Shirley challenges the traditional image of the fallen woman to suggest a different reading, one whose origins are embedded in the Magdalene of Roman Catholic tradition.

With a cult following on the continent – illuminated visually through the luminous Magdalenes of Carracci, Lanfranco and Gentilesco – St Mary Magdalene was held in special reverence by English Catholics. This is implied textually from Robert Southwell's frequently reprinted *St. Peter's Complaint and St. Mary Magdalens Funerall Tears* (1596, 1620); I. C.'s dramatic verse poem *Saint*

Marie Magdalens Conversion (1603) and John Sweetnam's *S. Mary Magdalens Pilgrimage to Paradise* (1617). Mary Magdalene was perceived as a markedly fitting paradigm for the English Catholic community. John Sweetnam openly recommended the Magdalene to a recusant readership, so that they might 'learne how to ascend from this vale of tears and misery, unto the toppe of all comfort and felicity'.[92] Likewise, the martyr Southwell depicted a figure especially attractive to the faltering church-papist:

> O Christian soule take B. Mary for thy mirrour, follow her affection that like effects may follow thyne. Learne O sinfull man of this once a sinfull woman, that sinners may find Christ, if their sins be amended. Learne that whom sinne looseth, love recovereth, whom faintnesse of faith chaseth away, firmnesse of hope recalleth.[93]

In particular Southwell viewed the Magdalene as a figure worthy of dramatic attention. He specifically argued how his own writings would be rewarded 'if it may woe some skilfuller pens from unworthy labour'; for 'Passion, and especially this of love, is in these dayes the chiefe commaunder of most mens actions, and the Idol to which both tongues and pennes do sacrifice their ill bestowed labours'.[94] Alison Shell has suggested that this literary directive was possibly aimed at Shakespeare himself, and ultimately rejected.[95] Yet in *The Wedding*, James Shirley adopts this revered martyr's counsel. Through the figure of Lucibel, he transforms the debauched figure of Rome, conjured up by Protestant polemic, into the saintly Magdalene of Roman Catholic tradition: a transition which is intensified (and made accessible) through the surprising parallels between Lucibel and the Magdalene of John Sweetnam's contemporary text.

Sweetnam begins his *Pilgrimage to Paradise* 'with mention of' the Magdalene's 'sinnes'. Focusing on the word 'peccatrix', he stresses: 'neither must we when we heare this word, *Peccatrix*, to wit a Sinner, have such imagination that she was a common Harlot, nor yet excuse her so much on the contraryside, that we say she sinned not at all but seemed a sinner'.[96] Similarly, Lucibel is neither innocent nor vicious; her only means of retribution is to make public her fall and, like the Magdalen, her actions throughout the text emphasise how her love was 'not idle, her Fayth dead, or her hope vayne, but all accompanied with so many good workes as her ability could affoard'.[97] Crucial to this textual reading is Lucibel's comment to the virginal Gratiana that their 'stories / Have [a] dependence' (IV.ii.7–8). This entwinement is underscored when, in reply to Gratiana's claim that her own sorrow 'is above / The common level of affliction' (IV.i.36–7), Lucibel observes: 'And yet I prophesy / There's something would make mine a part of yours / Were they examin'd' (IV.i.43–5). Turning again to contemporary devotional works we learn that the Magdalen was also perceived as a figure interdependent with that ultimate image of purity, the Blessed Virgin Mary. In his 1603 devotional treatise, I. C. presents a forceful symbol of the two Marys weeping at the foot of the cross.[98] Twenty-five years later the potency of this image remained. John Sweetnam elucidates how Christ left us

> two great lights, two holy MARYES above the rest, the Blessed Virgin MARY his Mother, and Saint MARY MAGDALEN, the one very bright and never loosing the light, the other farre inferior, and sometime eclypsed; the one signified by the Sunne, the other by the Moone, yet this moone is a great comfort to those who walke in the night: for by the light of her example they may easily find the way to Grace, which otherwise perhaps they might misse.[99]

The artist Gerard Seghers movingly illustrates this saintly entanglement through his contemporary compassionate depiction of *The Virgin and Child with St. Mary Magdalen* (1627).

By employing this popular dual image of the two Marys, Shirley engages with the late 1620s two-pronged Protestant attack on the integrity of the English Roman Catholic Church. Textually this directive is a success: the slander against the pure Gratiana is removed, and Marwood wishes to wed the fallen Lucibel. Francis Quarles declaimed in his contemporary rendering of the Song of Songs how 'the next way to the *Bridegroome* is the *Bride*'.[100] This sentiment is forcefully staged in the repentance of the profligate Marwood who welcomes Lucibel, the 'too much injured maid', both 'to [his] knowledge, and [his] heart' (V.ii.305–6). In Roman Catholic teaching Christ's bride is the institution of the Mother Church. Through the twinned figure of Gratiana/Lucibel, the Caroline stage explores the archetype of the Catholic Church as a force for good, outfacing critics in the established Church and embracing both recusant and church papist. For, as the bride declared in the Song of Songs:

76 *Staging the old faith*

> But you, my curious (and too nice) allyes,
> That view my fortunes, with too narrow eyes,
> You say my face is black, and foule; 'tis true;
> I'me beauteous, to my Love, though black to you;
> My censure stands not upon your esteeme
> He sees me as I am; you, as I seeme;
> You see the Clouds, but he discernes the Skie;
> Know, 'tis my mask that lookes so black, not I.[101]

A final layer emerges to *The Wedding* if we return to the proselytising mission of that other famous Roman Catholic bride of the 1620s, Henrietta Maria. Mary Magdalene was known to be the favoured saint of this French Queen Consort. Her own, likely, devotional image of the Magdalene was exhibited in 2001 at the Queen Elizabeth Jubilee Gallery, London (Figure 6). Henrietta

6 Hans Holbein the Younger, *Noli Me Tangere*, c.1524, likely devotional image of Queen Henrietta Maria.

Maria's confessor, Pierre de Bérulle, had penned a famous tract, *Élévation sur Sainte Madeleine* (1627), with the express intention of nourishing the Queen's own faith. In October 1626, as her letter to Fr Bérulle elucidated, Henrietta Maria was increasingly disheartened, for despite her efforts English Catholics faced continuing difficulties.[102] In his dedicatory epistle to *Élévation sur Sainte Madeleine*, Bérulle voiced his own anxiety, magnifying the Queen's 'état si périlleux' [perilous state] (*Sainte Madeleine*, p. 411). Equating England to 'un désert affreux' [an awful desert] which was 'stérile en grâce et fertile en iniquité' [sterile in grace and fertile in iniquity], Bérulle urged the Queen to mould herself in the likeness of the Magdalene, 'la plus éminente en l'école de son amour' [the most eminent in the school of love] (*Sainte Madeleine*, pp. 411–13). Recalling how in manuscript form this pamphlet was 'toujours entre vos mains; c'était votre soulas en vos ennuis, votre entretien en votre solitude' [always in your hands; it was your solace in your trials, your conversation in your solitude] (*Sainte Madeleine*, p. 413), Bérulle's hope was that through the Magdalene's example the Queen would find the strength for her own Counter-Reformation vocation. Illuminated from within by 'un feu céleste' [a celestial fire] (*Sainte Madeleine*, p. 413), crucially Henrietta Maria would bring light to a heretical country. By implication, through the figure of Lucibel in *The Wedding*, Shirley can also be seen to be encouraging his queen in her mission, a role which Henrietta Maria had herself signalled in her performance of *L'Artenice* in the nascent light of Candlemas Day.

The Grateful Servant: transforming 'the far-fetch'd bride'

With the assassination of the Duke of Buckingham in August 1628 the numinous possibilities inherent to the Queen's union with Charles I once more seemed plausible. Henrietta Maria had begun to grow significantly closer to her kingly husband. In September 1628 the Venetian ambassador, Alvise Contarini, commented how 'every day she concentrates in herself the favour and love that was previously divided between her and the duke'.[103] On 20 November 1629 Thomas Meautys was able to write to Jane, Lady Bacon how 'it beginnes to be currently spoken and believed that the Queene is with childe'.[104] The potential danger of spiritual repercussions from the Queen's budding sphere of influence caused consternation in godly circles. In pamphlet literature France was abruptly realigned with those traditional principal agents loyal to Rome: Spain and the Jesuits.[105] By 1629 the bells of Thomas Brewer's celebratory verse which had so joyfully welcomed Henrietta Maria to England's shores were silenced. A severe eruption of the plague which had marred the Queen's arrival in 1625 was now chronicled by George Wither in sinister terms, as an illness which was first discovered at:

> A *Frenchmans* house without the *Bishopsgate*,
> To intimate (perhaps), that such as be
> Our spirituall *Watchmen*, should the more foresee
> That they with discipline made strong the *Ward*,
> Which God appointed hath for them to guard;
> And chiefly, at this present, to have care,
> Lest now, while we, and *France* united are
> In bodily commerce; they bring unto us
> Those *Plagues* which may eternally undoe us.
> For, such like *Pestilences* soone begin;
> And (ere we be aware) will enter in,
> Unlesse our *Bishops*, both betimes, and late,
> Be diligent and watchfull at their *Gate*.[106]

Alarm was widely voiced that Henrietta Maria's presence might spiritually endanger the established Church of England. Henry Burton in *Truth's Triumph Over Trent* asked God: 'O strengthen our hearts and hands from the highest to the lowest, to cast out from among us our Idol-sins, and sinfull-Idols'.[107] William Crashaw openly prayed for Henrietta Maria's conversion:

> Thou that hast made her *His* make her also *Thine*, that so she may be a helpe to him, a blessing to us, a comfort to the distressed Churches of *France*, and a Ioy to the Christian World: Blesse therefore good Lord, and make powerfull all meanes of her Conversion publike and private, and for the setling of her Soule in thy holy Truth, and in the wayes of righteousnesse: And besides the Prayers of us ... dayly made for Her, we beseech thee graciously to regard the serious supplications which wee are sure his Majestie dayly powres out before thee, for her happie and speedie Conversion.[108]

Fear of the Queen's influence particularly dominated the puritan sphere of the established Church. Already concerned with the rise of avant-garde conformists, Burton with astonishing frankness reminded his reader of the 'remarkeable' example of 'Asa who in rooting out of *Idolatry*, spared not his own Mother *Maachah*, removing her from being *Queene*, because she had made *an Idol in a Grove*'.[109] Most extraordinary is Burton's appropriation in 1627 of the Queen's own Esther topos. In the *Baiting of the Popes Bull* he likened himself to the 'noble Queene *Hester*', who 'feared to hazard her person into the Presence *uncalled*' but chose 'death rather, than not to discharge the duty she owed to Gods people, now destinated, and doomed to destruction'.[110] In *The Grateful Servant*, Shirley reappropriates this Esther ideal through the redeeming figure of Leonora, urging his queenly patroness to reinforce her own efforts at this charged moment of renewed promise.

Licensed as *The Faithful Servant* on 3 November 1629, with all the inherent adumbrations surrounding the anniversary of the Gunpowder Plot, *The Grateful Servant* was published with its present title in 1630.[111] The plot revolves around the seeming rejection of the Duke of Savoy by Leonora, a Milanese princess. Stung by Milan's rebuff, the Duke vows to marry a native woman, Cleona, who is already privately betrothed to the noble Foscari. Leonora secretly attends the Savoy court through her disguise as Dulcino, male page to Foscari, where she is revealed as a purifying force both for the Duke and for his court.

Although the play is set within the safe confines of Savoy, direct parallels between Leonora and Henrietta Maria are suggested from the very first scene. Dismissing his former engagement to Leonora as a 'mere state trick' (I.i.149), the Duke proclaims:

> Give me a Lady born in my obedience,
> Whose disposition will not engage
> A search into the nature of her climate,
> Or make a scrutiny into the stars:
> Whose language is mine own, and will not need
> A smooth interpretator; whose virtue is
> Above all titles, though her birth or fortune
> Be a degree beneath us, such a wife
> Were worth a thousand far-fetch'd brides, that have
> More state, and less devotion. (I.i.152–61)

The image of a bride alienated from her adopted country's culture resonates with the difficulties known to have been experienced by Queen Henrietta Maria. Salvetti recounts how on her own arrival into England the Queen did not 'show herself much to the English ladies and gentlemen of her Court, probably because she cannot converse with them except through the unpleasant intervention of an interpreter'.[112] Likewise, Charles I's ignominious clash with his wife's French entourage was widely reported. In the summer of 1626 James Howell, writing to his brother the Bishop of Bristol, recounted how the king gave orders that:

> they must instantly away to *Sommerset* House, for ther were Barges and Coaches staying for them; and ther they should have all there wages payed them to a peny, and so they must be content to quit the Kingdom: This sudden, undream'd of Order, struck an astonishment into them all, both men and women; and running to complain to the Queen, His Majestie had taken her before into his Bed-Chamber, and lock'd the doors upon them, untill he had told her how matters stood; the Queen fell into a violent passion, broke the Glasse-Windows, and tore her Hair, but she was calm'd afterwards.[113]

Significantly, this negative view of such a foreign alliance is inverted in *The Grateful Servant*. Foscari eulogises how the disguised Leonora is 'full of excellent sweetness', with a 'fine' soul (I.ii.184, 178). Closely associated with the Roman Catholic Church, Leonora is first brought to Savoy by Father Valentino, a 'faithfull' Benedictine, whose integrity is in direct opposition to the rapacious caricatures of Protestant polemic. Moreover, like Henrietta Maria's own stage character Artenice, she (rather comically) contemplates entering the monastic life, before assuming her proper vocation of marriage to the Duke. Such uncompromising veracity forms a stark contrast to the seeming purity of the Duke's own court. Lodwick, the Duke's profligate brother, promotes Savoy as a site of overpowering morality, asking Cleona: 'do you think I [would] keep such a religious court and in this corner lodge a covey of Capuchins?' (II.ii.443–4). Yet one has to ask, is the Duke's court so 'religious'? Foscari paints a very different picture, where 'great men' dissemble:

> Pride, and court cunning hath *betray'd their faith*
> *To a secure idolatry*; their soul
> Is lighter than a complement. (I.ii.83–5, my emphasis)

As a contemporary audience would recognise, such a scornful indictment was by no means limited to Savoy. The Queen's confessor, Fr Bérulle, publicly warned Henrietta Maria against the glamour of court life reminding her that 'les beautés que vous voyez sont périssables et ne sont que des ombres de la beauté suprême et éternelle' [the beauties that you see are perishable and are only the shadows of the supreme and eternal beauty] (*Sainte Madeleine*, p. 413). John Donne in *Devotions Upon Emergent Occasions* regretted how '*Religion* is in a *Neutralitie* in the *World*', and lamented that one could 'make *new friends* by changing [the] *old religion*'.[114] In *The Grateful Servant*, in contrast to Savoy (and by implication the Caroline court) 'where men are but deceitful shadows' (I.ii.107), Leonora stands apart, rebuking Foscari's fears with the avowal: 'I hope you see not / Any propension in my youth, to sin / For pride, or wantonness' (II.ii.117–19). Such firm virtue highlights the deceit embedded within the Savoy court but also, and more provocatively, questions the actions of the Duke himself. Failing to reform his dissolute brother Lodwick, the Duke's pompous self-absorption reaches a climax in his manipulative wooing of Cleona. Tellingly, the Duke is able to realise his best self only when he is reunited with Leonora. In *The Grateful Servant* Shirley reminds the Queen of the possibilities imbued in the Catholic imagination when Henrietta Maria arrived on England's shores. On the Caroline stage at least this 'far-fetch'd bride' (I.i.160) is transformed from an alliance of 'dark ends' (I.i.149) to a source of reform both for the Duke and his court.

In these three early plays Shirley engages with the continued anxiety experienced within recusant circles. *The Witty Fair One* spotlights concern at the dilution of the language of the old faith and, by implication, the recusant's voice of opposition. Moving to *The Wedding*, the entwined agency of Gratiana and Lucibel both encourages the Queen in her Counter-Reformation mission and, simultaneously, defends the Roman Catholic Church against the insidious onslaught of insistent Protestant attack. Finally, in *The Grateful Servant*, Shirley overtly explores the renewed expectations surrounding Henrietta Maria as a potential source of salvation for both the recusant community and the English nation. From such a discussion it becomes increasingly apparent that Caroline theatre was neither ephemeral nor sterile. When read in the political context experienced by an alert Caroline audience, what Swinburne dismisses as 'vapid and colourless sketches' are revealed as rich discourses of challenging debate.[115] Likewise, language which has been criticised as dull and arcane can be more properly interpreted as a recusant voice of opposition and dissent.

Increasing division within the established Church, together with Henrietta Maria's growing influence with Charles I, warranted the real hope amongst the recusant community that the old faith might return. In his 1629 dedication to 'the Catholiques of England', Matthew Kellison praised his countrymen's tenacity, highlighting an unswerving loyalty to the 'true church':

> not withstanding their confiscations, confinings, Seizings, imprisonments, deaths (which you have heretofore endured, and yet some tymes endure) you are more encreased and multiplied ... we are so multiplied, that we maie be found in your courte, in your parlament, in your universities, amongst your nobilitie, amid your magistrates, yea ministers (if we regard their hartes) and in the thicke of your armies: no citie, no towne, no village, no Parish, no Prison scarse can you finde where Catholiques are not found, as your officers and Poursuivants can assure you.[116]

Such undaunted resolve, as Marwood comes to understand in *The Wedding*, evolved from the integral recusant belief that 'truth is ever constant / remains upon her square, firm and unshaken' (II.ii.51–2). This conviction energises Shirley's early texts, and as we explore in Chapter 3 is behind his continued encouragement of Queen Henrietta Maria to be both protector and liberator of the recusant community. Such stagings in turn bear witness to the martyr Robert Southwell's Roman Catholic appropriation, of Philip Sidney's observation in *The Defence of Poesy*, that 'in fables are often figured moral truths, and that covertly uttered to a common good, which without a maske would not find so free a passage'.[117]

Notes

1 Robert Southwell, *S. Peters Complaint and Saint, Mary Magdalens Funerall Teares. With Sundry Other Selected, and Devout Poems* (St Omer: 1596, 1620), pp. 51–2, my emphasis.
2 Arthur H. Nason, *James Shirley Dramatist: A Biographical and Critical Study* (New York: Arthur H. Nason Publisher, 1915), p. 3.
3 Edward Phillips, *Theatrum Poetarum: Or a Compleat Collection of the Poets, Especially the Most Eminent, of All Ages* (London: 1675), p. 80.

4 Marvin Morillo, 'Shirley's "Preferment" and the Court of Charles I', *SEL*, 1 (1961), 101–17, p. 103.
5 Algernon Swinburne, 'James Shirley', *The Fortnightly Review*, new series, 1 April (1890), 461–8, p. 461.
6 Arthur C. Kirsch, 'A Caroline Commentary on the Drama', *MP*, 66 (1969), 256–61, p. 260.
7 Butler, *Theatre and Crisis*, pp. 2, 6, 281.
8 Barroll, *Anna of Denmark*, p. 4; Julie Sanders 'Jonson's Caroline Coteries', in Takashi Kozuka and J. R. Mulryne (eds), *Shakespeare, Marlowe, Jonson: New Directions in Biography* (Aldershot: Ashgate, 2006), pp. 279–94, 280; Tomlinson, *Women on Stage*, p. 2.
9 Adolphus Ward, in Charles Mills Gayley, *Representative English Comedies*, 4 vols (London: 1914), 3, p. 555.
10 Anthony Wood, *Athenae Oxonienses*, 4 vols (Oxford: 1813), vol. 3, p. 737.
11 G. Barnett-Smith, 'James Shirley', *The Gentleman's Magazine*, 246 (1880), 584–610, p. 586; Joseph Gillow, *A Literary and Bibliographic History; Or Bibliographic Dictionary of English Catholics* (London: Burns and Oates, 1885–1902), vol. 4, p. 177. See also 'James Shirley', in William Devlin, *The Catholic Encyclopedia*, vol. 16 (New York: The Encyclopedia Press, 1914).
12 Ben Lucow, *James Shirley* (Boston: Twayne, 1981), p. 16.
13 *Ibid.*
14 G. M. S. Brooke and A. N. C. Hallen (eds), *Transcript of the Registers of the United Parishes of St. Mary Woolworth, S. Mary Woolchurch, Haw, 1531–1760* (London: 1886), p. 310; J. P. Feil, 'James Shirley's Years of Service', *RES*, new series, 8 (1957), 413–16. See also Burner, *James Shirley*, pp. 1–26.
15 Albert Baugh, 'Further Facts About James Shirley', *RES*, 7 (1931), 62–6; George Mackendrick Gregory, *Two Studies in Shirley* (Durham: University of North Carolina Press, 1935), p. 23; George Bas, 'Two Misrepresented Biographical Documents Concerning James Shirley', *RES*, 27 (1976), 304–6; Sandra Burner, *James Shirley: A Study of Literary Coteries and Patronage in Seventeenth Century England* (Lanham: University Press of America, 1988), p. 22.
16 Nicholas Tyacke, 'Lancelot Andrewes and the Myth of Anglicanism', in Peter Lake and Michael Questier (eds), *Conformity and Orthodoxy in the English Church, c.1560–1660* (Woodbridge: Boydell Press, 2000), pp. 5–34.
17 Burner, *James Shirley*, p. 24, my emphasis.
18 *Ibid.*
19 Peter Smart, *A Sermon Preached in the Cathedrall Church of Durham, July 7 1628* (London: 1628), p. 23.

20 Ray Armstrong (ed.), *The Poems of James Shirley* (New York: King's Crown Press, 1941), pp. 13, 67.
21 *Ibid.*, p. 95.
22 London, 11 April 1625, despatches of Amerigio Salvetti to the State of Florence, in Henry Barr Tomkins (ed.), *The Manuscripts of Henry Duncan Skrine, Esq., Salvetti Correspondence*, trans. Heath Wilson (London: 1887), p. 3. See also Charles E. Smith, *Religion Under the Barons of Baltimore* (Baltimore: E. Allen Lycett, 1899).
23 Wood, *Athenae Oxonienses*, p. 737.
24 Evelyn Shirley, 'Who Is Henry Shirley?', *N&Q*, 12 (1855), 27–37.
25 Anthony Parr (ed.), *Three Renaissance Travel Plays* (Manchester: Manchester University Press, 1999).
26 E. P. Shirley, *Stemmata Shirleiana: Or the Annals of the Shirley Family, Lords of Nether Etindon, in the County of Warwick, and of Shirley in the County of Derby* (London: J. B. Nichols, 1841), p. 64.
27 *Ibid.*, pp. 67, 88.
28 *Ibid.*, p. 94.
29 Richard Cust, 'Catholicism, Antiquarianism and Gentry Honour: The Writings of Sir Thomas Shirley', *Midland History*, 23 (1998), 40–70, pp. 57, 59.
30 Shirley, *Stemmata Shirleiana*, p. 89.
31 For the continued determination to celebrate the discovery of the powder plotters see Thomas Gataker, *An Anniversarie Memoriall of Englands Delivery from the Spanish Invasion* (London: 1626), especially sigs A3–A4.
32 Burner, *James Shirley*, pp. 97–102.
33 Armstrong, *Shirley's Poems*, pp. 9, 10, 12, 14, 15.
34 Habington wrote a commendatory verse for Shirley's *The Grateful Servant* (London: 1630). See Kenneth Allott (ed.), *The Poems of William Habington* (London: University Press of Liverpool, 1948), pp. xxviii–xxix.
35 Morillo, 'Shirley's "Preferment"', p. 102.
36 Burner, pp. 113–38; Allen Stevenson, 'Shirley's Years in Ireland', *RES*, 20 (1944), 20–2.
37 Marvin Morillo, '"Frier Sherley": James Shirley and "Mercurius Britannicus"', *N&Q*, new series, 7 (1960), 338–9, p. 339.
38 Donald Lawless, 'A Further Note on Shirley's Religion', *N&Q*, new series, 24 (1977), 543.
39 Armstrong (ed.), *Shirley's Poems*, p. 79.
40 Burner, *James Shirley*, p. 101.
41 Aline M. Taylor, 'James Shirley and "Mr Vincent Cane" the Franciscan', *N&Q*, new series, 7 (1960), 31–3.

42 Burner, *James Shirley*, p. 102.
43 Morillo, 'Shirley's "Preferment"', p. 103.
44 Sir Benjamin Rudyerd to Sir Francis Nethersole, December 1625. *CSP Dom 1625–1626*, p. 179.
45 John Pory to the Rev. Joseph Mead, 1 July 1626, Birch, *Court and Times*, vol. 1, p. 121.
46 Tabaruad, *Pierre de Bérulle*, vol. 1, p. 373.
47 *Ibid.*, pp. 373–4.
48 *Ibid.*, p. 374.
49 Hibbard, 'Translating Royalty', p. 23.
50 Birch, *Court and Times*, vol. 1, p. 121.
51 Tabaraud, *Pierre de Bérulle*, vol. 1, p. 360.
52 Rev. Joseph Mead to Sir Martin Stuteville, 3 October 1625, Birch, *Court and Times*, vol. 1, p. 50.
53 For further details regarding this new agreement see Havran, *Catholics in Caroline England*, pp. 47–50.
54 Tabaraud, *Pierre de Bérulle*, vol. 1, p. 384.
55 Havran, *Catholics in Caroline England*, pp. 112–14; AAW/A22, pp. 573–5.
56 Tomkins (ed.), *Salvetti Correspondence*, p. 25.
57 James Shirley, *Love Tricks* (London: 1631). William Gifford and Anthony Dyce (eds), *The Dramatic Works and Poems of James Shirley*, 6 vols (London: J. Murray, 1883), vol. 1, pp. 1–97. All subsequent citations refer to this edition and will appear in the text.
58 Juliet McGrath, 'James Shirley's Uses of Language', *SEL*, 6 (1966), 323–39, p. 323.
59 Shirley's fascination for language is reflected in *Via ad Latinam Linguam Complanata: The Way Made Plain to the Latine Tongue, the Rules Composed in English and Latine Verse for the Greater Delight and Benefit of Learners* (London: 1649); *The Rudiments of Grammar: The Rules Composed in English Verse for the Greater Benefit and Delight of Young Beginners* (London: 1656).
60 For further discussion on the distinctiveness of Protestant and Catholic language see Hopkins, *John Ford*, p. 99.
61 James Shirley, *The Witty Fair One* (London: 1633). Gifford and Dyce (eds), *Works*, vol. 1, pp. 273–362. All subsequent citations refer to this edition and will appear in the text.
62 Lodowick Carlell, *The Deserving Favourite* (London: 1629), I.i.413–15, sig. C3r.
63 Tomlinson, *Women on Stage*, p. 11.
64 Robert Lovell, *The High Way to Honor: As It Was Delivered (For Substance) In Two Sermons At All Hallowes, Barking* (London: 1627), pp. 14–15.

65 George Wither, *Britain's Remembrancer* (London: 1628), sig. P10r.
66 Thomas Loate to George Falcon, 2 April 1628, in *HMC Rutland*, vol. 1, p. 484.
67 William Prynne, *The Unlovelinesse of Love-Locks. Or, a Summarie Discourse, Prooving: The Wearing and Nourishing of a Locke, or Love-Lock, to Be Altogether Unseemely, and Unlawfull Unto Christians* (London: 1628), sig. A4v.
68 Robertus, Prior of Shrewsbury, *The Admirable Life of Saint Wenefride*, trans. John Falconer (St Omer: 1635).
69 Gee, *Foot Out of the Snare*, p. 38.
70 AAW/A20, Ed Pennant, about the school at Greenfield, Holywell, p. 291. See also the beautifully embroidered 'St Winefride's Chalice Veil', c.1610–1640, which was created as a thanksgiving following a miraculous cure at the Holywell shrine, within Maurice Whitehead (ed.), *Held in Trust: 2008 Years of Sacred Culture* (Stonyhurst: St Omers Press, 2008), pp. 84–5.
71 Andrew Gurr, *Playgoing in Shakespeare's London* (Cambridge: Cambridge University Press, 1996), pp. 182–96.
72 Tomlinson, *Women on Stage*, p. 81; Lisa Hopkins, *The Female Hero in English Renaissance Tragedy* (Basingstoke: Palgrave, 2002), p. 119.
73 Bossy, *Catholic Community*, p. 158. See also Betty S. Travitsky, '"A Pittilesse Mother"? Reports of a Seventeenth-Century English Filicide', *Mosaic: A Journal for the Interdisciplinary Study of Literature*, 27 (1994), 55–76.
74 James Shirley, *The Wedding*, ed. Sister Martin Flavin (New York: Garland Publishing, 1980), II.ii.42–3. All subsequent citations refer to this edition and will appear in the text.
75 Humphry Sydenham, *The Athenian Babler: A Sermon Preached At St Maries in Oxforde, the 7th of July 9. 1626* (Oxford: 1626), p. 41.
76 Henry Burton, *Babel No Bethel: That Is the Church of Rome No True Visible Church of Christ* (London: 1629), dedicatory preface to Parliament, sig. ¶2r.
77 For a detailed examination see Milton, *Catholic and Reformed*; Tyacke, *Anti-Calvinists*.
78 Wither, *Britain's Remembrancer*, sig. T9r.
79 Ralphe Mab, *The Character of A Christian: As Hee Is Distinguished From Hypocrites and Heretickes* (London: 1627).
80 John Cosin, *A Collection of Private Devotions: In the Practice of the Ancient Church Called the Houres of Prayer* (London: 1627).
81 William Prynne, *A Briefe Survay and Censure of Mr. Cozens His Couzening Devotions* (London: 1628), p. 3.

82 Henry Valentine, *Noahs Dove: Or a Prayer for the Peace of Jerusalem* (London: 1627), pp. 8–9. See also James Baillie, *Spiritual Marriage: Or the Union Betweene Christ and His Church* (London: 1627), p. 14.
83 Wither, *Britain's Remembrancer*, sig. T9r.
84 Joseph Hall, *The Olde Religion: A Treatise Wherein Is Laid Down the True State of the Difference Betwixt the Reformed, and Romane Church* (London: 1628), pp. 14–15. See also Hugh Cholmley, *The State of the Now-Romane Church* (London: 1629).
85 Francis Rous, the elder, *Testis Veritatis: The Doctrine of King James Our Late Soveraigne of Famous Memory* (London: 1626), p. 105.
86 Robert Butterfield, *Maschil: Or, a Treatise to Give Instruction, Touching the State of the Church of Rome Since the Councell of Trent, Whether Shee Be Yet a True Christian Church* (London: 1629), p. 107.
87 William Shakespeare, *Much Ado About Nothing*, ed. J. Waters-Benett (Harmondsworth: Penguin, 1969). All subsequent references are to this edition and appear in the text.
88 John Cameron, *An Examination of Those Plausible Appearances Which Seeme Most to Commend the Romish Church, And to Prejudice the Reformed* (London: 1626), p. 153 – my emphasis.
89 Henry Hawkins, *Partheneia Sacra: Or the Mysterious and Delicious Garden of the Sacred Parthenes; Symbolically Set Forth and Enriched with Pious Devices and Emblems for the Entertainement of Devout Soules; Contrived Al to the Honour of the Incomparable Virgin Marie, Mother of God* (Rouen: 1633), p. 213.
90 William Bedell, *An Examination of Certaine Motives to Recusancie* (Cambridge: 1628), pp. 1–2.
91 *Ibid.*, p. 60.
92 John Sweetnam, *S. Mary Magdalens Pilgrimage to Paradise* (St Omer: 1617, 1627), p. 10.
93 Southwell, *Magdalens Funerall Tears*, p. 154.
94 *Ibid.*, pp. 45–6, 49.
95 Alison Shell, 'Why Didn't Shakespeare Write Religious Verse?', in Kozuka and Mulryne (eds), *Shakespeare, Marlowe, Jonson*, pp. 85–112.
96 Sweetnam, *Pilgrimage to Paradise*, pp. 27–8.
97 *Ibid.*, p. 57, see also p. 61.
98 I. C., *Saint Marie Magdalens Conversion* (printed secretly in England: 1603), sig. C3v, verse 83, my emphasis.
99 Sweetnam, *Pilgrimage to Paradise*, p. 63.
100 Quarles, '"Sions Sonnets", Sung by Solomon the King', *Divine Poems*, sonnet 18, p. 300.

101 *Ibid.*, Sonnet 1, verse 4, p. 272.
102 Tabaruad, *Pierre de Bérulle*, p. 384.
103 Alvise Contarini to Giorgio Zorzi, 26 September 1628, *CSP Ven*, 1628–1629, pp. 310–11.
104 Thomas Meautys to Jane, Lady Bacon, 20 November 1629, Richard Griffin (ed.), *The Private Correspondence of Jane, Lady Cornwallis, 1613–1644* (London: 1842), p. 217.
105 Lewis Owen, *Speculum Jesuiticum* (London: 1629); Joseph Hall, *An Answer to Pope Urban His Inurbanity, Expressed in a Breve Sent to Louis the French King, Exasperating Him Against the Protestants in France* (London: 1629), especially sig. A3 and p. 7.
106 Wither, *Britain's Remembrancer*, sig. D10r.
107 Henry Burton, *Truth's Triumph Over Trent: Or the Great Gulfe Between Sion and Babylon* (London: 1629), sig. *3r.
108 William Crashaw, *Englands Lamentable Complaint to Her God* (London: 1629), sigs C5r–v.
109 Henry Burton, *Israels Fast: Or a Meditation Upon the Seventh Chapter of Joshuah: A Faire Precedent For These Times* (London: 1628), p. 32.
110 Henry Burton, *The Baiting of the Popes Bull: Or An Unmasking of the Mystery of Iniquity* (London: 1627), sig. ¶1r.
111 Gifford and Dyce (eds), *Works*, 2, p. 10. All subsequent references are to this edition and appear in the text.
112 Tomkins (ed.), *Salvetti Correspondence*, p. 25.
113 'Letter to my Brother (after) Dr *Howell*, now Bishop of *Bristol*', undated, within Howell, *Ho-Elianae*, section 4, p. 36. For a further account of intrigue within the Queen's household see John Dauncey, *The History of the Thrice Illustrious Princess Henrietta Maria de Bourbon, Queen of England* (London: 1660), pp. 42–4.
114 John Donne, *Devotions Upon Emergent Occasions* (London: 1626), p. 333. For ease of reference see Anthony Raspa (ed.), *Devotions Upon Emergent Occasions* (Oxford: Oxford University Press, 1987), p. 74.
115 Swinburne, *Fortnightly Review*, p. 461.
116 Matthew Kellison, *A Treatise of the Hierarchie and Divers Orders of the Church Against the Anarchie of Calvin* (Douai: 1629), sigs a3r–a4r.
117 Southwell, *Magdalens Funeral Teares*, p. 52; Philip Sidney, 'The Defence of Poesy', in Katherine Duncan-Jones (ed.), *Sir Philip Sidney* (Oxford: Oxford University Press, 1992), pp. 212–50, p. 223.

3

'A Case of Conscience': issues of allegiance and identity, 1630–1633[1]

In September 1632 a reported two thousand people gathered at Somerset House to witness the momentous event of the laying of the foundation stone of the first purpose-built Roman Catholic church within the heart of London since the Reformation. With Queen Henrietta Maria as both the principle participant and sponsor, bringing all her understanding of effective performance to enrich the occasion and enrapture the senses, this was very much a 'living spectacle'.[2] As Father Cyprien of Gamache records, the ceremony, specifically performed on the Feast of the Holy Cross, was strikingly lavish and overtly public:

> a plot of ground, on which the chapel was to stand, was very tastefully fitted up in the form of a church; rich tapestry served for walls; the most costly stuffs for roof; the floor was strewed with flowers, which diffused an agreeable odour. At the further end was seen an altar, garnished with magnificent ornaments, with large chandeliers of silver gilt, and with a great number of vases, the costliness and workmanship of which rendered them worthy of being compared with those of Solomon's Temple.[3]

The earthly focal point of this 'Temple' for those who flocked to attend would have been Henrietta Maria herself, and this is reflected in the careful choreography of the Queen's movements within the ceremony. First she 'knelt upon a cushion of crimson velvet' under a specially erected dais whilst her grand almoner freely 'performed high mass with solemnity' and 'harmonious music ravished the heart'. Then, under the gaze of the multitude, the Queen was led with great ceremony

> to the place where she was to lay the first stone, which she touched with her royal hand; . . . laying hold of a trowel, the handle

of which was covered with fine fringed velvet ... and taking mortar from a large glittering basin of silver gilt, and with a grace which imparted devotion to the people, she threw it ... three times upon the stone.[4]

To accompanying shouts of 'long live the Queen' from well paid workmen, who 'were so satisfied that they gave a thousand blessings to the Queen', and with the air ringing from cannon fire, this spectacle evoked a coronation-like atmosphere, perhaps suggesting a Catholic alternative to the official Protestant ceremony of 1626 at which Henrietta Maria had refused to be present. Jubilant celebrations continued into the evening on the Thames riverbank. The newly dedicated foundations of this blatantly Roman Catholic 'temple' were a blaze of light, causing the astonished public to wonder how 'nuict estoit un plain jour, & que l'element de l'eauë alloit estre consumé par celuy du feu' [night had become plain day and how the element of water had been consumed by that of fire].[5]

Notably, French accounts perceived this event as a personal triumph for Henrietta Maria, a 'singulier monument de sa pieté' [a singular monument of her piety].[6] The disarming image of how she begged Charles, 'avec tant de respect, d'amour & de larmes' [with so much respect, love and tears], to allow her to build a chapel is very much in accord with her self-professed vow to act as a second Esther to the English Catholics.[7] However, within the Protestant imagination, the inherent danger of France's professed hope, that through such an action the English monarchs would 'á l'advenir qu'une mesme Religion' [in the future have the same Religion], is implied in a description of this same solemnity by the geographer and traveller John Pory.[8] Curiously, Pory, in his newsletter to Sir Thomas Puckering, ignores such popish opulence to focus on the seemingly more mundane specifications of the two square corner stones which Henrietta Maria had laid with such ceremonious devotion. In particular, Pory spotlights the silver dedicatory plaque which had 'caused to be engraven upon the upper part of that plate *the pictures of their majesties, as founders*, and the lower side of the capuchins, as consecrators' (my italics).[9] Pory's fascinating detail of an engraving of Charles and Henrietta Maria as visible joint founders of the Capuchin chapel complicates any easy reading of a Roman Catholic spectacle exclusive to the Queen's household. Rather, such a Janus image hints at the growing concerns within

1630s England over the increasing fluidity of religious identity. Entangled with this re-emergence of court Catholicism under the guidance of Henrietta Maria was the growth of Laudianism within the Protestant establishment, a movement which further destabilised the religious landscape. With the tentacles of Catholicism straddling the monarchy, Pory's letter not only suggests an unease at the continued incursion of the recusant faith into the heart of Caroline society but insinuates the betrayal of militant Protestant hopes by Charles I, the former White Knight of Middleton's *A Game at Chesse*.

The anxiety which enveloped such a shifting and multilayering of religious identities is revealed in the vigorous debates which thundered from the pulpit and the printing press. Despite the flamboyance of the Queen's 'piety', which so exacerbated godly alarm, English Catholics continued to find their own practising of the old faith forbidden. In his texts of 1630 to 1633 Shirley explores and reworks this troubling (and state-manipulated) 'case of conscience': moving from the ambiguity surrounding the ideal of religious constancy in *Changes, Or Love in a Maze* (licensed 1632, published 1632) to the image inherent within popular Protestant thinking of the scheming, treacherous Roman Catholic in *The Traitor* (licensed 1631, published 1635) and *The Young Admiral* (licensed 1633, published 1637). Probing this complex issue of recusant allegiance and treason, Shirley raises a central question regarding Henrietta Maria's key role as defender of the English Catholics. Was she successful in her position as champion of the English recusants? Henrietta Maria's own positive assertion is explored in her fascinating performance as Bellessa in Walter Montagu's *The Shepherds' Paradise* (performed 1632, published 1659). But Shirley's response, teased out in *The Bird in a Cage* (licensed 1633, published 1633), is more equivocal. At a moment when the recusant body was undermined by an increasingly influential Laudian movement, and with matters further complicated through the Queen's association with a Puritan cabal, Shirley (as a true son of Ben Jonson) continued to urge Henrietta Maria to become her best self.

Love in a Maze: staging the early modern temporiser

In his 1633 text *Puritanisme the Mother, Sinne the Daughter* the English recusant B. C. jubilantly recorded the conversion of 'one

Doctour Pryce, Deane of *Hereford*, who dyed Catholike'.[10] Stressing Pryce's high profile within the Protestant establishment, how he was 'particularly knowne and respected by his Majesty', B. C. took great relish in describing the Dean's deathbed conversion, allegedly quoting verbatim Dr Pryce's final remonstrance with a Protestant Bishop:

> O my good Lord, these your wordes are but health-discourses. If you did lye in that case, in which I now am, (and your Lordship must once come to this) at what tyme the veyle of all transitory motives must be drawne asyde, you would no doubt discover your selfe to be of a different opinion in religion . . . For I must tell you plainely, I am persuaded, that there is never a learned Bishop, nor learned Devine in England (if so he hath spent much tyme in the study of Controversies) but that he is inwardly, and in soule a Catholike, howsoever he may be content to dissemble his Religion, through the temporall Motives of Wyfe, Children, Riches, honour, and the lyke.[11]

With reports of Charles I's royal image etched on the foundation stone of the Queen's Capuchin chapel, Dr Pryce's reproach would seem to strike at the heart of Caroline government, supporting Michael Questier's argument that 'when an individual converted to Rome, he demonstrated the existence of a hidden fund of latent popery about which Protestants had every reason to be anxious'.[12] Prominent Whitehall figures such as Francis Cottingham and Thomas Wentworth immediately spring to mind. However, unease over effectively managing this dormant Popery was not exclusive to the established Church. As explored in Chapter 1, from the mid-1620s there had been anxiety in recusant circles regarding the impact on the church-papist of the attractive irenicism emerging from parts of the established Church. By 1633, with the appointment of William Laud to the See of Canterbury, reformed Catholicism (with its focus on the primitive church, and emphasis on the beautification of churches and church ceremony) had moved to the centre of Caroline worship. Traditionally, such Laudianism has been viewed purely from the puritan perspective, embodied in vivid attacks which repeatedly denounced these 'pur-blinde, squint-eyed, ideall Arminian Novellists'.[13] But as the conformist writer William Page intimated, Puritanism was not the only ideology to be alarmed: 'the Spouse of Christ is so prickt, goared, wounded, and molested betweene two Wild factions, of the furious Novelist and the firy Recusant, that a modest, sober, moderate, and peaceable Christian scarce now dares shew his head'.[14] Edward Knott clearly illuminates such recusant hostility towards this encroachment of Laudianism on traditions associated with the old faith. In the aptly named *Charity Mistaken*, he deliberately rejected such irenicism whilst pointedly delineating the differences which continued to separate the two Churches:

> who perceaves not at the first sight, that we resolutely differ from one another, in the prime and maine points of Christian Religion? We embrace not all the same *Scriptures*; we differ about no fewer than *five Sacraments*... we differ about the authority of *all traditions unwritten*, which is the very foundation of our beliefe of the *holy Scripture* itself... We differ aboute *the Primacie of S. Peter*... *the justification of soules*... the *Communion of Saincts*... And we differ not... as men who ar ready to relinquish their opinions, if they be commanded; but we ar on both sides resolved to persist.[15]

Tellingly, Knott reinforces this view by suggesting how the very culture of the Protestant establishment has forced England's Catholics into a position of opposition, a critique which bears reading in full:

> for the finall proofe of this last point according even to their practise as well as ours: let my Reader but looke upon the body of their lawes made against us... wherein they plentifully show how hateful an opinion they have of our Church; Let him looke upon the severall Acts of State, which have issued from my Lords of the Counsell; Let him looke upon the proclamations, which have beene made and published from time to time; Let him looke upon the large commissions, which have beene granted to Pursuivants, whereby that scume of the world, hath been and is enabled, both to ransome & ransacke us at their pleasure; Let him looke upon those speeches, which have been uttered in both houses of Parliament, not only against the professours, but even the profession it selfe of our Religion; and how his most excellent Majestye, hath been importuned by their Petitions, to add more weight to our miseries: for thus it will easily be seene, how false, how rotten, how superstitious, how Idolatrous, how detestable, how damnable, and even destructive of all truth and goodness. they professe themselves to esteem our Religion, and in fine that we carry such a marke of the Beast in our foreheads as must needs, in their opinion, shut up the gates of Heaven against us, and

set open the jawes of Hell to devoure and swallow us up. So that certainly we are no more of one Church with them in their opinion, then they are of one with us in ours.[16]

Such a vehement protestation of religious difference questions the validity of the harmonised image of Henrietta Maria and Charles I etched on the corner stone of the Queen's Capuchin chapel. This tenacious insistence on a recusant 'otherness' becomes an informing dynamic of James Shirley's early 1630s texts.

Shirley's own perspective on the value of an integral recusant honour is overtly implied in his choice of patron for the masque *A Contention for Honour and Riches* (1633). In dedicating this work to Edward Golding of Colston Bassett in Nottinghamshire, Shirley publicly celebrates Golding's 'act and virtue'.[17] This most likely refers to Golding's documented refusal to compromise his recusant beliefs. In honouring such unwavering religious allegiance, Shirley's sentiments are in accord with a noticeable trend within Roman Catholic tracts of the period. In 1631 a paradigm of constancy was urged upon the laity in the form of the martyr Thomas More. His priestly grandson reminded his readers how this Saint 'was raysed by God to be one of the first famous warriours in this our long persecution. Wherefore he may worthily be sett before our eyes, as a perfect patterne and livelie example to be imitated by us: for he had more to loose, then most men in the land.'[18] Similarly *Fuga Saeculi* (1632) extolled the steadfast merits of seventeen saints who had likewise 'delighted in their paynes'.[19] This saintly ideal urged by recusant thinkers found a living embodiment in the resolve of men like Golding, and Shirley engages with this 'act and virtue' in *Changes, or Love in a Maze*. Adopting the motto 'Deserta per avia dulcis / Raptat Amor', Shirley urges fidelity in a text which closely mirrors the adamant sentiments of the 1631 recusant press.[20] Yet, as Shirley himself remarked in his preface to the *Works of Beaumont and Fletcher*, the poet must have 'more than the instruction of libraries (which of itself is but a cold contemplative knowledge)'.[21] As he observes in the prologue to *The Cardinal*, the 'poet's art is to lead on your thought / Through subtle paths and workings of a plot'.[22]

Licensed by the Master of the Revels in January 1632, *Love in a Maze*, as its alternative title *Changes* suggests, focuses on inconstancy in love; juxtaposing the fickleness of the male suitors Gerard and Thornay against the unwavering loyalty of Yongrave. Foregrounded in the text is the pain and unease found in such inconstancy. Gerard himself admits in the opening act: 'I am divided, / And like the trembling needle of a dial / My heart's afraid to fix' (I.ii.424–6). Indeed he vacillates so frequently between the twins Aurelia and Chrysolina that when Gerard finally decides to wed Aurelia she remains unconvinced of the validity of his loyalty, evocatively remarking how 'language is no clue to guide us to / The knowlege of your heart' (III.iii.231–2). Shirley intensifies this pervasive sense of mistrust surrounding the shadowy figure of the temporiser-lover through the actions of Thornay who for worldly gain rejects Eugenia and attempts to woo Chrysolina. In doing so, Thornay breaks an oath of a religious quality, as Eugenia reminds him:

> Tell him I had the promise of his faith,
> When I gave up my heart, in the presence of
> A thousand angels, that will witness it. (II.i.112–4)

In many ways such jejune scenes are typical of the criticisms levelled at Caroline drama by critics from Swinburne to Harbage, encapsulated by Clifford Leech's complaint about these playwrights' 'romantic escape into a world where there were none of the threats that they themselves knew but instead elegant menaces that were foreign to them'.[23] Yet read against the religious polemic of the time, these seemingly vapid exchanges simmer with contemporary concern surrounding the amorphous figure of the neuter, temporiser, church-papist whose heart was also hidden. This anxiety which Aurelia articulates, and Eugenia echoes, studded early modern society. Gerard's fluctuation finds a parallel in the 'neuter' criticised by Thomas Adams in *A Commentary: Or, Exposition Upon the Divine Second Epistle Generall, Written By the Blessed Apostle St. Peter* as 'of either side, of neither side; today a Romist, tomorrow a Protestant, next day no man can tell what, nor himselfe'.[24] Likewise Thornay's abrupt rejection of Eugenia for a more profitable bridal choice in Chrysolina is matched in the temporiser of Brathwaite's *Whimzies*, who 'a *Conscience* (saith he) I professe; but yet I would not have it so nicely scrupulous, as to reject opportunitie of profit'.[25]

In the liberating space of the Caroline stage Shirley confutes this chameleon image to suggest an alternative model of constancy. From *Love in A Maze*'s opening scene Yongrave is presented as unswerving in his loyalty to Eugenia, even though his love is unrequited and brings him little personal profit. He refuses to enter the home of the twins as: 'I must not yield to that / Will bring my faith and honour into question' (I.i.42–3), and he vows to free Eugenia from the malevolent guard of her Uncle Woodhouse. Such selfless fidelity wins the love of Chrysolina and influences Thornay to honour his initial commitment to Eugenia. Engaging with the neuter's 'wonder' through Yongrave's 'act and virtue', *Love in a Maze* highlights the transforming effect on the faltering temporiser of such a staunch recusant model. When Woodhouse appeals against the deception of Eugenia's secret marriage to Thornay crying out 'there is law', Yongrave retorts, 'And there is conscience' (V.v.159–60). Such an equation encapsulates the dilemma embodied by Dr Pryce's alleged deathbed confession: how, as George Wither damningly observed, 'for wives, for wealth, and for our vaine delights / We change *Religion*, like the *Sichemites*'.[26] This championing of Yongrave's rectitude on the Caroline stage is further endorsed by Shirley's choice of patron for his printed play. *Love in a Maze* is dedicated to Lady Dorothy Shirley, publicly praised in Torsellino's *Admirable Life of St. Francis Xavier* (1632) as one whose 'firm and immoveable' profession of the 'Catholike Romane Faith' was 'famous over all our Land'. Like Edward Golding in Nottinghamshire and Yongrave in the fictitious world of *Love in a Maze*, Dorothy Shirley was similarly renowned for her implacable '*Resolution* and *Constancy*' which as Torsellino praised had stood 'firme, and immoveable in the Profession of the Catholike Roman Faith' even 'in the middst of strongest Reasons, Tryalls and Provocations to the contrary'.[27]

The Traitor: probing the politics of temporal and spiritual allegiance

The predicament of the temporiser, caught between 'law', and 'conscience', which is so neatly summed up in the closing lines of *Love in a Maze* is crucial to any understanding of the practising of Roman Catholicism in early modern England. Yongrave might, ultimately, dismiss the 'law' but this brooding presence (documented in the 1606 Oaths of Supremacy and Allegiance) haunted the recusant community. Despite the lavish and seemingly accommodating public dedication ceremony of the Queen's chapel at Somerset House, spiritual allegiance to England's old faith remained inextricably entwined in the wider Protestant consciousness with treason against the state and monarch. Certainly most venom was directed towards the treacherous wiles of the Jesuits.[28] Conformists like George Synge freely admitted 'who knoweth not *Papists* have their kindes? . . . some wee tearme *treacherous* and *disloyall*, their deserts merite it. That others we acknowledge loyall and faithfull, our experiences approve it.'[29] Yet the possibility, that an English Catholic could be deceived by the 'devilish practices' of the Jesuits and in times of national crisis defect to Rome, refused to disappear.[30] As Anthony Cade disturbingly probed in *A Justification of the Church of England*: 'consider well, whether they that perswade you to be absolute *Roman* Catholikes, doe not in deed and effect perswade you to be traytors, troublers of the world, cursed and devilish people!'[31]

However, this potentially vengeful, popish spectre of Protestant nightmare was as misleading as the state's promulgation of the Oath of Allegiance as a simple profession of civil loyalty. Rather, as Michael Questier has argued, from its very initiation in 1606, this oath set out to fracture the recusant community internally. Archpriest Blackwell immediately prophesied such an internecine struggle, remarking how 'we shall in tyme fall into horrible schismes and divisions among ourselves', and that 'if any be once discontented and cannot have his will, he presently beginneth to imagine his flight to the enemie'.[32] As the notorious Widdrington tracts illuminate, such 'schismes' were deliberately exacerbated by the Protestant establishment.[33] Ostensibly the most formidable Catholic defence of the Oaths, these 'recusant' tracts on closer examination reveal a more subversive dynamic. Roger Widdrington was in fact the pseudonym of the Benedictine monk Thomas Preston. Imprisoned in the Clink for his defence of the faith, this seeming epitome of recusancy had become a protégé of Archbishop Abbot of Canterbury. Elaborate intrigues were developed to maintain public belief that the pamphlets were written by an independent Roman Catholic. Abbot even threatened death to the printer if any of Widdrington's 'sheets' were 'pirated', and instructed Sir Thomas Edmondes, the English ambassador in Paris, to 'picke out some nimble fellow who may cunningly convay this booke to the Nuntio, not as from you, but as being some Papist come lately out of England'.[34]

This deliberate attempt to splinter the core of the recusant community by subtly manipulating the recusant's belief in his ability to maintain separate political and religious allegiance fired contemporary debate. During the early 1630s there was 'much talke' amongst recusants regarding issues of temporal and spiritual allegiance, focusing in 1631 on the imminent arrival of the Bishop of Chalcedon and, in 1634, on William Howard's *A Patterne of Christian Loyaltie*.[35] For English Catholics the alternative to recusancy, the unknowable allegiance of the temporiser, had a potentially devastating implication, as the *Lay Catholics Declaration* manifests:

> there are so many lamentable examples among us, not only of friends who have discovered and betraied other friends for receaving Priests, eyther for interest, licentiousnesse of lyfe, revenge, frailty, or for some other passion; but of Servants, who have betrrayed their Maysters, Nephews, Uncles, Grandchildren & children their Parents, Daughters their very Mothers, yea and even Priests themselves sometymes, who have fallen and betrayed Catholikes.[36]

Shirley engages with this thorny debate in *The Traitor* (1631) and *The Young Admiral* (1633). Abandoning the arid distinctions of polemical writing, Shirley explores the ambiguities surrounding the cross-confessionalism of everyday life; both revealing the complexity behind this stereotype of the traitorous English Roman Catholic and exposing the inner turmoil which such oaths inflicted on the Catholic community.

Licensed in 1631, *The Traitor* plunges immediately into the multi-faceted concept of allegiance.[37] An insidious unease pervades the play, for Florentine society, like Caroline London, is shot through with temporisers. Pisano and Cosmo break the commitment of betrothal, the people of the crowd are dismissed as 'the giddy multitude' (IV.i.17), and the Duke himself hovers between the virtue of Amidea and the scheming wiles of Lorenzo, his favourite and kinsman. The focus of this text is on the political machinations of the arch-temporiser Lorenzo, who aims to kill the Duke and win Florence for himself. Lorenzo's impenetrable cunning is established from the first act when he convincingly refutes the charge of treachery, sententiously musing, 'have I a soul / To think the guilt of such a murder easy, / . . . a parricide!' (I.ii.123–7). Yet these raptures and proofs of loyalty are punctured by the muttered commentary of Depazzi, Lorenzo's pawn, who privately denounces him as an 'Admirable traitor' (I.ii.169).

Such stage language of regicide is closely paralleled in contemporary writings which warned against the insidious threat of the perfidious papist. Henry Burton in a direct 'advertisement' to those 'my Countrymen whom the Pope calleth his *Catholicke Sonnes*', warns against becoming so 'farre besotted and infatuated with Jesuiticall Illusions, that treason & rebellion against your Soveraine Prince' appear 'meritorious'.[38] In *The Traitor* such a potential rebel is immediately suggested through the figure of Sciarrha. Manipulated into revenge against the Duke by the seemingly loyal Lorenzo, who warns him of the Duke's plans to rape his sister, Sciarrha declares how there is only one 'cure for this great state / Imposthume' to 'lance it' (II.i.118–21). Significantly Lorenzo (who has actually encouraged the Duke's vicious attack) feeds Sciarrha's beliefs: 'I applaud the wisdom of my stars / That made me for his friendship who preserves / The same religious fire' (II.ii.146–8). Such rhetoric engages Sciarrha's trust, to launch him upon a desperate regicidal path.

This extreme image of regicide is tempered in *The Traitor* by Sciarrha's virtuous sister Amidea, who suggests in her own encounter with the Duke an alternative model of loyalty. When the Duke attempts seduction, Amidea appears to threaten him with a poniard, stating:

> Although I bow in duty to your person,
> I hate your black thoughts; tempt not my just hand
> With violent approach, I dare, and will
> Do that will grieve you, if you have a soul. (III.iii.106–9)

In the hands of a Protestant polemicist this would be the cue for recusant regicide, but on the platform of the Phoenix theatre Shirley stages the possibility of displaying loyalty to both temporal and spiritual rulers:

> *Duke*: Thou dar'st not kill me.
> *Amidea*: True, but I dare die.
> *Duke*: Be thine own murderer?
> *Amidea*: Rather than you should be my ravisher . . .
> *Duke*: I'll not believe –
> *Amidea*: Let this deserve your faith I dare be just
> 　　　　　　　　　　　　　[*she wounds her arm*]
> 　　　　　　　　　　　　　(III.iii.110–25)[39]

Through Amidea's self-mutilation, all are reconciled. The Duke is 'sorry, sorry from my soul' and 'bleed[s] inward' (III.iii.144–5), and Sciarrha, 'all joy' in his liege's 'conversion' (III.iii.176–7), looks upon him 'with new obedience' (III.iii.203). In her own search for justice Amidea challenges the veracity of this recusant spectre, taught as Humphrey Lynde sensationally wrote 'to *eate your God, and kill your King*'.[40] Simultaneously, Shirley's heroine recalls the paradigms of constancy urged upon the recusant community, such as the contemporary hagiography of St Thomas More, who his readers are told 'did . . . willingly forgoe all, yea life it selfe rather then to wrong his Conscience, in consenting to anie thing against the law of God and Justice'.[41] For Catholics, spiritual allegiance to the 'old faith' by no means had an inevitable correlation with temporal disloyalty to the reigning monarch. Indeed, as the 1631 *Declaration of the Lay Catholickes of England* makes explicit, one reason for the rejection of a resident Catholic bishop in England was the impact of his projected clerical court: 'controversies of this nature have mixture with temporall Authority, concerning our temporall Fortunes . . . all which are so already setled, as innovation is most dangerous'.[42]

The Traitor could end here, but curiously Shirley insists on a virtual re-run of the whole plot. Again, Lorenzo manipulates Sciarrha, and the Duke reattempts his seduction of Amidea. Such refusal of an easy textual resolution tightens the play's focus on the danger posed to the state by the temporiser's impenetrability. Ultimately the traitor in this play is not Sciarrha but Lorenzo, whose daily ritual of stabbing the Duke's portrait achieves reality in the regicide of the final scene. Far from having converted, as implied in Act III, Lorenzo is 'but cunning in this shape of honesty', and his soul remains a 'traitor' (IV.i.384). There is a pervading bleakness in this text where the Duke dies having made Lorenzo his 'altar', Cosmo assumes power having earlier forsaken Oriana for temporal gain and Sciarrha stabs Amidea to preserve her honour. In death Amidea, the staunch heroine, becomes a 'pale relic' (V.i.242), a 'martyr' (IV. i.150), a 'red letter' (IV.i.149) – a specific reference to the Catholic custom of printing the feast days of the martyrs in red letters on the calendar – whose integrity questions the persistent papist threat invoked by alarmist Protestant polemic. Intriguingly, theatre legend and *The Traitor*'s reprint of 1692 suggest that this play was only 'ushered' on to the stage by Shirley.

The actual author was one Mr Rivers, a Jesuit languishing in Fleet Street gaol and thereby a member of the most feared Catholic community in early modern England.[43] Most likely this is pure rumour, especially as no mention of such a partnership emerges until some forty years after the play's premiere. Yet the anecdote itself adds another frisson to this reading. In a play which debates the nature of treason, the popularly perceived gap between a recusant's temporal and spiritual allegiance is bridged. Instead, the danger of temporising is foregrounded, a perilous state which the Catholic community perceived to be encouraged by the Oaths of Allegiance and which was widely acknowledged to be embedded throughout Caroline society.

The Young Admiral: re-imagining the recusant traitor

Continuing to pit the Catholic imagination against the Protestant, Shirley re-engages with the concept of the recusant traitor in *The Young Admiral*. Licensed in July 1633 and published in 1637, *The Young Admiral* is known to have been staged on 'tusday the 19th of November, being the king's birth-day' and was 'acted at St. James by the queen's players, and likt by the K. and Queen'.[44] Focusing on the systematic alienation of Vittori, Admiral of the Fleet of Naples, King Charles sees played out before him the agony of a subject whose innate loyalty is complicated by state intervention. Indeed, a certain irony becomes apparent as *The Young Admiral* allows both Charles and his Queen a powerful insight into the recusant conscience and the turmoil rendered in Stuart England by the enforcement of the Oaths of Allegiance and Supremacy.

Unlike the hot-headed Sciarrha of *The Traitor*, Vittori is from the outset contextualised as a loyal subject of Naples. When his officers contemplate insurrection, Vittori counsels how 'Subjects are bound to fight for Princes, they / Not bound to the reward of every service' (I.ii.47–8). Accordingly on the King's arrival he proffers his 'duty' (I.ii.218). The Prince's rebuffal of this symbolic ritual catapults Vittori into the physical torments of banishment and shipwreck. Yet more agonising is his mental torment as he scrutinises the issues surrounding allegiance. Intriguingly, the state, speaking through Prince Cesario, intrinsically misjudges this concept. Criticising his father's decision to banish Vittori, Cesario claims that banishment, like any form of marginalisation, 'disengages' the 'relation and tie of subject' (II.i.91–2). However, as Vittori makes clear, issues of loyalty are not so unambiguous. When the King of Sicily suggests that the banished Vittori should revenge himself against 'Naples ingratitude' (III.iii.219) by becoming 'our soldier' (III.i.222), Vittori finds such an action untenable:

> Does he call treason justice? Such a treason
> As heathens blush at; nature and religion
> Tremble to hear: to fight against my country!
> 'Tis a less sin to kill my father. (III.i.237–40)

Stating, 'I must not make a desperate shipwreck of / My piety' (III.i.257–8), Vittori finds loyalty to his country etched in his very being: 'It was / Articled in the creation of my soul / I should obey, and serve my country with it / Above myself' (III.i.258–61). And he seeks relief in death, declaring that he will 'die my country's martyr' (III.iii.286).

This insistence upon the inextricable union of an individual's ties of religion and state allegiance compellingly questions Protestant England's continued promulgation of the Oath of Allegiance as an uncomplicated profession of civil loyalty. Thomas Preston claimed in 1634, writing under a new pseudonym of William Howard, that the Oath simply made a *'true distinction, not betwixt* Catholikes *and* Protestants, *but betwixt* Catholikes *of quiet disposition, and in all other things good Subjects, and such other* Catholikes *as in their hearts maintained the like violent bloudie Maximes, as the Powder-traytors did'*.[45] Rather, such renewed government manipulation further reinforces Michael Questier's argument that these Oaths deliberately challenged the 'always uneasy determination of English Romanists to keep consciences away from the prying eyes of the Protestant state' for 'in questioning Papal power, the Oaths [struck] at the heart of the Roman Catholic faith, potentially alienating all English recusants'.[46] In November 1633 these matters were firmly to the fore of the national consciousness. Notably, in the very same week that Shirley's *The Young Admiral* was performed at court for the King's birthday, a Dominican friar, Arthur Geoghegan, was actually being tried for 'treasonable words' regarding the deposition of heretical kings. Charles 'himself did not think much of the proofs against him and was disposed to pardon him, or to punish him lightly'.[47] Yet, on 27 November, Geoghegan died a traitor's death at Tyburn.

Shirley tightens this focus on issues of loyalty through the structure of *The Young Admiral*; as in *The Traitor* any simple resolution is denied. The King of Sicily uses Vittoria's beloved Cassandra as a decisive bargaining pledge. Weighing his devotion to Cassandra against his instinctive fealty to his country, Vittori voices his inner turmoil in military terms: 'I cannot hold, this conflict is more fierce / Than many thousand battles' (III.i.326–7). Echoing Sciarrha in *The Traitor*, Vittori adopts the language of the sea: 'I am in a tempest, / and know not how to steer; destruction dwells / on both sides' (III.ii.349–51). Ultimately, Vittori chooses to 'take arms' (III.i.354), the overriding fear of Protestant England. Yet it is with agonising remorse that Vittori chooses to let Cassandra live, crying:

> forgive me then,
> Great Genius of my Country, that, to save
> Her life, I bring my honour to the grave. (III.i.354–6)

Moreover, Vittori is not the only character in *The Young Admiral* forced by state machinations to re-examine issues of loyalty. Alphonso, Vittori's father, is also falsely accused of treason, causing him to ponder in anguish, 'Is obligation of a parent, more / Than that we owe our country?' (IV.ii.19–20). Provocatively Cassandra elucidates the potential self-inflicted damage to the establishment inherent in such intrusion into a subject's conscience. This loyal and honourable noblewoman is so disturbed that she momentarily realigns her own ties of allegiance, wishing 'for the punishment of Naples / More cruel than our enemies' (III.i. 340–1) for 'Naples has been injurious, and we made / No solemn vow to love what hath betrayed us' (III.i.252–3).

In dedicating this play to George, Lord Berkeley, Shirley's patron choice adds a further layer to the issues explored on the stage. On the one hand this might seem fairly unremarkable; Lord Berkeley was a popular patron. Amongst others John Webster, Robert Burton and Philip Massinger all dedicated works to one who, as Mary Fage ruminated in *Fames Roule*, 'ever doth breed the Muses great delight'.[48] Yet, digging a little deeper, it is perhaps with no great surprise that the Berkeley family emerges with a very clear recusant-cum-church-papist lineage. George Berkeley's great-grandmother, Anne Savage was renowned for her constancy to the Catholic faith, 'which was the cause why Queene Mary and the Clergy of her time exceedingly favoured her'.[49] Rumours of church-papism clung around Berkeley's grandfather, Henry, who was a key figure in aiding Queen Mary in the Wyatt rebellion. Indeed, towards the end of Elizabeth I's reign Henry Berkeley received a letter from the Archbishop of Canterbury:

> greatly advising him to take notice of the dispositions of his servants, and his wife's wayting-women, in the matter of their conformity in religion, and how comely and honourable it would be to see himself and his wife attended upon at service and sacraments by his whole family; prayinge his Lordship to take from him the occasion of a second admonition.[50]

More contemporarily, George Berkeley's Aunt Frances, youngest sister of his father, had married into the Warwickshire Shirleys, whose coat of arms James Shirley had so boldly appropriated (as depicted in Figure 3). Frances's recorded deathbed wish was that her three children should be 'instructed and brought up in the fear of God, and true Catholick religion'.[51] That this desire was apparently fulfilled is evident from her eldest son Henry, first cousin to George Berkeley, choosing as his wife the same Dorothy Shirley famed by Torsellino for her recusant constancy, and to whom James Shirley dedicated *Love in a Maze*. During this period George Berkeley was the target of Protestant writers offering him guides to proper living such as Anthony Stafford's *Guide of Honour*.[52] In *The Young Admiral*, James Shirley offers George Berkeley an alternative code, reminding him, through this exploration of recusant allegiance, of the difficult choices his ancestors made, and to which some family members continued to adhere.

If we return to the actual staging of *The Young Admiral* and remember how this play is known to have been performed before Shirley's key patroness, Queen Henrietta Maria, it is remarkable how Vittori is finally saved from betraying his country through the salvatory figure of Rosinda, daughter of the King of Sicily. This outside force who brings resolution and reform has a 'bearing ... above the common spirit' (V.ii.117), a eulogy culminating in the King of Naples's comment: 'with what eyes could he look / Upon this beauty, and not love it' (V.ii.226–7). Yet, as Vittori proclaims, Rosinda's 'beauty is her least perfection' (V.ii.228). More remarkable is her courage in reforming the wayward Prince and uniting the states of Sicily and Naples. Crucially, Rosinda dissolves the inextricable tensions surrounding the issues of treason and allegiance, an especially potent trope when performed before this Roman Catholic Queen Consort. In the context of Vittori's image of shipwreck Rosinda proves to be a true 'star of the sea'. The Roman Catholic resonance of such language and imagery would not be lost on Catholic members of Shirley's audience, as is evident from John Brereley's popular *Virginalia* of 1632, where the opening sonnet states:

> MARIA, glorious sea-starre; thy cleare sight
> Guides us upon the world's tempestuous waves; ...
> Help me ô then, sinn's dang'rous shelves to shunne.[53]

Deeming Rosinda a 'religious treasure' (V.iv.28), Cesario admits 'there's virtue in that excellent princess / to stock two kingdoms' (V.iv.22–4). Such a conclusion surely recalls the adumbration within Roman Catholic Europe of Queen Henrietta Maria's vocation to restore England's old faith, a mission which, if successful, would have instantly dispelled the English Catholic's inner turmoil.

The Shepherds' Paradise: Queen Henrietta Maria's remodelling of her Counter-Reformation vision

But one has to ask how comparable was this reforming figure of Rosinda to Shirley's key patroness, Queen Henrietta Maria? The Queen's own perception of her success is suggested from her self-presentation in a Van Dyck portrait completed in 1632, where she gazes serenely out of the canvas, gently cradling a rose, the symbol of England (Frontispiece). In a painting of such dark hues, from the richly muted backdrop to the black patina of the Queen's elegant gown, the eye is repeatedly drawn to the blush of damask pink at the painting's centre. With several rosebuds peeking from the foliage, at its most obvious level this rose represents Henrietta Maria's success at fulfilling her main duty as Queen Consort, that of providing a royal heir. By 1632 the young Prince Charles was two years old and most likely Henrietta Maria was expecting Princess Mary while sitting for this portrait. Yet for Henrietta Maria the rose had an added significance. Pope Urban VIII had given his goddaughter a rose of gold on her wedding day.[54] Notably, in 1627 Fr Bérulle employed this floral emblem (signifying both the Queen's new homeland and her papal mission) to deplore England's state of religion:

le rosier de cette île a changé de nature lorsqu'elle a changé de créance. Et il ne porte que des épines très poignantes. Les rosiers avant le péché (ce dit saint Basile) portaient des roses sans épines. Mais l'hérésie qui est le comble du péché, fait que les rosiers de cette île ne portent que des épines sans roses, de sorte que leurs armes anciennes leur manquent aussi bien que la foi et piété ancienne.[55]

[The rose tree of this Island changed in nature when belief changed. And it only bears very sharp thorns. The rose trees before the fall (according to St Basil) bore roses without thorns. But heresey which is the crown of sin, made the rose trees of this island bear only the thorns without the roses, so that England's ancient coat of arms are missing faith as well as the old piety] (*Sainte Madeleine*, p. 411).

As this Van Dyck portrait displays, by 1632, in the nurturing hands of Henrietta Maria, once more the rose was in full bloom. John Brerely's 'Rosa Mystica', a contemporary setting of the Litany of Loreto, illuminates how the rose was closely associated with the Blessed Virgin Mary, to whom Henrietta Maria had a special devotion.[56] With the Queen's new chapel openly dedicated 'sous le très-heureuse auspices de la très hereuse Vierge Marie, sa Patronne' [under the very happy auspices of the very blessed Virgin Mary, her Patroness], it certainly seemed that, as Fr Gamache recorded, the Queen's 'piety' had begun to displace those 'thorns of heresy' from 'when the religion was changed in this unhappy kingdom'.[57]

However, the simple iconography of this painting also resonates with an image of a different English Queen; that of Elizabeth I. Nicholas Hilliard's beautiful miniature of the Virgin Queen from c.1575 displayed in Figure 7 depicts Elizabeth I in sumptuous costume, elegantly poised with a full-blossomed rose. In appropriating such a dynamic image of Gloriana, the embodiment of Protestant England, Henrietta Maria can be seen to be positioning herself at the heart of the nation. As Malcolm Smuts has argued in an influential article, Henrietta Maria by no means simply surrounded herself with a coterie of court Catholics.[58] During the early 1630s especially she deliberately allied herself with a cabal whose anti-Spanish policies complemented her own pro-French, anti-Richelieu sentiments. Such a position anomalously encouraged strong links with privy councillors renowned for their godly sympathies such as the Earl of Pembroke and Sir Dudley Carleton.[59] Through the image of the rose Van Dyck's portrayal of

7 Nicholas Hilliard, *Queen Elizabeth I*, c. 1575.

Henrietta Maria allowed the Queen to reach out visibly to both her Catholic and her Protestant subjects. This seeming complexity is perhaps rooted in the Queen's growing understanding of her mother's advice on departing from France: 'n'oubliez-pas non plus les autres pauvres Anglais' [do not forget those other poor [i.e.

non-Catholic] English subjects].[60] With the Laudian blurring of traditional religious boundaries, and the accommodating dedication ceremony of the Queen's flagrantly Roman Catholic chapel, the possibilities behind such gentle proselytising would have seemed especially tantalising. In 1632 this nascent promise overflowed on to the elite Caroline stage. Henrietta Maria once more assumed the mantle of actress to perform the lead role of Bellessa in Walter Montagu's *The Shepherds' Paradise*. Building from *L'Artenice*, where Henrietta Maria had asserted her own model of her status as Queen Consort, *The Shepherds' Paradise* enabled the Queen to reaffirm and refashion this ideal. Just as her provocative portrayal of Artenice had offset a period of difficulties for the Queen, so too the timing of *The Shepherds' Paradise* neatly redirected attention away from the accusations of intrigue which surrounded Henrietta Maria in the early 1630s. Abruptly thwarted in her attempts to unseat Cardinal Richelieu, and with the Catholic community somewhat unnerved by her public scheming with puritan sympathisers, the stage role of Bellessa allowed Henrietta Maria to showcase a renewed vision for her position as Queen Consort.

Recently, *The Shepherds' Paradise* has received substantial scholarly attention.[61] Previously considered as a theatrical curio, with most critics astounded by the Queen and her ladies' ability to deliver nearly four thousand lines of dialogue, *The Shepherds' Paradise* is worthy of attention for its place in the annals of stage history alone. As Sophie Tomlinson asserts, not only is Walter Montagu the first known English playwright to stage a play specifically for an all-female cast, but this is also the first play in which a reigning Queen Consort sang as well as acted.[62] Originally scheduled to be delivered on the King's birthday in November 1632, the royal performance was delayed until early in the New Year. Reports of lengthy rehearsals under the tutelage of the actor Joseph Taylor underscore the importance which the Queen placed on this staging.[63] The results of such exactitude are recorded in Salvetti's diplomatic accounts of the evening:

> the scenic apparatus was very lovely, but so was the beauty of the performers, and of the queen above all the rest, who with her English and the grace with which she showed it off, together with her regal gestures ... out did all the other ladies though they too acted their parts with the greatest variety.[64]

The play itself is a romance pastoral, that genre most conducive to Henrietta Maria's theatrical tastes. Within the safe confines of this Shepherds' Paradise, Bellessa, the elected queen of the community, is wooed by Moramente, which in this play of multiple disguise in fact unites the Princess of Navarre with Prince Basilino of Castile. As Karen Britland has argued, *The Shepherds' Paradise* 'resonates' with its time of composition, refusing to be constricted to one specific political allegory.[65] From the romance of Bellessa and Moramente allusions are positively encouraged to Henrietta Maria's own wedding narrative, whilst the sudden discovery of the Prince Palatine in the play's final scene is a far from oblique reference to the continued plight of Elizabeth of Bohemia. Emphasising these tiers of political and allegorical nuances, contemporaries are known to have been eager to study this pastoral in some detail. Sarah Poynting documents how Lucius Cary, Viscount Falkland, was particularly keen to gain a manuscript copy:

> I have here returned, what I had much rather have kept, but that I am enjoyned to restitucon, & my comfort is that the parteing with this, will purchase me the readeing of the rest, if I valued it so high at the single hearing, when myne eares could not catch halfe the words, what must I do now, in the reading when I may pause uppon it, but what should I doe if I might enjoy a Coppy of it, or have leave to Coppy it, which favour I hope I shall one day obtaine, for it is not twice or thrise reading this peece, that will sufficiently satisfie a well advised reader.[66]

One such known 'well advised reader' was Lady Dorothy Shirley, that renowned recusant whom, in this instance, Cary describes as longing 'extreamely to read it, and hath sent to beg a sight of it'.[67] It can be presumed that equally enthusiastic readers were the Tixalls, a firmly Catholic Staffordshire family, as the surviving manuscript which provides the basis for Sarah Poynting's excellent edition of the text is likely to have belonged to them.[68] The question asked here is what such early modern recusant readers would have thought as they avidly devoured this manuscript play of wandering pilgrims, where Fidamira the alter-heroine, whose name literally means 'miracle of faith', finds sanctuary in a paradise ruled by Bellessa, a part written for and acted by that most visible of Catholics in Caroline England, Queen Henrietta Maria.

At essence this paradise is a place of refuge, 'a peacefull ... receptacle of distressed mindes, & sanctuary against fortunes severest executions' (854–5). The anguished Prince of Castile specifically visits this 'peacefull harbour' (469) because of its fame for 'the strange repair of wrack't / & hopeles fortunes' (470–1). With members taking vows and assuming habits on joining the community, it is a space moreover which evokes rituals of living closely associated with the old faith. Erica Veevers suggests how the Paradise's 'vows, ceremonies, priests, altar, temple and prayers' are celebrated with a 'religious solemnity'.[69] Karen Britland documents how the election rules for the Queen of this paradise appear to be rooted in the rules of the Visitandine nuns, whom Henrietta Maria herself patronised in the 1650s.[70] John Peacock perceives an 'atmosphere which is recognisably and peculiarly Catholic'.[71] Moreover, the elaborate cupola and flamboyant architecture of the pastoral's Temple in Inigo Jones's designs (Figure 8) evokes the baroque Catholicism of the Counter-Reformation which Henrietta Maria was effectively introducing to England through her own Capuchin chapel. It is into such a 'Center', where 'all the extended / lynes of vertue, that are in this worlds Circumference' (2263–4) meet, that Fidamira flees, beset by the unwelcome passions of both the King and Prince of Navarre. Engaging with the anxiety surrounding issues of constancy explored on the commercial stage, Fidamira is established as the quintessence of fidelity in a world marked by the 'vicissitude of Change' (2829). The once loudly voiced passions of both the Prince and Agenor for Fidamira falter under the charms of Bellessa, but her own love for Agenor remains 'unmov'd' (2834). Indeed, as Fidamira remarks, 'it is I then for being constant / among these Changes am unnaturall' (2835–6).

Strikingly, throughout the play, it is Bellessa who reminds the audience of Fidamira's inherent value. Chancing upon Agenor gazing upon a miniature of Fidamira which he first suggestively terms 'a litle Manuall of Devotion' (2722), only to dismiss it abruptly as of little consequence, Bellessa rebukes him and urges him in his 'private / Devotion' to 'recant this dissembling' (2758–9). Likewise when Moramente questions the election of Fidamira (freshly disguised as the Mooress Gemella) into the community, Bellessa censures him, asking 'whoe knowes what one day may be called beauty? / since wee see the opinion of it alter every day' (1784–5). The close links between Fidamira and Bellessa are further

'A Case of Conscience' 111

8 Inigo Jones's sketch of *A Temple* for Walter Montagu,
The Shepherds' Paradise, 1632.

suggested in Agenor's comment when he mistakes Fidamira for an angel: 'Thou / Must needs know her if Angells knowe one another, for / She is our delegate here on earth' (3224–6). As Sophie Tomlinson asserts, Bellessa's integrity and her underlying role of protector to Fidamira culminate in the play's final scene, for crucially it is the Queen who 'transforms Gemella from blackness to beauty'.[72] In a staged action which resonates with the language of the Song of Songs, 'know tis my Veil looks black, not I', Bellessa rips away 'Gemella's' dark veil to reveal Fidamira's natural beauty, declaring 'Thus I justefy my choice, expecting / Admiration, not exception' (3713–14).[73] That Fidamira, ultimately named as Miranda, flourishes under the protection of Queen Bellessa is at the very least wondrously suggestive – especially as, if the rehearsal schedule had gone according to plan, this royal performance would have occurred barely two months after the Queen's other much reported event of 1632/3, the public dedication ceremony of her Roman Catholic 'Temple'. Indeed, highlighting the theatrical element of Henrietta Maria's religious preferences, John Pory brackets the Queen's enthusiastic preparations for this elite performance in the same letter as he reports on the laying of the foundation stone for her Capuchin chapel.[74]

Such allusions are heightened if we truncate that 'moment of disbelief' inherent to any performance to consider the actress beneath Fidamira's disguise. From surviving cast lists, as Sarah Poynting has established, the role of Fidamira is known to have been played by Sophia Carew or, more properly, Sophia Neville owing to her wedding in December 1632 to Richard Neville, a gentleman of the King's Chamber.[75] As a daughter of the Carew/Godolphin families, Sophia had strong links with the established Church, comprising the full spectrum of both conformist and puritan sympathies.[76] However, her husband's family name of Neville is redolent with connections to the old faith and previous notorious attempts at restoration. Most blatant was the attainder in 1570 of Sir Charles Neville, Earl of Westmorland, for plotting to put Mary Queen of Scots on the throne, precisely because 'divers disordered and evil disposed persons about the Queens Majesty have by their subtle and crafty dealings, to advance themselves, overcome in this realm the true and Catholic religion'.[77] Some thirty years later Sir Charles died in exile, having survived on a 'miserable pittance allowed him by the King of Spain'.[78] Yet, according to the letters of Tobie Matthew, the Bishop of Durham, Westmorland's daughters, Margaret and Katherine, who remained in England, were renowned for their maintenance of recusant networks and the harbouring of priests.[79] Likewise in the junior Abergavenny branch to which Richard Neville belonged, papism was still deeply rooted. His first cousin Anne was Abbess of a convent in Pontoise, France, whilst on the death of his uncle, Lord Henry Abergavenny, his Aunt Frances had married the leading Catholic Sir Basil Brooke.[80] Further embedding these recusant networks, Richard Neville's cousin Margaret had married her stepfather's son, Thomas Brooke.[81]

Contemporary readers like the Tixalls would have been only too alert to such nuances. The political implications for England's old faith deepen in a play where both Bellessa and Fidamira repeatedly encourage the shepherds in one of the three cardinal virtues integral to Catholic teaching, namely hope. Fidamira urges the despairing Moramente, Prince of Navarre, to 'learne of me to hope' (2808). And Bellessa advises her servant Martiro to 'measure time' with 'your soule, not your sence' (1261), warning him: 'you must not Antedate your desires soe as time may seeme / too slow to bring you them' (1262–3); 'If you must needs / wish something without your selfe, let it be somewhat you / may hope for; nothing takes more from time, then that' (1267–9). Such a virtue was particularly pertinent to the longsuffering recusant community. Where Sarah Poynting has argued that this paradise is largely secular, Karen Britland suggests the pastoral's 'religious vision' is 'allusive'.[82] Yet, for the Catholic reader like Lady Dorothy Shirley, the inherent religio-political possibilities of the oath which Bellessa swears upon her election as queen of this paradise would have been more than 'allusive'. Bellessa emphatically vows *'To keepe the honour & the Regall due: / Without exacting any thing that's new'* (719–20). But the additional clause, that as queen she will *'assume . . . no more, then must / Give me the meanes & power to be just'* (721–2), implies some leverage within the defined oath. Such brokerage is intensified through her pledge to *'Reserve noe power to suspend the Lawes'* (724), again with the fundamental exception, *'but for Charity & mercies Cause'* (723). Bellessa's manifesto in this staged coronation suggests the agency which Henrietta Maria as Queen of England might affect in the patriarchal arena of Caroline England. Such intervention was of particular interest to the Catholic community. Contemporary reports are dotted with proven instances of the Queen's intercession for the English recusants. Fr Cyprien of Gamache records Henrietta Maria's actions when some thirty papists were apprehended. Amongst them was a 'very virtuous young lady, big with child' who:

> was dragged thither with such violence that she was extremely ill in consequence, and was delivered before her time of a dead infant. The zeal of the Queen was kindled by this affair, of which she made grievous complaint to the King, obtained an order for the release of the Catholics from prison, and the confinement there of the persecutors by whom they had been consigned thither with such inhuman violence.[83]

Indeed, the potential strength of this queenly influence is suggested in the trajectory of Sophia Neville herself. Whatever her own religious inclination before 1632, by the 1650s Sophia was a known recusant whose faith prevented her from attending her own son's wedding.[84]

The emblem of the rose in the Van Dyck portrait of 1632 signalled Henrietta Maria's positioning of herself at the heart of the English nation, reaching out to all her subjects although especially mindful of the Catholic community. Significantly the Shepherds' Paradise is also clearly defined as a space

> Whose peacefull bounds have that strange vertue
> From the Gods, as to include all those that are admitted
> There, in peaceful acquiesence. (1876–8)

Yet, as Bellessa's vow enunciates even within such an inclusive paradise, the shepherds' queen adheres to the right to protect those persecuted by unjust laws. Moreover, she guarantees this vow by her own hopes '*to rise / From this unto an higher Paradice*' (725–6) and specifically goes off to pray to find the strength to keep this resolve. Such a stage role allowed Henrietta Maria to quite literally recreate herself before her elite audience: revoicing and developing her own position as Queen Consort. In this pastoral, a genre defined by George Puttenham as being able to 'insinuate and glaunce at greater matters', the figure of Bellessa might well give hope to those recusant readers, such as the Tixalls, that their community was protected by a Queen governed by the virtues of mercy and charity.[85] In turn this adds an additional frisson to Martiro's final blessing to Bellessa in the play's concluding couplet. His wish that '*when Heavens heate shall draw you to the skye*', Bellessa, like the saintly paradigms of the Virgin Mary and St Mary Magdalene, may also '*transfigur'd not disfigur'd dye*' (3858–9).

The Bird in a Cage: a synthesis of early modern Catholic cultures

Although Henrietta Maria was content in her role as Queen Consort, and the elite ideal expressed in *The Shepherds' Paradise* resonated with hope for the Catholic community, more militant recusants might legitimately question this harnessing of queenly influence for the Catholic faith. Undoubtedly Catholicism appeared to be flourishing within the immediate confines of the Queen's court circle. But the brimming possibilities of such religious fervour seemed limited exclusively to the Queen's immediate vistas. Even the triumph engulfing the creation of the Queen's Capuchin chapel was somewhat muted by contemporary Catholic accounts which highlighted the continued plight of the non-elite English recusant as having 'much ado to heare Masse in a corner, as private as may be, without discovery'.[86] As documented in Chapter 2, 1629 had seen an increase in fines against recusancy: the harsher measure both quieting puritan anxiety and supporting the Stuart belief that spiritual allegiance to Rome could be better tolerated on a full exchequer. By no means suggesting an Inquisition-like persecution, just a couple of isolated instances in a single year such as 1633 serve as a reminder of the unrelenting punishments inflicted upon those who continued in their allegiance to the old faith. Lady Wotton was publicly fined £500 for inscribing on her husband's tomb that he 'died a true Catholic of the Roman Church', whilst the Irish Dominican Arthur Geoghegan was hanged for treason.[87]

Noticeably in the recusant writings of this period the drive to incite the laity to a renewed constancy was mirrored by Catholic polemicists urging upon Henrietta Maria the exemplar of Queen Esther. In his 1631 dedication to *A Hive of Honie-Combes*, Br Antonie Batt openly declared his wish to

> move your Majestie, like a second Hester, that having such power with our great Assuerus, as your lovely vertues, strengthtened with the hopefull seale of marriage (which is a Prince of Great Britaine, proceeding from both your loines) do afford you: you would after her imitation, as hitherto you have done, reconcile his favour and mercie to youre poore afflicted subjects the Catholiques of England: not to have power and leave to defend themselves against their enemies; but to be freed and secured from vexation in their faith.[88]

The devotions within *A Hive of Honie-Combes* encourage an unyielding practising of recusancy: 'he hath powred forth his blood for thee: do thou in like sort powre forth thine by daily affliction of thy bodie'.[89] The 'reward' for such adversity 'is to see God, to live with God' in comparison to which 'the love of riches and possessions, the affection of kindred, the desire of honours, the pleasure of the flesh is bird lime'.[90] In the face of such uncompromising devotion, from an English recusant perspective, Henrietta Maria's own potential as an Esther figure remained tantalisingly unfulfilled. Fr John Southcot, in a letter to Peter Biddulph in August 1633, voiced his own support for Henrietta Maria's 'good offices' for English Catholics, but recounted how

> some of the Jes[uits'] followers here do observe as a great wonder that, since the queen came in, none of the ladies at court are become catholickes, and I heard my self a Jes[uit] speake this openly, as it were to the queens disgrace, in a gentlemans house in the country.[91]

In a dispatch to Cardinal Richelieu the French ambassador Châteauneuf hinted at the Queen's deliberate reluctance to exploit her influence: 'every time she wants to speak to [the King] he listens and replies: but as she does not apply herself and worries very little about things, and does not know how she must speak, it does little good, and is regarded by the English ministers as of no importance'.[92] Such apathy is in direct opposition to the courageous actions of the Old Testament heroine Esther. As Francis Quarles's contemporary exploration of the Esther story reiterated, this Old Testament prototype led a proactive and uncompromising campaign. Galvanised into action by Mordechai's suggestion that 'her feare' was *'too great'*, her zeal *'too small'*, Esther had made full use of her prime position *'bosom'd in* [the King's] *heart'* to free her people from oppression.[93]

A possible root of this conflict between Henrietta Maria's vision of her role as Queen Consort and the part imagined for her by the English militant recusant can be identified from her inculcation in, and practising of, a French style of Catholicism. The ideal of Catholic femininity emerging from contemporary French devotional works is one of gentle passivity. Francis de Sales advocates the need for his female reader to be cordial to all: 'to gentlie and sweetlie follow on their way', to 'show in everie enterprise Obedience and Charitie', for 'Blessed are the pliable hearts, for they will never break'.[94] Similarly, Nicolas Caussin advises that she 'who well obeyeth, commandeth wel', with the rider 'when we once have surprised the hart of a man, there is not any thing resisteth our wils'.[95] Caussin in *The Holy Court* even suggested a new model for Henrietta Maria in the figure of Clotilda, the first Catholic Queen of France, who converted her husband Clodeus rather 'by the example of a good life, & her humble prayers presented on Aultars, then by any other way'.[96] The parallels with Henrietta Maria are suggestive: 'so many poore Catholiques, as were then in France, beheld [Clotilda] as the dawning of the day, which came to charme their cares, wipe away their teares, breake their fetters, & guild the tymes with the lustre of her Majesty'.[97] Significantly, in the light of Henrietta Maria's recent construction of a Catholic chapel, Clotilda makes

> a little Oratory, as *Judith* in the royall Palace, where she attended, as much as tyme would permit to prayers, and mortifications of flesh . . . Yet did she manage all her actions with singular discretion, that she might not seeme too austere in the eyes of her Court . . . It was an Angelicall Spectacle to see her present at Masse; and dispose hereselfe to receyve the blessed Sacrament, which she very often frequented, to draw grace and strength from its source.[98]

Accordingly, as Erica Veevers has discussed, the type of Roman Catholicism which appealed to Henrietta Maria, and which was integral to her preferred theatrical experiences, focuses on the subtle power of women as beautiful creatures whose example can lead to conversion from within. Such shimmering divinity was the antithesis of the more active virtue which had, for reasons of survival alone, from necessity been practised by the females of the oppositional community of English recusants. In the 1630s this difference in experience of French and English Catholicism was bridged in recusant writing by an attempt to cross-fertilise the two cultures. Thus, *The Treatise of the Love of God* by Francis de Sales with its emphasis on beauty as a potential force for conversion was very apposite to Henrietta Maria. As Veevers seems not to notice, this tract is dedicated to Elizabeth Dormer, daughter of the archetypal Elizabethan recusant matriarch, the redoubtable Lady Magdalen Viscountess Montague. The translator of Francis de Sales's, work, Miles Car, magnifies the vigorous zeal of the Montague family. Elizabeth's mother 'strooke even heretikes with astonishment', her father was renowned for his 'undaunted Zeale', whilst her own 'performances' as a recusant had taught 'Forrainers to speake and use your HONOR'S name in termes of respect and honour'.[99] Such interaction suggests, at the very least, an attempt to provide understanding of the Queen's own Roman Catholicism. And this cultural chasm is highlighted by a timely reminder in at least one recusant tract of the time: 'let our care be, in the sight of God, unpartially to consider, and with indifferency to desire, what may be most expedient for Catholickes, not in *France, Spayne, Italy*, and other Countreyes, happy with peaceable possession of Ecclesiasticall splendour; but in *England* blessed only with joyful suffering alonge continued persecution'.[100]

This inherent belief in the singularity of the recusant position within Christendom defines the thinking of the English Catholic. Significantly, this 'otherness' so essential to the recusant's sense of identity had been nourished by a strong matriarchy. Almost as a literary Mordechai, Shirley through the feminocentricity of his texts can be seen to be urging Henrietta Maria towards a similarly redoubtable leadership of this Catholic community. Shirley's heroines succeed in their endeavours not through divine beauty alone but through a forceful zeal which openly converts. Vittori highlights in *The Young Admiral* how Rosinda's beauty is 'her least perfection'. Reflecting the synthesis of cultures within the recusant press, Shirley fuses in his heroines the transforming beauty which was so attractive to Henrietta Maria, with the steadfast fervour inherent to the old faith. Rosinda, Amidea, Penelope, Gratiana and Lucibel are all renowned for their near-celestial attractiveness, yet they are firmly cast in the mould of gritty virtue which was so vital to the early modern recusant woman. Such resourceful tenacity was encapsulated in the contemporary actions of Agnes Rosendale, whom John Falconer celebrated in his *Mirrour of Created Perfection* (1632). Thwarted by her family in her desire to become a nun, Agnes fled to the English Carmelites at Antwerp, and achieved her aim only by putting herself 'in to a small Wheele, serving (as the manner is) to take in and out things needful for the inclosed, left at that tyme by a rare chance unlocked'. Such an intrepid arrival 'no lesse amazed the Reverend Mother, and Sisters to see a person of your knowne quality, kneeling almost naked before them, with flowing teares begging their holy habit, then it joyed your selfe to have gotten in so among them'.[101]

This tale of recusant ingenuity neatly juxtaposes the gulf between the determination of the more fervent recusant and Henrietta Maria's passive zeal. In the 1630s the Catholic community's demand for an ardent champion was exacerbated by the disconcerting advance of Laudianism within the Caroline court. Shirley explores the complexities of this cultural moment in perhaps his best known play, *The Bird in a Cage*.[102] Originally entitled *The Bewties*, this play has been widely perceived as an animated defence of Henrietta Maria against the open invective of William Prynne's notorious *Histriomastix*.[103] Yet on closer examination, the dynamic which energises *The Bird in a Cage* is in essence rooted in the same protest as its seeming opposite *Histriomastix*, resistance to the dominant Caroline establishment. Through the figure of Eugenia, Shirley urges Henrietta Maria to overreach the boundaries within which she had complacently settled herself, and to reinvigorate her Counter-Reformation mission which she had first avowed in *L'Artenice*, some seven years earlier.

In his dedication of *The Bird in a Cage* to William Prynne, Shirley markedly draws attention to the shifting intricacy of religious realignment within the established Church. Newsletters from early 1633 were bursting with news of Prynne's imprisonment. As Sir George Cresley announced, Prynne was to be arraigned

> for publishing a book, a little before the queen's acting of her play, of the unlawfulnesse of plays; wherein in the table of his book and his brief additions thereunto he hath these words, 'women actors notorious whores': and that St. Paul prohibits women to speak publicly in the Church, 'and dares then', saith he, 'any christian woman be so more than whorishly impudent, as to act, to speak publicly on a stage (perchance in man's apparel and cut hair) in the presence of sundry men and women?' Which words, it is thought by some, will cost him his ears, or heavily punished, and deeply fined.[104]

Yet to Justinian Paget, corresponding with James Harrington, the issue appeared more complex: 'I do not conceive this to be the only cause why he is called in question, but rather some exorbitant passage concerning ecclesiastical government; for I hear he compares the playing on the organs between the first and second lesson, to interludes and stage playes.'[105] William Sanderson supported this conclusion, reporting how Prynne's 'invective against *Stage-plays*' was as much against 'the solemn *Musick* used in the *Cathedrals* and the *Royal Chappels*', as against '*Masques*' and '*Dancings* at *Court*'.[106] In his dedication to Prynne, Shirley addresses both issues. Undoubtedly, as Sophie Tomlinson argues, Shirley berates Prynne's attack on the stage and women-players. But equally as prominent is his acknowledgement of Prynne's reputation as an avid puritan polemicist, whose work emphatically denounced Rome and the rising swell of the Laudian movement. Declaring in his preface that the title of his own play was an open 'imitation' of Prynne's own 'ingeniously fancied' tracts, Shirley forcefully censures any link between Laudianism and Rome as 'errata' (preface).[107] Engaging with what he deemed Prynne's secular 'Roman constancy' (preface), Shirley in *The Bird in the Cage* creates a recusant model of fortitude which distinctly differentiates between the Roman Catholic and the established Churches. Just as Prynne had hoped his own tracts would advance puritanism and galvanise Charles I to reform within the established Church, so in this staging Shirley clearly aimed to inspire Henrietta Maria by spotlighting the insidious encroachment of this troubling 'new court catechism' (preface) upon England's old faith.

The Bird in a Cage revolves around the Duke of Mantua's enclosure of his daughter Eugenia within the New Prison. The Duke aims to preserve Eugenia from the attempts of suitors such as the banished Philenzo, disguised as Rolliardo, to free her and win her love. The tyranny of the Duke's original act of entrapment immediately becomes apparent. Fulvio, loyal kinsman to Philenzo, comments how 'the Duke will be censured for this act' (I.i.158), whilst Philenzo fights against such oppression which views Eugenia's chaste love for him as treason. Repeating the successful formula of *Love in a Maze*, Shirley, through the banished Philenzo, creates a figure like Yongrave whose devotion to Eugenia is the embodiment of 'Roman constancy'. Again conflict, as in *The Traitor* and *The Young Admiral*, is initiated by government manipulation which requires the active zeal of the virtuous heroine to dissolve tensions between the state and the subject. However, a crucial difference emerges within *The Bird in a Cage*. Philenzo's masquerade as Rolliardo allows him the freedom of the role of court cynic. This part reverberates with both recusant and puritan concerns to suggest, as the disguised Philenzo succinctly remarks, that 'we are all infidel that won't believe the court catechism' (III.ii.66–7).

The Bird in a Cage is studded with references to Prynne's multi-level and multi-volume attack on what he deplored as a morally corrupt Caroline government.[108] Shirley by no means completely distances himself from such condemnation. In the very first lines the nobleman Orpiano tells the courtier Morello that 'your amorous lock has a hair out of order' (I.i.23). Such a comment is on one level an obviously facetious sweep at Prynne's voluminous tract *The*

Unlovelinesse of Love-Lockes (1628). With typical verbosity, and in a complaint which encompasses Charles I himself, Prynne had railed against the nobility's fashion for

> Womanish, Sinfull, and Unmanly Crisping, Curling, Frouncing, Powdring, and nourishing of their Lockes and Hairie excrements, in which they place their corporall Excellencie, and chiefest Glorie... the Barber is their Chaplaine; his Shop their Chappell; the Looking-glasse, their Bible... Are they not in dayly thraldom, and perpetual bondage to their curling Irons... now so vaine and idle, that they hold a Counsell about every Haire, sometimes Combing it backe, another time Frouncing, and spredding it abroad.[109]

Yet Morello's response 'Um! What an oversight was this of my barber! I must return now and have it corrected' (I.i.24–25), and Fulvio's commentary, 'here's a courtier that will not miss a hair of his compliment' (I.i.26), in fact underscore Prynne's criticism of the establishment. Ridiculous as Prynne's fears seem, the possible dangers of such frivolous obsessions are enacted in *The Bird in a Cage*. Morello is so obsessed by his immaculate love-lock that he misses the public encaging of Eugenia, the pivotal scene in the play, as Fulvio aptly remarks: 'Signor Morello, is your lock rectified? You have missed your lady but a hair's breadth' (I.i.169–70).

Philenzo's opposition to the 'court catechism' continues through his oblique criticism of a court ruled by money. His one condition on accepting the Duke's challenge to gain access to Eugenia is that he has 'money enough', for 'Money it opens locks, draws curtains, buys wit, sells honesty, keeps courts, fights quarrels, pulls down churches and builds almshouses' (I.i.249–51). As Julie Sanders suggests, this is a direct allusion to the myth of Danae which is so central to the play, whereby Jupiter breaks through Danae's incarceration in an impregnating shower of gold.[110] Yet, as we have seen, from a recusant viewpoint, money – or the lack of it – seemed to rule temporal existence. Jane Owen reiterates this shattering equation in her contemporary tract *Antidote Against Purgatory*, remarking how 'Catholickes throughout England pay yerely great sommes of money for their Recusancy' causing 'divers of these poore men and women [to] have forsaken already (contrary to their conscience) externally their Religion, and... to come to the Protestant Church'.[111] Reminding the wealthier members of the Catholic community how *'the chiefest help for the preventing of the paines of* Purgatory, *is the practice of* Workes *of* Almes-deeds' Owen urges assistance for those struggling with the financial difficulties of recusancy, advising the Catholic 'rich in temporall state . . . to lay out his wealth to an infinite increase of spirituall gayne. O how many peculiar *Advocates* and *Intercessours* . . . might a rich Catholike purchase to himself, by this former meanes thereby to pleade his course before the Throne of Almighty God.'[112] With similar intuition Philenzo uses his freedom with the Duke's exchequer to 'send to all the prisons i' th' city and pay the poor men's debts' (II.i.553–4). As he perceptively concludes: 'since I fail in my other ends I will do some good deeds before I die, so shall I be more sure of prayers than if I built a church, for they are not so certain to continue their foundation' (II.i.555–8). With this reference to specific traditions of the old faith (praying for the dead and corporal works of mercy) highlighted by the mocking insinuation regarding the flux of established religion, Philenzo can be seen to be operating against the values of the Mantuan court. This trajectory of opposition culminates in Philenzo facing death to free Eugenia. Invoking his imprisoned lover as 'blessed Eugenia', to 'whose memory my heart does dedicate / Itself an altar' (V.i.101–3), he scornfully derides the mocking courtiers:

> . . . You may think
> I've made a sorry bargain for my life:
> Let scorners know, in aiming at her only
> My memory after death receives more honour
> Than all your marble pinnacles can raise you. (II.i.517–21)

Such language, by no means uncommon to Caroline love scenes, gains an additional dynamic when repositioned within contemporary religious polemic. As Jane Owen remarked, it was such fervent belief, 'this Zeale of many good Catholikes', which had been 'the fuell, that hath nourished, and kept in, the fyer of Catholike Religion in our owne Country for many years past'.[113] These parallels are intensified through the language of martyrdom: 'it is not life / I'll ask, for that I give up willingly' (V.i.275–6). Such a statement of 'Roman constancy' (preface) rings throughout recusant history. Indeed, as Richard Cust has shown, recusants such as the antiquarian Thomas Shirley glorified martyrdom as the greatest Catholic privilege. Thomas Shirley freely praised men like William Macclesfield who in sheltering a Jesuit had been 'ever readie by his death to have given the last proofes of his constancy and perseverance in the catholike faith'.[114] Indeed, perhaps it is no accident that – in an echo of the recusant's familiarity with the need for disguise – we learn of Philenzo's true identity only in the play's final Act.

Typically of the heroines of Shirley's romances, Eugenia's beauty and virtue are quickly established. The Duke deems her 'a miracle', a figure 'too precious for man's eye' and commands that she be 'shut up, where / a guard more watchful than the dragon's did / forbid access to mankind' (I.i.304–7). This curious image resonates with allusions to the apocalyptic vision of the Book of Revelation.[115] Moreover such spiritual references deepen. In Catholic tradition the Virgin Mary was herself likened to a tower, emphasising her protective role within the Church. John Brereley in his sonnet 'Turris Davidica', begs the Virgin to 'succour the weake & those who humbly weepe / And flye to thee'.[116] Yet, in reference to Eugenia, such an image of strength is inverted into one of encasement and powerlessness. In contrast to other Shirley heroines whom we have examined, Eugenia is not without criticism. Her ladies openly complain: 'Madame, you are too passive; if you be dejected what must we, whose hopes and blisses depend upon your fortune' (III.iii.1–2). And when they decide to enact a play to pass away the time Eugenia accepts the traditionally submissive role of Danae.[117] Indeed, it is only with the arrival of Philenzo, hidden within the framework of the bird-cage, that Eugenia emerges from such passivity to assume her proper role. Injected with a new-found strength Eugenia, like the Ivory Tower of Brerely's Litany, provides 'succour' against 'the fierce assaults' of the 'ne're resting foe'.[118] Ready to face death with Philenzo, when this is denied she preserves Philenzo's life and brings her father to repentance. Awaking from a drugged sleep to find a remorseful Duke asking him to 'call me father' (V.i.402), Philenzo deems such a transformation 'a miracle' (V.i.404), one which Eugenia confirms: 'Thou art, Philenzo, and all this is truth; / My father is converted' (V.i.403–4). This in turn fulfils Philenzo's depiction of Eugenia as a 'glorious building' (IV.ii.331) with the connotations in recusant terms of the ultimate shelter of the Virgin Mary.

Sophie Tomlinson perceives a deep-rooted ambivalence in *The Bird in a Cage* which she suggests stems from Shirley's equivocal concern surrounding the concept of the female actor so provocatively embodied in Henrietta Maria's elite performances.[119] Yet perhaps it is as much the religio-political message within such stagings which caused Shirley such anxiety. Through this awakening of the virtuous Eugenia from passive encasement to active freedom, Shirley can once more be seen to be encouraging Henrietta Maria to achieve her Counter-Reformation potential; synthesising in his heroine the beauty of French Catholicism with the redoubtable zeal of the recusant matriarchy. As the Catholic thinker Richard Broughton explained, by adopting this dynamic role, Henrietta Maria would gain her own place in 'auncient histories', in a kingdom which is still known today as 'THE DOWRIE OF MARIE, the Mother of God':

> Which perchance is the cause why it hath beene so fortunate in Queen MARIES, as in Queene MARIE who restored the Catholike Religion after the death of her brother King EDWARD the sixt; and in Queene MARIE our souueraignes grand-mother, who sanctified our Land with her bloud shed for defence of the Catholike Faith: and lastlie by your Majestie our last Queene MARIE, by whom this land is blessed by a royall issue, and as we hope shall in time be made happie by restitution of the Catholike Religion, eyther in your owne, or your childrens dayes.[120]

Such consistent exhortation by recusant polemicists of the Queen's Catholic mission stimulates Shirley's texts of the early 1630s. Adopting the role of a dramatic Mordechai, his feminocentric plays, rooted in the historicity of the English recusant community, engage with Henrietta Maria's own stage ideals to effectively critique her leadership of the English Catholics. Ultimately it seems likely that such militant recusancy cost Shirley his post as favourite dramatist to the Queen. With some bluster, Shirley himself claimed that he 'never affected the ways of flattery'.[121] By the mid-1630s, as we explore in Chapter 4, Shirley was eclipsed by a new dramatist, William Davenant, whose moderate approach celebrated the Queen's role in 'the old faith's' survival, advising negotiation rather than resistance at a time of Laudian ascendancy.

Notes

1 Walter Montagu, *The Shepherds' Paradise*, ed. Sarah Poynting (Oxford: published for the Malone Society by Oxford University Press, 1997), line 1097. All subsequent references are from this edition and are in the text.

2 Barbara Ravelhofer, *The Early Stuart Masque: Dance, Costume, and Music* (Oxford: Oxford University Press, 2006), p. 269.
3 'Memoirs of the Mission in England of the Capuchin Friars of the Province of Paris, from the year 1630 to 1669 by Father Cyprien of Gamache', Birch, *Court and Times*, vol. 2, p. 308.
4 *Ibid.*, p. 308.
5 *Les Royales Ceremonies Faites en l'Edification d'une Chappelle de Capucins à Londres en Angleterre, dans le Palais de la Royne* (Rheims: 1633), p. 13.
6 *Ibid.*, p. 11.
7 *Ibid.*, p. 7.
8 *Ibid.*, p. 14.
9 John Pory to Sir Thomas Puckering, 20 September 1632, within Birch, *Court and Times*, vol. 2, p. 176, my emphasis.
10 B. C., *Puritanisme the Mother, Sinne the Daughter* (St Omer: 1633), appendix, p. 113.
11 *Ibid.*, p. 121.
12 Questier, *Conversion, Politics and Religion*, p. 8.
13 William Prynne, *Anti-Arminianisme: Or the Church of Englands Old Antithesis to New Arminianisme* (London: 1630), sig. a3v.
14 William Page, *A Treatise or Justification of Bowing at the Name of Jesus* (Oxford: 1631), sigs ¶2r–v.
15 Edward Knott, *Charity Mistaken With the Want Thereof Catholikes Are Unjustly Charged: For Affirming As They Doe With Grief That Protestancy Unrepented Destroies Salvation* (London: 1630), pp. 46–7. See also Lawrence Anderton, *The Progenie of Catholicks and Protestants. Whereby On the One Side Is Proved the Lineal Descent of Catholicks For the Roman Faith and Religion . . . And On the Other, the Never-Being of Protestants* (Rouen: 1633), p. 239.
16 Knott, *Charity Mistaken*, pp. 98–9.
17 Sandra Burner cites an entry from the Middlesex Sessions Rolls on 3 December 1633 for 'Edward Gouldinge late of Colston Bassett Co. Nottingham Gentleman' in *James Shirley*, pp. 100–1.
18 Cresacre More, *The Life and Death of Sir Thomas Moore* (Antwerp: 1631), pp. 9–10.
19 Giovanni Maffei, *Fuga Saeculi: Or the Holy Hatred of the World*, trans. Henry Hawkins (Paris [St Omer]: 1632), sig. é4v.
20 James Shirley, *Love in a Maze* (London: 1631). Gifford and Dyce (eds), *Works*, 2, pp. 269–364, p. 270. All subsequent references are to this edition and are in the text.
21 Anon., 'The Dramatic Works and Poems of James Shirley, Now First Collected', *American Quarterly Review*, 16 (1834), 103–66, p. 166.

22 James Shirley, *The Cardinal*, ed. E. M. Yearling (Manchester: Manchester University Press, 1986), V.i.275.
23 Leech, *Shakespeare's Tragedies*, p. 173.
24 Thomas Adams, *A Commentary: Or, Exposition Upon the Divine Second Epistle Generall, Written By the Blessed Apostle St. Peter* (London: 1633), p. 393.
25 Richard Brathwaite, *Whimzies: Or, a New Cast of Characters* (London: 1631), p. 101.
26 Wither, *Britain's Remembrancer*, sig. P4r
27 Orazio Torsellino, *The Admirable Life of S. Francis Xavier*, trans. Thomas Fitz-Herbert (Paris [St Omer]: 1632), sigs A1r–A2v.
28 Henry Mason, *The New Arte of Lying, Covered By Jesuites Under the Vaile of Equivocations* (London: 1634); William Freake, *The Doctrines and Practices of the Society of Jesuites* (London: 1630). For an alleged Jesuit plot in March 1628 see Havran, *Catholics in Caroline England*, pp. 66–8.
29 Synge, *Rejoynder to the Reply*, pp. 6–7.
30 John Clarke, *Holy Incense for the Censers of the Saints: Or a Method of Prayer, With Matter, and Formes in Selected Sentences of Sacred Scripture* (London: 1634), p. 220.
31 Anthony Cade, *A Justification of the Church of England: Demonstrating It to Be a True Church of God, Affording All Sufficient Meanes to Salvation*, 2 vols (London: 1630), vol. 2, p. 106.
32 Cited by Michael Questier, 'Loyalty, Religion and State Power in Early Modern England: English Romanism and the Jacobean Oath of Allegiance', *HJ*, 40 (1997), 311–29, p. 316.
33 Roger Widdrington, aka Thomas Preston, *A Theologicall Disputation Concerning the Oath of Allegiance* (London: 1613).
34 Archbishop Abbot to Sir Thomas Edmondes, 25 August 1613, cited by W. K. L. Webb (SJ), 'Thomas Preston O.S.B; alias Roger Widdrington, 1567–1640', *Biographical Studies*, 2 (1953), 216–60, pp. 232–3. See also Havran, *Catholics in Caroline England*, p. 63.
35 William Howard, *A Patterne of Christian Loyaltie: Whereby Any Prudent Man May Clearely Perceive, in What Manner the New Oath of Allegiance, and Every Clause Thereof, May in a True, and Catholike Sense, Without Danger of Perjury, Be Taken by Roman Catholikes* (London: 1634).
36 *The Declaration of the Lay Catholikes of England, Concerning the Authority Challenged Over Them, By the Right Reverend Lord Bishop of Chalcedon* bound with *The Attestation of the Most Excellent, and Most Illustrious Lord, Don Carlos Coloma, Embassadour Extraordinary for Spayne* (Brussels: 1631), p. 10.

37 James Shirley, *The Traitor* (London: 1631). Gifford and Dyce (eds), *Works*, vol. 2, pp. 94–187. All subsequent references are from this edition and are in the text.
38 Burton, *Popes Bull*, p. 76.
39 For a parallel tempering of this popular image of the regicidal recusant see Samuel Rowley, *The Noble Spanish Souldier* (London: 1634), especially the advice of Baltazar in Act V.i.
40 Humphrey Lynde, *Via Devia: The By-Way: Misleading the Weake and Unstable Into Dangerous Paths of Error* (London: 1630), sig. a6v.
41 More, *Thomas Moore*, p. 10.
42 *Lay Catholikes Declaration*, p. 21.
43 For a full discussion of this legend see James Shirley, *The Traitor*, ed. John S. Carter (London: Edwards Arnold, 1965).
44 Bawcutt, *Records of Sir Henry Herbert*, p. 184; James Shirley, *The Young Admiral* (London: 1633) within Gifford and Dyce (eds), *Works*, vol. 3 pp. 92–181. All subsequent references are from this edition and are in the text.
45 Howard, *Christian Loyalty*, p. 10.
46 Questier, 'Oath of Allegiance', pp. 327–8.
47 Godfrey Anstruther, *A Hundred Homeless Years. English Dominicans, 1558–1658* (London: Blackfriars Publications, 1958), pp. 143–6.
48 Mary Fage, *Fames Roule: Or the Names of Our Dread Soveraigne Lord King Charles, His Royall Queen Mary, and His Most Hopefull Posterity: Together with, the Names of the Dukes ... of England, Scotland and Ireland: Annarammatiz'd and Expressed by Acrosticke Lines on Their Names* (London: 1637), sig. M2v.
49 John Smyth, *The Berkeley Manuscripts: The Lives of the Berkeleys, Lords of the Honour, Castle and Manor of Berkeley In the County of Gloucester from 1066 to 1618*, 3 vols (Gloucester: John Bellows, 1883), vol. 2, p. 253.
50 Thomas Fosbroke, *Berkeley Manuscripts: Abstracts and Extracts of Smyth's Lives of the Berkeleys* (London: John Nichols and Son, 1821), p. 203.
51 Shirley, *Stemmata Shirleiana*, p. 66.
52 Anthony Stafford, *The Guide of Honour: Or, the Ballance Wherin She May Weigh Her Actions* (London: 1634), dedicatory preface.
53 J. B., aka John Brereley, aka Lawrence Anderton, *Virginalia. Or Spirituall Sonnets in Prayse of the Most Glorious Virgin Marie, Upon Everie Severall Title of Her Litanies of Loreto* (Rouen: 1632), sonnet 1, p. 5.

54 Gordon Albion, *Charles I and the Court of Rome: A Study in Seventeenth Century Diplomacy* (London: Burns, Oates and Co., 1935), p. 77. The papal envoy on presenting the rose spoke of Henrietta Maria as 'inter spinas hebraicae iniquitas flos de radice Jesse'.

55 Bérulle, *Sainte Madeleine*, p. 411.

56 Brerely, *Virginalia*, sonnet 26, p. 30. See also Hawkins, *Parthenaie Sacra*, pp. 17–27.

57 *Royales Ceremonies*, p. 12; Gamache, 'Memoirs of the Mission', p. 308.

58 R. Malcolm Smuts, 'The Puritan Followers of Henrietta Maria in the 1630s', *EHR*, 93 (1978), 26–45.

59 *Ibid.*, p. 29.

60 Tabaraud, *Pierre de Bérulle*, p. 360.

61 Britland, *Drama at the Courts*, pp. 111–30; Barbara Ravelhofer, 'Bureaucrats and Courtly Cross-dressers in the *Shrovetide Masque* and *The Shepherds' Paradise*', *ELR*, 29 (1999), 75–96; Sarah Poynting '"In the Name of All the Sisters": Henrietta Maria's Notorious Whores', in Clare McManus (ed.), *Women and Culture at the Courts of the Stuart Queens, 1603–42* (Basingstoke: Palgrave Macmillan, 2003), pp. 163–85; Sophie Tomlinson, 'Theatrical Vibrancy on the Caroline Court Stage: *Tempe Restored* and *The Shepherds' Paradise*', in McManus (ed.), *Women and Culture*, pp. 186–203.

62 *Ibid.*, p. 187.

63 John Pory to Sir Thomas Puckering, 3 November 1632: 'Mr Taylour the Player hath also the making of a knight given him for teaching them how to act the Pastorall', cited by Poynting, *Shepherds' Paradise*, p. viii.

64 Translated by John Orrell in 'Amerigo Salvetti and the London Court Theatre, 1616–1640', *Theatre Survey*, 20 (1979), 1–26, p. 18.

65 Britland, *Drama at the Courts*, p. 121.

66 Poynting, *Shepherds' Paradise*, p. xiv.

67 *Ibid.*, p. xiv, footnote 41.

68 As Poynting carefully documents, this manuscript was housed in the library of Sir Walter Aston (1589–1639) at family estate at Tixall, Staffordshire. Inscribed on the flyleaf are the words 'The Lady Persall's book' dated 1653. This refers to Lord Walter Aston's daughter, Lady Frances, but, as Poynting points out, 'this was twenty years after the first performance', so the manuscript 'could have been copied for Lady Persall, or her father (or indeed some other member of the family)', *Ibid.*, p. xvi. See also Deborah Aldrich Larson, *The Verse Miscellany of Constance Aston Fowler: A Diplomatic Edition* (Tempe, Ariz.: Arizona Centre for Medieval and Renaissance Studies, 2000).

69 Veevers, *Images of Love*, pp. 44.
70 Britland, *Drama at the Courts*, pp. 127–8.
71 John Peacock, 'The French Element in Inigo Jones's Masque Designs', in David Lindley (ed.), *The Court Masque* (Manchester: Manchester University Press, 1984), pp. 149–68, p. 156.
72 Tomlinson, 'Theatrical Vibrancy', p. 195.
73 See Chapter 2, note 100.
74 Birch, *Court and Times*, vol. 2, p. 176.
75 Poynting, 'Notorious Whores', p. 170.
76 M. Coate, *Cornwall in the Great Civil War and Interregnum, 1642–1660* (Oxford: Clarendon Press, 1993); Anne Duffin, *Faction and Faith: Politics and Religion of the Cornish Gentry Before the Civil War* (Exeter: University of Exeter Press, 1996); F. G. Marsh, *The Godolphins* (New Milton: privately printed, 1930); W. H. Tregellas, *Cornish Worthies*, 2 vols (London: 1884).
77 Daniel Rowland, *An Historical and Genealogical Account of the Noble Family of Nevill, Particularly of the House of Abergavenny* (London: Samuel Bentley, 1830), p. 44.
78 *Ibid.*, p. 53.
79 *Ibid.*, pp. 51–3.
80 *Ibid.*, p. 168.
81 *Ibid.*
82 Sarah Poynting, 'A Critical Edition of Walter Montagu's *The Shepherds' Paradise*, Acts 1–3' (PhD dissertation, University of Oxford, 2000), pp. 156–7; Britland, *Drama at the Courts*, p. 127.
83 Cyprien of Gamache, 'Memoirs of the Mission', p. 303.
84 Poynting, 'Notorious Whores', p. 179; Whitelocke's diary entry reads: 'his mother was not present att her sons marryage att Chelsey, which she excused by extraordinary occasions att that time, butt afterwards Which found the reason to be because she was a Popish Recusant', Ruth Spalding (ed.), *The Diary of Bulstrode Whitelocke, 1605–1675* (Oxford: Oxford University Press, 1990), p. 466.
85 George Puttenham, *The Arte of English Poesie, 1589* (Menston: Scolar Press, 1968), p. 31.
86 L. B., *The Answere of a Catholike Lay Gentleman, to the Iudgement of a Devine, Upon the Letter of the Lay Catholikes to the Sayd Lord Bishop of Chalcedon* (Bruxelles: 1631), p. 89.
87 Sir George Gresley to Sir Thomas Puckering, 6 February 1633, within Birch, *Court and Times*, vol. 2, p. 227.
88 St Bernard, *A Hive of Sacred Honie-Combes, Containing Most Sweet and Heavenly Counsel: Taken Out of the Workes of the Mellifluous Doctor S. Bernard, Abbot of Clareval*, trans. Antonie Batt (Douai: 1631), sig. *3.

89 *Ibid.*, p. 15.
90 *Ibid.*, pp. 18, 47.
91 John Southcot to Peter Biddulph, 16 August 1633, AAW/B47, no. 42 – although Southcot himself supports Henrietta Maria's 'good offices . . . both for Catholickes and priests . . . which are not few in number, nor of small regard'. *Ibid.*
92 Cited by Smuts, 'Puritan Followers', p. 28.
93 Quarles, *History of Queene Ester*, pp. 134, 148.
94 Francis de Sales, *Delicious Entertainments of the Soule*, trans. Agnes More (Douai: 1632), pp. 14–15.
95 Nicolas Caussin, *The Holy Court. Or, the Christian Institution of Men of Quality*, trans. Thomas Hawkins, 2 vols (Paris [St Omer]: 1626), vol. 2, p. 497.
96 *Ibid.*, p. 517.
97 *Ibid.*, p. 516.
98 *Ibid.*, p. 518.
99 Francis de Sales, *A Treatise of the Love of God*, trans. Miles Car (Douai: 18th edition, 1630), sigs a4–a5.
100 A. B., aka Matthew Wilson, *A Defence of Nicholas Smith Against a Reply to His Discussion of Some Pointes Taught by Mr. Doctour Kellison in His Treatise of the Ecclesiasticall Hierarchy* (Rouen: 1630), p. 15.
101 John Falconer, *The Mirrour of Created Perfection: Or the Life of the Most Blessed Virgin Mary, Mother of God* (St Omer: 1632), sig. *3v.
102 James Shirley, *The Bird in a Cage*, ed. Julie Sanders, in *Three Seventeenth-Century Plays on Women and Performance*, eds Hero Chalmers, Julie Sanders and Sophie Tomlinson (Manchester: Manchester University Press, 2006). All subsequent references are to this edition and are in the text.
103 William Prynne, *Histriomastix: The Players Scourge or Actors Tragaedie* (London: 1633). See also Kim Walker, '"New Prison": Representing the Female Actor in Shirley's *The Bird in a Cage*', *ELR*, 21 (1991), 383–400.
104 Sir George Gresley to Sir Thomas Puckering, 31 January 1633, within Birch, *Court and Times*, vol. 2, p. 224.
105 Justinian Paget to James Harrington, 28 January 1633, *ibid.*, p. 222.
106 Sanderson, *Compleat History*, p. 196.
107 The title of *Bird in a Cage* also resonates with Racan's *L'Artenice*. Alcidor in his opening speech claims how his love is 'n'est pas de ces oyseaux, que l'on enferme en cage' [not like the birds who are enclosed in a cage] (I.i.83).

108 See Sophie Tomlinson '"She that Plays the King": Henrietta Maria and the Threat of the Actress', in Gordon McMullan and Jonathan Hope (eds), *The Politics of Tragicomedy: Shakespeare and After* (London: Routledge, 1992), pp. 189–207; Valerie Traub, 'The (In)significance of Lesbian Desire in Early Modern England', in Susan Zimmerman (ed.), *Erotic Politics: Desire on the Renaissance Stage* (New York: Routledge, 1992), pp. 136–57.
109 William Prynne, *Unlovelinesse of Love-Locke*, sigs A3r–A4v.
110 Julie Sanders, '"Powdered with Golden Rain": The Myth of Danae in Early Modern Drama', *Early Modern Literary Studies*, 8 (2002), 1.1–23.
111 Jane Owen, *An Antidote Against Purgatory* (St Omer: 1634), pp. 229–30.
112 *Ibid*., sigs *5r–*6v.
113 *Ibid*., p. 205.
114 Cited by Cust, 'Writings of Sir Thomas Shirley', p. 58.
115 Revelations, 12: 1–6.
116 Brerely, *Virginalia*, 'TURRIS EBURNEA', sonnet 28, p. 32; see also 'TURRIS DAVIDICA', sonnet 27, p. 31.
117 Sanders, 'Powdered with Golden Rain', pp. 1.4, 1.22.
118 Brerely, *Virginalia*, sig. B8v.
119 Tomlinson, *Women on Stage*, p. 92; see also Sanders (ed.), *Bird in a Cage*, pp. 25, 27–8.
120 Richard Broughton, *The Judgement of the Apostles* (Douai: 1632), sigs *7r–v.
121 See James Shirley's dedication to Henry Osborne in *The Maid's Revenge* (London: 1639), sig. A2r. See Gifford and Dyce (eds), *Works*, vol. 1, pp. 98–185, p. 101.

4

William Davenant: the chimera of religious reunion, 1634–1637

> how, all the *Daughters*, of the SPOUSE *Divine*
> Might Reconciled be.[1]

From the mid-1630s contemporary reports reveal Queen Henrietta Maria's persistent association with an increasingly favoured playwright, William Davenant (Figure 9). In June 1634 James Howell gossiped how

> the Court affords little news at present, but that ther is a Love call'd *Platonic* love, which much swayes there of late ... This love sets the wits of the Town on work, and they say ther will be a Mask shortly of it, whereof Her Majestie and Her Maids of Honour will be part.[2]

Despite James Shirley's success with *The Triumph of Peace*, a masque commissioned by the Inns of Court in February 1634 and presented before the royal couple to great acclaim, this privilege was granted to William Davenant. Where Shirley had protested an incapability to practise the 'court sinne of flattery', Davenant deftly entrenched himself within the elite milieu of the Queen's court circle.[3] Pursuing every opportunity to gain notice, Davenant addressed several New Year's Day poems to Henrietta Maria and dedicated his play *The Just Italian* (licensed 1629, published 1630) to the Earl of Dorset, head of the Queen's household.[4] He courted her favourite Henry Jermyn with poems and a dedication in *The Platonic Lovers* (licensed 1635, published 1636). And, intriguingly, he even altered the typography of his own name from the unobtrusive Davenant to D'Avenant, to suggest an elusive French origin.[5]

As Shirley's own trajectory revealed, the Caroline stage was very much a way to courtly preferment and Davenant's efforts were

9 'Sir William D'Avenant, Crowned with Bays', frontispiece to William Davenant, *Works* (London: 1673).

gradually rewarded. In 1633 his prologue was sung for the royal performance of Fletcher's *Faithful Shepherdess* (1608) at Somerset House. By 1634, having been commissioned by Henrietta Maria to collaborate on the staging of her latest masque *The Temple of Love* (1635), Davenant appeared for the first time on a printed title page as 'her Majesties Servant'. Nurturing this honour, Davenant's continued quest for the Queen's patronage was boldly announced in the evolutionary title of his next play *Love and Honour* (licensed 1634, printed 1649). Initially entitled *The Courage of Love*, and then renamed *The Nonpareilles; or The Matchless Maids*, this search for a title which best suited the Queen's preferred stage experiences further illuminates Davenant's open courtship of Henrietta Maria's patronage. His success is strikingly apparent from the Queen's unusual appearance, disguised as a citizen's wife, in the audience of his next masque *The Triumphs of the Prince d'Amour* (1636). This obvious 'pretence' fooled nobody as Sir John Finet wryly commented, likening his Queen to 'that bird, which thrusting but her head into a bush, is said then to think all her body hidn'.[6] With such overt royal affirmation, Davenant openly put himself forward as very much the unofficial spokesman of the court. Indeed, Joseph Mead's eagerness to acquire his mock epic ' "Geffreidos", describing a combat between Geoffrey, the queen's dwarf, and a turkey-cock at Dunkirk' neatly encapsulates Davenant's public familiarity within the Queen's court circle.[7]

The creative rivalry between Davenant and Shirley, evident as early as 1630 from the acerbic commendatory verses accompanying Shirley's *The Grateful Servant* (licensed 1629, published 1630) and Davenant's *The Just Italian*, simultaneously highlights an internecine struggle within the Caroline theatre itself. Shirley's advocates such as Joseph Hall revealingly present the commercial stage as a medium 'abused' by the 'swelling words' of courtier playwrights.[8] As Alan Fletcher suggests, Shirley's decampment to the Werburgh Street Theatre in Dublin in 1636 was most likely a reaction both to his enforced competition with Davenant and the prevailing fashion for 'gilded' pastorals.[9] Henrietta Maria's intense fascination for all things theatrical was not satisfied by court productions alone. The 1630s witness the Queen branching out from the royal environs of Somerset House and Whitehall to grace the private theatres with her patronage, in particular Blackfriars. In 1634 Henrietta Maria attended *Cleander* by Philip Massinger, the following year she watched a performance of *Arviragus* by Lodowick Carlell, and she was again at Blackfriars, in 1638, for a staging of Davenant's *The Unfortunate Lovers* (licensed 1638, published 1643). With a newly gained esteem associated with dramatic performance, Harbage correctly observes a 'social evolution' in the approach of courtiers to drama.[10] Writing a fashionable play became a proven means to gain preferment and social prestige, embodied by courtiers such as William Habington, John Suckling and Lodowick Carlell. These gentlemen of independent means (though of varying incomes) all had minor roles of office within the court; Carlell, for example, in 1629 was Gentleman of the Bows to Queen Henrietta Maria and Groom of the Privy Chamber to Charles I. Notably, each of these courtiers was to successfully present a play, not merely within the amateur confines of the court but on the public stage of the Blackfriars theatre. As Prusias slyly remarks in William Cartwright's *The Siege* 'hee's scarce a Courtier now, that hath not writ / His brace of Plaies'.[11] Suckling even provided spectacular costumes and scenery for the staging of his play *Aglaura* in 1638; the costumes alone, according to John Aubrey, were 'very rich; no tinsell, all the lace pure gold and silver'.[12]

This remarkable theatrical departure has led critics such as Keith Sturgess to assume that Henrietta Maria saw the Caroline stage both 'amateur and professional as what it undoubtedly was, an adornment of court life'.[13] In consequence Sturgess detects a shift from the Jacobean audience, which he argues had an 'intellectual, even radical bias', to 'an increasingly cavalier, courtly and fashionable audience of the 1630s for whom theatre provided less the stimulation of provocation and debate, more a form of cultivated recreation'.[14] With some inevitability William Davenant, the playwright whom Harbage accorded the dubious distinction of being 'the dramatist who showed the most skill in keeping one foot in the public theatre and the other in the royal banqueting halls', has served as a theatrical yardstick by which to mark the extent of such dramatic decadence.[15] Yet, as is now recognised, this critique of the experience of the Caroline theatregoer is so reductive as to be unhelpful. Martin Butler was the first not only to reassert the breadth of viewpoint of this politically alert and involved audience but to strongly emphasise the variety of Caroline drama; there were seven stages competing in 1630s London, with each theatre 'straining to excite the attention and interest of as many spectators as possible'.[16] More recently, Julie Sanders in her explorations into Caroline theatre emphasises 'the subtle play of intersection, interaction and influence' between public and private (especially courtly) drama.[17] Undoubtedly influenced by the Queen's theatrical preferences, commercial theatre was far from subsumed and by no means subservient to Whitehall. Despite his opportunistic self-positioning within the Queen's household, William Davenant did not refuse his commercial drama a political edge. As we will explore through *Love and Honour*, Davenant, like his rival Shirley, immersed himself in the debates of the day and used the vibrant space of the Blackfriars stage to explore and exchange ideas.

In examining the theatrical rise of William Davenant, one crucial difference emerges from the direct parallels which can be drawn with James Shirley. Whereas Shirley's independently formed, staunchly Catholic beliefs led to favour with the Queen, Davenant's gradual inclination towards Rome was very much influenced by the court. For Davenant, Shirley's court niche had a glitter all of its own. Indeed, during the early 1630s, Davenant was more famous for the loss of his nose from syphilis than for any religious fervour. Interestingly, Davenant equates his recovery from this near-death experience with two men, both of whom had strong links with the febrile Catholicism of Henrietta Maria's circle, which suggest that the seeds of Davenant's own apostasy were planted at this juncture.[18] Sir Thomas Cademon, the Queen's doctor, was documented as a practising Catholic, and Endymion Porter, a gentleman of the King's Chamber and key patron of Davenant, was renowned for his intensely Catholic wife Olivia, a major proselytising force within Whitehall.[19] By the 1640s, Davenant's leanings towards Catholicism (and his close links with the court Roman Catholics) were publicly emblazoned through typically abusive parliamentarian epithets such as 'Popish dog and Curre of Rome'.[20] Finally, during the 1650s, with Henrietta Maria's court in exile, Davenant officially converted to Rome, together with a sizeable number of others.[21] This gradual apostasy, fostered from within the court, provides a key to any understanding of Davenant's own beliefs. Contrary to a fierce recusancy, Davenant's conversion was secured by a more flexible combination of compromise and negotiation. Indeed such a religious paradigm was embodied in the powerful example of his beloved patron Endymion Porter who, despite his own papist inclinations, continued to receive Anglican Communion in the King's chapel. This concession within religious affairs surfaces in Davenant's own behaviour. In a detailed account from 1650, Jean Chevalier recounts Davenant's preparations for his voyage from the Channel Islands to the New World, to assume his short-lived sinecure as Lieutenant-Governor of Maryland. Apparently two French friars accompanied Davenant on his abortive travels, one of them being Father du Plessis, a priest ejected from Henrietta Maria's court in 1626. Primarily they sailed as missionaries yet, as Chevalier records, they also acted as 'chaplains and confessors to Sir William's Frenchmen and to Sir William himself'.[22] However, when Dr. Halle, a minister of the established Church, conducted a service in St. Helier, Davenant freely 'partook of the eucharist'.[23] Such compromise in matters of religion percolates through Davenant's mid-1630s texts to fill the sophisticated space of the Blackfriars theatre with an undeniably subversive charge. The rise of Laudianism within the established Church mirrored an ever more fashionable practising of Roman Catholicism within Whitehall. Increasingly the imponderable and politically explosive debate regarding the possibility of religious union between England's Protestant King and his Roman Catholic Queen was becoming progressively urgent. George Wither succinctly articulated such concern:

> For, as you, *Both*, Prime *Children* are of these
> Two *Sister-Churches*, betwixt whom, yet, growes
> Unseemely *strife*; So, *You*, perhaps, may be
> An *Emblem*, how these MOTHERS may agree
> And, not by your *Example*, onely, show
> How wrought it may be; but, effect it so.[24]

Where better to express ideas regarding such a defining discourse in Caroline culture than in the energetic space of its theatres?

The consecration of the Queen's Capuchin chapel: a Counter-Reformation spectacle

From the perspective of the godly puritan, even the faintest prospect of such a union between the Protestant and Catholic Churches would have seemed unthinkably perilous – acutely so when, on 8 December 1635, Queen Henrietta Maria flamboyantly celebrated the solemn consecration of her Capuchin chapel. With her customary panache for the spectacular, the Queen had 'resolved that the first mass should be held there with all possible pomp and magnificence'.[25] The extraordinary planning to achieve this dazzling spiritual event in the court calendar quite possibly surpassed the strenuous efforts and the dedicated rehearsals for the Queen's theatricals. The visual focal point of this occasion was the Holy Sacrament itself. Indeed, the Capuchins deliberately enlisted the aid of the 'eminent sculptor' François Dieussart to create a 'machine' to 'exhibit' the Sacrament so as 'to give it a more majestic appearance'.[26] George Gerrard articulated Protestant disdain, commenting how the

> ceremonies lasted three days, massing, preaching and singing of litanies, and such a glorious scene built over their altar, the Glory of Heaven, Inigo Jones never presented a more curious piece in any of the masques at Whitehall: with this our ignorant papists are mightily taken.[27]

The impact of such a ravishing 'scene' would undoubtedly have astonished the spectators, as the intricate detail of Fr Cyprien of Gamache's report makes clear:

> Behind the altar was seen a Paraclete, raised above seven ranges of clouds, in which were figures of archangels, of cherubim, of seraphim, to the number of two hundred, some adoring the Holy Sacrament, others singing and playing on all sorts of musical instruments, the whole painted and placed according to the rules of perspective. The Holy Sacrament formed the point of view, with hidden lights, but which kept increasing, so that the distance appeared very great, and the number of figures double what they were, deceiving, by an ingenious artifice, not only the eye but also the ear, all conceiving that, instead of the music, they heard the melody of the angels.[28]

Such theatricality was further heightened as this stunning vision was only revealed once the Queen had assumed her own central position within the congregation: 'as soon as she had taken the place prepared for her, the curtains being drawn back, all at once gave to view those wonders which excited admiration, joy, and adoration in her Majesty'.[29] For the assembled worshippers, and curious courtiers, the intense effect of this focal line of visual interplay, between the shimmering brilliance of the Holy Sacrament and a Queen whose living faith had achieved such a celebration, was provocatively symbolised in the 'tears of joy [which] seemed to trickle from the eyes of the Queen, considering, in this pious and striking ceremony, the grace which God bestowed on her to erect a church where would thenceforth be celebrated all the divine services which heresy had banished from England'.[30] After dinner the Queen promptly returned to the Chapel to 'attend vespers, complins and the sermon' which Monseigneur du Peron appropriately delivered on the Psalm 'This is the Lord's doing, and it is marvellous in our eyes' – before she retired for the evening 'with the applause of the whole audience, which was very large'.[31] Fr Cyprien was himself astounded by the 'crowd of people who were bent on forcing their way in to see the magnificence displayed there. The crush last[ing] so long that it was impossible to close the doors of the church till the third night.'[32] Ultimately, the success of the Capuchins' endeavours was apparent from Charles I's comment 'that he had never seen anything more beautiful or more ingeniously designed'.[33]

So, despite the nexus of anxiety explored in Shirley's texts, the passive zeal intrinsic to Henrietta Maria's brand of French Catholicism had an undoubted puissance. From a courtly perspective at least, such proselytising was greatly enhanced by the sympathy of the King's court for the baroque splendours of the Counter-Reformation. Having recovered from the ignominy of the Richelieu debacle of the early 1630s, the Queen was becoming bolder in her aims for a Catholic renewal. In 1633 she informed the Duc de Griegny, the French ambassador, of her ambition to work 'pour le bien et consolation des Catholiques de ce pays' [for the well-being and consolation of the Catholics of this country].[34] This integral image of the Queen as mediatrix to her Catholic subjects was supported by Peter Fitton's advice to de Griegny:

> le souhaict de la Reigne sont preféré a celluy des autres Catholiques Anglais pour deux raisons particulierement. La premiere est a cause quelle est chef de tous le Catholiques d'Angleterre, et que comme Mere commune de tous elle n'est point attachée d'affection particuliere a aucun ... mais elle regarde en cela simplement la gloire de Dieu et le bien de tous. La seconde est quelle scaiet tres bien quels sont les sentiments du Roy en cette affaire, et de son conseil, et que par consequant elle peut mieux juger que aucun des choses qui peuvent servir au bien des Catholiques.[35]

> [the wishes of the Queen are to be preferred to those of other English Catholics for two particular reasons. The first is because she is the chief of all the English Catholics, and as the Mother of all the

community, she is not particularly attached in affection to any individual . . . she is simply concerned with the glory of God and the well being of everyone. The second reason is that she knows very well the sentiments of the King in this affair, and his understanding, so that consequently, she can judge better than anyone those things which will best serve Catholic needs].

Accordingly, when convinced of the need for a Roman Catholic bishop to minister to the recusant flock, Henrietta Maria 'tooke occasion to speake much in the commendation of the Bishop of Calcedoine' to Charles I.[36] She was directly involved in the visit of Sir Robert Douglas to Rome in October 1633 which, with the tacit permission of the King, urged upon the Pope the need for a bishop to unite English recusants and suggested that this was a symbolic moment to raise an Englishman to the Cardinalate.[37] By February 1634, after painful negotiations, the Curia had agreed to an exchange of papal agents between the Pope and the Queen. Urban VIII also assented to send an agent with the precise role of solving the dissension within the English clergy. The latter, Gregorio Panzani, arrived in December 1634. By May 1635 King Charles had approved this exchange of agents, the first since the break with Rome, with the stipulation that he should nominate the individual and that it should remain a close secret. In June 1635, with Sir Robert Douglas appointed as the Queen's papal agent and George Con as the Vatican's English agent, the Queen's confessor, Fr Phillip of Sanquhar, was heard to declare that within three years Rome would have England back within its fold.[38] The expectation expressed in these sentiments was not without some foundation. In June 1636 the Queen's agent arrived in Rome and in July, George Con landed at Rye and immediately set off for the royal court at Windsor. The potential of such an exchange in the eyes of Roman Catholic Europe is best summarised by the Spanish ambassador: concerned by this sudden rapport between the Courts of Rome and England, and jealous of such harmony, he announced that Con was 'coming in great pomp to receive the King into the Church'.[39]

The success of the Queen's (seeming) influence within the Vatican was mirrored in Whitehall. During this period Roman Catholicism positively flourished in court, illuminated by a steady stream of noble converts. In July 1634 William Laud recorded the conversion of two daughters of Lord Falkland; Easter 1635 saw the apostasy of Walter Montagu; the following March, Kenelm Digby returned to the Roman Catholic fold, swiftly followed by the very public apostasy of Lady Purbeck; and 1637 witnessed an incredible flurry of conversions linked with the missionary fervour of Olivia Porter.[40] Crucially, such an open practising of Roman Catholicism could not be limited to the confines of Henrietta Maria's court. Powerful symbols of England's old faith would have confronted Londoners on an almost daily basis. As early as 1632 the Queen's Capuchin priests had become prominent visual figures in the city. Fr Cyprien, with some bias, records how

> the Catholics looked with joy upon the Capuchins as men sent by Heaven to show, in the profession of their life, the truth of the faith which they had received from their ancestors, and who had always boldly maintained it, at the expense of their fortunes, their honour, and their blood. They could not turn their eyes from that dress, in which they contemplated the poverty of Jesus Christ... They compared this simplicity with the luxury of the ministers, and thanked God for having kept them in that religion of which their fathers were genuine professors.[41]

The arrival of papal agents 'with permission to profess [their religion] publicly' was a further, potentially inflammatory, symbol of overt Catholicism:

> These nuncios had successively their chapels open to all the Catholics, to the great discontent of the Puritans... From morning till noon, masses were continually said in their chapels; the Catholics attended them: there were no pursuivants to hinder any persons or to oppose their devotion. The nuncios paid their Court to the King and to the Queen. They were known to every body. Their carriages rolled along the streets of London, without any one daring to say a word against them.[42]

By February 1637 petitioners complained about the alarming spread of popery in St Giles Parish where the Catholics were 'so exceedingly multiplied that in that part of the parish called Bloomsbury there are as many or more than Protestants'.[43] Indeed, by the mid-1630s the effects of court Catholicism were even reported outside London. Undoubtedly with some prejudice, the papal envoy, Panzani, writing to Cardinal Barberini in Rome, intimated how even country folk flocked to see the Queen's chapel when her household left London. Many were 'surprised, after the scandals they had heard preached about the Papists, to find nothing evil in the place. Others sighed that they could have no such beautiful things in their own churches.' As Gordon Albion translates, Panzani was staying in Northhampton:

> a centre of Puritanism ... not at Court but with a non-Catholic lady, who not only gave him candles and wine for his Mass, but wanted to go to confession! As someone remarked to him, these people were no heretics, but Christians badly catechised.[44]

As the Roman Catholic community increasingly acknowledged, Henrietta Maria was instrumental to any sustained revival of the Roman Catholic faith. In the 1635 instructions for the agent at Rome, the Queen's 'religious zeale and constant devotions' were extolled.[45] Described as one who has 'purchased unto herselfe love and admiration from all the court and kingdome and unto the Catholique Religion ... great respect & honor', Henrietta Maria was lauded as 'una beata de Casa' [a blessed house] for 'whose sake Heaven [I] hope doth intend many blessings'.[46] Essential to this model of Roman Catholic renaissance within England was Henrietta Maria's role as mediator with Charles I. As the Roman Catholic priest Mr Morgan commented in February 1634:

> let it bee considered, that our gratious soveraine is of a most mild and mercifull spirit, howsoever hee may bee disposed in religion. And our most vertuous and Catholike queene beeing soe deere unto him, in so much that the reciprocall love betweene them is admired by all, it cannot be imagined, that hee will bee cruell to any of her religion, especially to those who jumpe with her in religious obedience to God and king.[47]

The tangible effects of such queenly influence are documented by the papal agent's private figures on the number of known recusants: where Panzani in 1637 recorded 150,000 recusants, by 1638 George Con estimated a figure nearer to 200,000, neither of these figures including the shadowy group of church-papists.[48] In 1634 George Leyburn assured the Bishop of Chalcedon that for English Roman Catholics 'there was never too great hopes of wished tymes as now ther are'.[49] To mark this defining cultural moment, Henrietta Maria once more turned to the stage. *The Temple of Love*, a collaboration between William Davenant and Inigo Jones, reaffirms the Queen's ultimate ambition of engendering 'a generation not of bodies but of souls'.[50]

The Temple of Love: performing a daring ambition of a kingly apostasy?

Performed as the Queen's Shrovetide Masque on 10 February 1635, *The Temple of Love* was the final masque to be danced in the splendour of the magnificent Whitehall Banqueting Hall. It was received with much acclaim, and even the Venetian ambassador, Angelo Correr, who was no novice to the splendour of court ritual, was full of praise, reporting to the Doge and Senate how 'the Court has been fully occupied . . . with the representation of a masque, which the queen has repeated three times, set out with the most stately scenery, machines and dresses'.[51] Such an emphasis on the mechanics of the masque perhaps explains why, to the modern reader, *The Temple of Love* can be deemed as the epitome of apparent meaningless spectacle. Indeed, Graham Parry frankly describes this masque as 'an empty exercise in Caroline neo-platonism'.[52] Equally as curious is Stephen Orgel's reading of the masque purely from the King's perspective.[53] For this masque, paid for by the Queen and performed possibly four times at Court, was very much Henrietta Maria's direct assertion of herself. Securely anchored in its occasion, *The Temple of Love*, as Erica Veevers first argued, celebrates the Queen's success as a Counter-Reformation champion and encapsulates her anticipation of a deeper and permanent revival of the old faith.[54] Textually the language is of 'miracle' and 'prophecy'; of 'Fate' and of 'time prefixed'; all of which are resolved when Indamora, Queen of Narsinga, re-establishes 'the Temple of Chaste Love' (*The Temple of Love*, the argument, 1–41). It is surely no coincidence that, at the very moment Henrietta Maria was dancing this title role of Indamora, her own Capuchin chapel, often referred to as a 'Temple', was being richly furnished in readiness for the reinstitution of those Catholic ceremonies which, although never forgotten, had similarly 'been abolished and forbidden for so many years'.[55]

The power of neoplatonic love is integral to Indamora's role in *The Temple of Love*. This elevated ideal of womanhood had been popular as a reforming force within the debauched court of Henri IV of France when Henrietta Maria had been an impressionable princess.[56] As Queen of England, she eagerly translated this chivalric notion of chaste love to the Caroline court, to create a cult which has often been disparaged as mere affectation. J. B. Fletcher declares that it inclines 'to the silly and dangerous' whilst E. C. Marchant frankly dismisses it as 'TOSH'.[57] Undoubtedly the concept can be easily accused of irrationality and unnaturalness. As Davenant gently satirises within the masque itself: 'there will be / Little pastime upon earth without bodies / Your spirit's a cold companion at midnight' (197–9). Moreover, the courtiers beneath the masquing disguise were by no means beacons of chastity.[58] Yet for Henrietta Maria the ideal was far from frivolous. The Queen's understanding of the concept was rooted in the devout humanism of Catholic thinkers such as St Francis de Sales, where a woman was worthy of such faithful devotion because of her innate ability to draw her suitors towards God, her beauty encouraging the platonic lover to moral excellence.

Erica Veevers has perceptively argued how direct connections can be drawn between this emphasis in the Queen's masques on the power of platonic love, and that ultimate ideal of female love and beauty in the Catholic faith, the Virgin Mary. Such parallels are particularly apposite to an understanding of the Queen's own faith. Fr Cyprien de Gamache noted how the Queen 'always regarded the most Blessed Virgin as her good mistress and her dear Mother'.[59] During the 1630s she led something of a cult, holding weekly meetings of the Confraternity of the Rosary, where 'the litanies of the Blessed Virgin . . . were sung with great solemnity in that chapel dedicated to the glory of that celestial lady, who was held in such great veneration by the Catholics, French and English'.[60] As contemporary writings such as Henry Hawkins's *Partheneia Sacra* (1633) illuminate, the Virgin was clearly associated with images of light (the moon and stars), and beauty (gardens, flowers and fountains).[61] Thus the defining radiance of the Queen's masques not only suggests Henrietta Maria's embodiment as the ideal of platonic love but also encourages her identification as a queen who actively formed herself in the image of that ultimate mediatrix, the Virgin Mary.[62] Such an association was keenly encouraged by her Catholic subjects, as is foregrounded in N. N.'s dedicatory preface to Henrietta Maria in *Maria Triumphans*: 'thus will *Mary* intercede for *Mary*; the *Queene of Heaven*, for a great *Queene* upon *earth*'.[63] In *The Temple of Love* these interconnections are signified precisely through such images of light, beauty and succour. The power of Indamora's 'beauty's light' (131) is a healing and cleansing force, and Indamora's purpose is to guide men 'to see and know what they should love' (90).[64]

For the Caroline spectator the focus of this courtly performance was Henrietta Maria's vivid stage entrance as the exotic Indamora (Figure 10). Davenant heightens this sense of expectation by bestowing goddess-like attributes upon Indamora which are repeatedly invoked to create an awe-inspiring aura of sanctity and prophecy. The masque opens with Divine Poesy conferring upon Charles the exalted news 'That Fate hath made thy reign her choice' (122) for Indamora's advent. The magicians of the antimasque are appalled by the approach of this 'delight of destiny' (186), whilst the Persian masquers, Orpheus and the priestly Brachmani eagerly await her arrival as 'More welcome than the wand'ring seaman's star / When in the night the winds make causeless war' (427–8). With Inigo Jones's unerring eye for visual effect, Henrietta Maria's stunning appearance as Indamora, complete with feathered headdress to befit her role of Queen of India, is intensified by her arrival in a specially crafted chariot, 'the back of which was a great scallop shell' (415–16). The prominence of this highly visible scallop shell, a traditional Catholic symbol both of pilgrimage and baptism, would have further enhanced the contemporary religious allusions within this courtly spectacle, whose argument pivoted on an Indian Queen who (like this living French Princess) had crossed seas and left her homeland to reinstate a mystical Temple.

The Temple of Love's assertion of Henrietta Maria's queenly identity is deepened by the positive promulgation of values intrinsic to her French Catholicism. The ideal of the male bending to the female had particular force for Henrietta Maria through her belief in Frances de Sales's concept of the 'honnête femme'. As we examined in Chapter 3, de Sales promoted the feminine qualities of piety, chastity and compassion as a valuable means of converting unbelieving spouses. To some English recusants this had seemed unacceptably passive. Yet, as Henrietta Maria's flourishing court Catholicism makes clear, de Sales's archetype of the 'honnête femme' was imbued with an undeniable power and is central to *The Temple of Love*. King Charles is warned by the Poets that on seeing Indamora he must 'Take leave now of thy heart' (136), and this paradigm for union is reiterated in the duet between Sunesis and Thelema. This is emphasised structurally within *The Temple of Love* through the unusual feature of two groups of masquers. Indamora, Queen of Narsinga, rules her own train of female beauties and also bears sway over the cluster of male masquers disguised

10 Inigo Jones's sketch for the costume of *Indamora, Queen of Narsinga*, played by Queen Henrietta Maria in *The Temple of Love*, 1635.

as Persian youths, a departure which strengthens her regal authority. Through what Sarah Cohen terms 'the politics of dancing', Indamora's female cohort subdue these Persian masquers, leading them in 'various figures meet' (445) so each shall have a 'lawful though a loving heart' (454).[65]

Indamora's dynamic stage presence reaches its zenith when, upon her dazzling arrival, the central conceit of the masque, the Temple of Love itself, becomes fully visible. Although there is no extant sketch of this Temple, the detailed commentary supplied in the masque text evokes a curious mix of architectural styles. The foreground has mythical overtones, 'instead of columns' teams of 'young satyrs' bear up 'the returns of architrave, frieze and cornice' (459–60). Yet 'the further part of the temple running far from the eye was designed of another kind of architecture, with pilasters, niches and statues . . . all which seemed to be of burnished gold' (461–5). Such a richly decorated Temple suggests the baroque magnificence of Henrietta Maria's own nearly completed Capuchin chapel. Veiled allusions to specifically Catholic sites of worship deepen, for as the magicians of the antimasque make clear this Temple had always existed on the island. Mists have simply hidden it from the 'sinful use' (172) of the magicians who have 'seduced the more voluptuous race / Of men to give false worship' (173–4). The parallels both with an unbroken (though furtive) history of recusancy in England, and Henrietta Maria's current vibrant celebration of the Roman Catholic faith, would have been unmistakable to her elite audience. Indeed the blending of architectural styles within the Temple itself quite possibly signifies the grafting of Henrietta Maria's opulent Counter-Reformation Catholicism upon England's ancient faith. For although Veevers does not recognise the crux of the 'unbroken existence' of the Temple, as she rightly emphasizes, 'the near completion of a Catholic chapel' would have been a source of intense interest 'either as a good omen or a bad' to everyone at court.[66] Evocatively, both the prayers from the chorus 'to make this union thrive' (487) and Sunesis and Thelema's wish that the royal couple will 'become one virtuous appetite' (479) are proclaimed from within this Temple's holy sanctuary.

This suggestive Counter-Reformation vision is strengthened through the banished figures of the antimasque which include a token puritan, debauched lovers and the magicians themselves who had established their own 'gay Altar' (245). The puritan and the debauched lovers of the antimasque are self-explanatory. More enigmatic is the meaning behind the banished 'gay altar' of the false magicians. James Shirley in his late play *The Cardinal* (licensed 1641, published 1653) specifically uses the word 'gay' in a passage which denounces a Cardinal with more than a passing resemblance to Cardinal Laud.[67] According to the *Oxford English Dictionary*, one meaning of the word 'gay' at this time was 'brilliant', 'showy'. Quite possibly, this bogus imitation of the true Temple of Love is a reflection upon the increasing intensity of Laudian policy concerning the beautifying of churches within the Protestant establishment, specifically their reappropriation of the concept of the altar as opposed to the communion table.[68] From the recusant point of view, these avant-garde reformers were perceived as impinging on accepted Roman Catholic territory. Moroever, Henrietta Maria had little affection for Archbishop Laud. Fr Peter Fitton records their wranglings in 1636: 'Mr Montagu tells mee that *the king for the present will nott permit a* [Catholic] *Bishop in* England, and that the Bishop of Canterburye tould the Queen *plainely, when she spake* to him about it, that he would oppose *it as much as he could.*'[69] All these forces can be seen to attack the values which Henrietta Maria cherishes. Their dismissal, on the arrival of Indamora, heralded by the harmonies of Orpheus (who has himself been likened by Veevers to Cardinal Panzani), is very much an idealised depiction of England's own second Esther, Queen Henrietta Maria.

The final tableau lingering in the collective memory of *The Temple of Love*'s audience would have been that of the befeathered Indamora, sitting 'under the state' (457) with King Charles I, lauded by Amianteros as the 'emblem' of his 'deity' namely of 'chaste love' (499–500). The triumph of such love over illicit passion was the determining trope linking all the masques of Charles I's reign, reflecting and celebrating his happy marriage with Henrietta Maria. But in this masque, a direct assertion of Henrietta Maria's royal self, this regal image of chaste love projects the potentially explosive symbol of religious union. Just as Sunesis bends to the will of Thelema, and the Persian masquers have been subdued by Indamora's train, Indamora has filled King Charles heart 'with her own' (141). It is impossible to overestimate the electrifying power of this closing vision; of Charles 'the Royal Lover' at the side of the omniscient Indamora, celebrating the re-establishment of her Temple. Precisely because of the Queen's unrivalled position as the 'darling of his breast' (512) contemporary pamphlet literature was riddled with accounts of Henrietta Maria's influence upon Charles I. Puritans feared a malign manipulation. As one writer boldly opined, if 'ordinary women, can in the Night time perswade their husbands to give them new Gowns or Petticoates, and make them grant their desire; and could not Catholik Queen *Mary* (think ye) by her night discourses, encline the King to Popery?'[70] Inevitably, the Catholic community literally bombarded the Queen with saintly paradigms of virtuous wives who had successfully secured kingly conversions. In 1635 Cardinal Barberini reminded Henrietta Maria how 'St. Urban desired nothing more of St. Cecily than the conversion of Valerian her husband. This is all the present pope expects from her Britannic majesty.'[71] In this powerful, concluding spectacle of *The Temple of Love*, the hopes of Roman Catholic Europe are displayed, and potently intensified through Sunesis's reference to the couple's 'offspring' (515): a 'generation' of 'bodies' which recusant polemicists consistently viewed as a potential 'generation' of 'souls' (Argument of *The Temple of Love*). Notably, despite Prince Charles's christening within the rites of the established Church, William Sanderson recorded how the 'Puritan party' were conspicuously 'shut up, as on the day of general mourning'.[72] This godly anxiety regarding the Queen's insidious sphere of influence is an acute reflection of Henrietta Maria's position, which Frances Dolan describes, as a 'symbolic figurehead for Catholicism's generativity and motherhood's ascendancy'.[73] Before his arrival in England, Panzani had been warned by Cardinal del Bagno that 'Henrietta Maria 'could of course do much' as the King 'was devoted to her', but 'she and her ladies were fully occupied with dancing and balls'.[74] In *The Temple of Love* Henrietta Maria answers her critics by flamboyantly showcasing her daring Counter-Reformation ambitions. In this spectacle collaborated upon by Davenant, the ultimate aim of the prophetic Indamora, this 'delight of destiny' (186), was indeed to bestow upon her royal lover an '*eternal* growth to love' (510 my emphasis).

Untangling the complexities of the wider religious landscape, 1634–1637

Such an explosive image of religious union gains further currency when properly contextualised within the wider religio-political landscape. During the period 1634 to 1637 the thriving Roman Catholicism sustained from within the Queen's court was mirrored by a deepening entrenchment of Laudianism within the King's court and the established Church. Central to Laud's thesis, as he himself explained, was 'the reducing of the [Reformed Church] into *Order*, the upholding of the *Externall Worship* of *God* in it, and the setling of it to the *Rules* of its *first Reformation*'.[75] Laud's supporters vividly translated this vision into contemporary pamphlet literature. Robert Skinner in a sermon originally preached before the King questioned:

> do wee not finde ourselves otherwise affected, when we come into a naked, deformed, ruinous Temple, adorned with nothing but dust and cobwebs, and when we come into a goodly reverend beautifull Church ...? Doth not the very Fabricke and fashion, and solemne accommodation beget in our hearts a religious regard, and venerable thoughts?[76]

The extent to which these avant-garde reformers strayed into territory traditionally associated with Rome is manifest in Prideaux's sermon *The Patronage of Angels* and Anthony Stafford's treatise *The Female Glory: or the Life and Death of Our Blessed Lady*.[77] Such slippage within the orthodoxy of the established Church was underlined through changing attitudes towards, previously, fiercely defended essential doctrinal differences. Building on the problematic language used by John Cosin in *Private Devotions*, Henry Valentine in his 'Directions for the due receiving of the Sacrament of the Lords Supper' provocatively suggests that communion should be received not

> as our common, ordinary, and daily bread, but as the *body of Christ Sacramentally*. We must consider the *wine*, not as the bloud of the *grape*, but as the *bloud* of Christ in a true, yet *sacramentall* maner. Christ is truly present in the Sacrament; it is the eating of his flesh, and the drinking of his bloud.[78]

With this flux surrounding the concept of orthodoxy within the established Church, the gulf widened inexorably between what can be loosely termed the Laudian and puritan factions. To John Pocklington, the puritans were little more than 'wandring starres, and disastrous planets, who have and doe blast the most flourishing and glorious Church under the cope of Heaven'.[79] Most worrying, this 'fretting canker' of godly ministers' actions was infectious.[80] Francis White, the Bishop of Ely, remarked in his dedication to William Laud how '*By* these mens positions, and irregular proceedings, many of our people are infected with dislike and hatred of the godly forme of our Church-Service'.[81] Such disaffection was illuminated in Peter Hausted's exhortations to his congregation

> not to stay lurking at your houses till the *Confession* and *Absolution* be past, nay many times till the *Psalmes* be done, because yee would prevent the standing up at the *Doxologyes* betwixt them, nay sometimes till the *Lessons* and the *Popery* of the *Letanie* (as yee call it) be over, and then come stealing in, as if yee were sent for Spyes, to see what Religion we are of.[82]

William Quelch crystallised the effects of dissension within the established Church:

> We cannot chuse but see, unless wee wilfully shut our eyes, how much our adversaries are enriched by these *contentions*: how many good professors upon these grounds have leapt aside into the tents of Popery: how many quiet and peaceable congregations have been torne and distracted into sundry factions; how many zealous and painfull labourers onely for the cause of their bare conformity are growne suspected to their owne flockes: and which is most to be lamented, many a faithfull and learned Prelate that should be counted worthy of double honour, is traduced as a favourer of Popish tyranny, because he labours and strives ... to beate downe these fond and trifling *quarrels*.[83]

Yet the puritan response to this insidious projection of Laudianism as the ideal of Protestant orthodoxy demonstrates that this was no 'trifling quarrel'. Utilising the traditional weaponry of the established Church, nonconformist tracts insistently attacked not only Roman Catholicism but the dangerously papist tendencies within the establishment. Thomas Taylor published his sermons in the hope that this

> might be a meanes to restraine our *declining times* from gazing and doting on that pompous Harlot, the Church of Rome. For when our nation shall see, and consider afresh, how insatiable she hath alwaies beene of blood, and English blood! I cannot thinke we can be so inconsiderate, as to dreame of any toleration, much lesse any sound reconcilement with so implacable an enemie.[84]

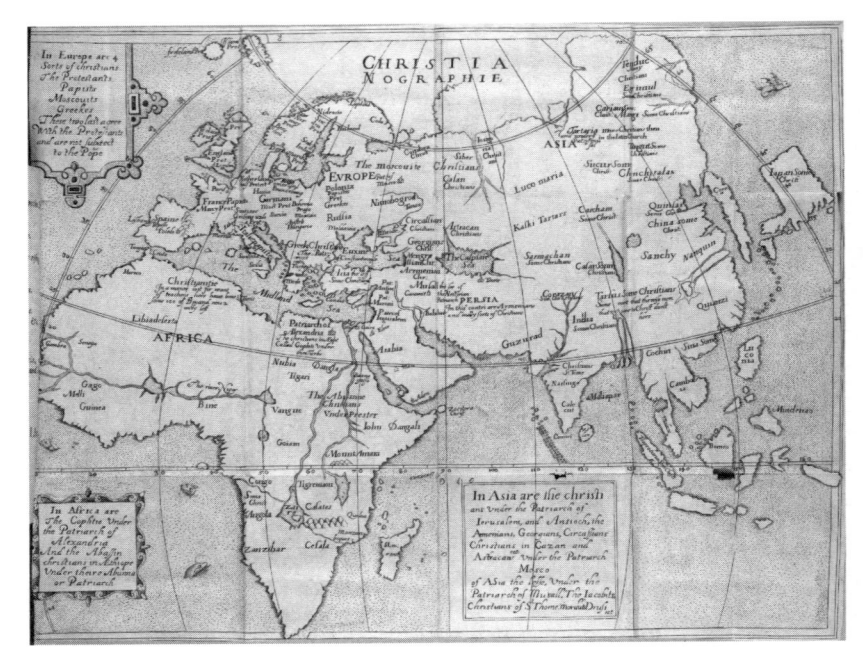

11 Frontispiece to Ephraim Pagitt, *Christianographie: Or the Description of the Multitude and Sundry Sorts of Christians in the World Not Subject to the Pope* (London: 1635).

As Figure 11 illustrates, Ephraim Pagitt literally provided the reader of *Christianographie* with a global map which depicted how 'many millions of Christians' actively dissented from Rome.[85] Indeed, the mid-1630s erupted with a flood of textual reprints which reasserted the heritage of the Reformed Church as a force pitted against the Vatican. Thomas Becon warned from the bloody days of Queen Mary how 'yee have heard, that the Masse is the fountain, well, head-spring, and originall of all Idolatry, superstition, wickednes, sin & abomination'.[86] John Rhodes's popular anti-papist doggerel verse of 1588 reappeared.[87] And the ghostly voice of Lady Jane Grey counselled against those 'who rent and teare the most precious body of our Saviour Christ with ... bodily and fleshly teeth'.[88] Repeatedly, in censuring Rome, puritans decried the 'ADVANCING OF POPERY' within the established

Church.[89] For William Prynne the 'bringinge in of bowinge to *Altars, Images*, the *Hoste, Transubstantiation* and *Masse* . . . the turning of Communion Tables to Altars or Altaringe, everywhere' could only mean the 'erectinge of Popery'.[90] Speaking of alarm in the hearts of 'Loyall Subjects' at 'an approaching alteration of Religion, and totall Apostasie unto the Sea of Rome', Prynne accused Laudians of hardening Catholics in 'their Antichristian Errours', for as 'they see us runnning, if not flying so fast of late, that they say they need not come towards us, since wee are posting so fast to them'.[91] Changes within the Common Prayer Book completed the puritans' oppositional status, leading William Odell to entreat Elizabeth of Bohemia for succour, through the very 'Esther' topos appropriated by militant recusants.[92] In short, as William Prynne indignantly expressed, the 'Lord Prelates' were now implementing strategies against the puritans which had previously been reserved for papists, 'hunting after them with their blood-hounds, the Pursevants, and rifling and breaking up their howses, Studies, Coffers, with unheard of violence, as if they were the archest Traytors breathing'.[93]

Yet puritan concern at these 'Romish Innovations' found a startling echo in the tracts of the godly's religious opposite, the militant English Catholic.[94] Significantly, in the period 1634 to 1637, the recusant's own ideal of showing strength in adversity continued to be advanced. Wadding's overriding desire in his *History of the Angelicall Virgin Glorious St. Clare* was 'that others be excited to the imitation of . . . Heroicke actions'.[95] Jane Owen dedicated her *Antidote Against Purgatory* to the 'worthy and constant Catholickes'.[96] And Edward Lechmere in his dedicatory preface to an unnamed church-papist insisted 'go the Catholike waie: that, is secure. Seek no by-waies'.[97] Twinned with this recusant valour was a sustained attempt to capitalise upon the undermining divisions within the established Church. B. C. directly addressing the 'learned Protestant Wryters', speculated:

> can it be thought, that [God] would institute a Religion for the saving of Mans Soule . . . which consisteth of such *Heterogenious* and different doctrines (as *Protestancy* is found to be) . . . the Professors thereof tearing asunder each others reputation and honour, with their violent Philippicks and declamatory Satyrs? It is not probable; It is not credible; It is not possible.[98]

Matthew Wilson acknowledged the rise of Laudianism: 'doe not their Churches beginne to looke with another face? their walles to speake a new language? their Preachers to use a sweeter tone?'[99] Yet he solemnly insisted that Protestants must absolutely capitulate to Rome: 'wee then are safe by your owne confession; but you cannot be so, without repentance, and reunion to our Church'.[100]

However, alongside this adamant reaction of hardened recusant polemicists, there existed more flexible groupings of English Catholics who were responsive to change within the established Church. Thomas Doughty went so far as to openly align with Rome those 'moderate Protestants', who 'after a sort confesse, both the reall and substantiall presence of the Sonne of God in the Sacrament of the Altar, and also the visible Sacrifice in the Church of God'.[101] With some naivety, Panzani gathered information on all the English bishops in an effort to judge their attitude towards Rome. By July 1635 he had high hopes of a spiritual reunion between the courts of Rome and England.[102] As *Information Touching the Present State of the Catholic Church in England* suggested, such a prospect was 'conceaved' with 'much the more hope' because the King

> loveth the Queene tenderly by whose power, diligence, and zeale the said union and reconciliation is principally to be wrought in this Court and wee hope that there would not want [men] of worth and power to second her Majestie... & to serve her willingly in so good a busines'.[103]

More progressively, some English Catholics held the radical view of a mutual compromise between the Churches of Rome and England, rather than the orthodox expectations of a complete Protestant apostasy. In December 1634 Leander Jones, President General of the Benedictine Order, Prior of Douai and university friend of Archbishop Laud, was sent from Rome to appraise the situation.[104] In a memorandum to the Holy See he advised the Vatican to be careful not to 'vex moderate Catholicks, by censures or disgraces, since their end is to please God and the King, and promote the union of the Catholick religion'.[105] The Benedictine General boldly reformulated a milder version of the Oath of Allegiance in an attempt to foster such rapprochement which caused him great personal difficulties. As he commented to Wentworth: 'I do much fear, lest the various surmises of men... may doe me some harm either in magnifying my favours received, as if they were due to my endeavours; or in mistaking my endeavours, as if I performed but weakly the part of a good Catholick.'[106] This belief in a mutual accommodation was shared by one of Henrietta Maria's chaplains, Christopher Davenport, known as Francis à Sancta Clara, a convert to Roman Catholicism who remained in close contact with such central reformers as Richard Montague, William Laud and John Cosin. Davenport's controversial tract *Deus, Natura, Gratia* (1634) examined the Thirty Nine Articles to reveal the proximity, rather than the distance, between the two Churches. As Davenport commented: 'I beheld Christ divided... who would not mourn such a sight? Who would not advise reunion? Who would not persuade it by every means he could?'[107] Leander Jones openly supported Davenport's treatise, whilst opposing the missionary William Courteney who was languishing in prison for asserting that Roman Catholics should refuse to take the Oath of Allegiance. One priest, Mr Wilford, corresponding with Leander Jones from Rome, begged him 'to engage yourself no further in writing of this argument of the oath... You know this is so ticklish an argument, that it is hard, if not impossible, to please all parts.'[108] At the heart of this more moderate Catholic position was a growing insistence that the Vatican ought to comprehend, and attempt to alleviate, the difficulties faced by an English Roman Catholic. In 1634 a stir was caused at court over Sir Richard Lashford's refusal to take the Oath of Allegiance. Leander Jones immediately appealed to Rome to temper its own uncompromising position, but this conflict was resolved only when the King insisted that he simply required temporal obedience.[109] As one Catholic commentator observed: 'there were better hopes of good for religion in England if in Rome they were made to understand rightly, the condition thereof, and what cause they might... yet take to advance it'.[110]

This daring possibility of religious reunion was accentuated through the conciliatory attitudes which emanated from some quarters within the Laudian movement. Robert Shelford in his sermon *Antichrist Not Yet Come* preached that although 'Papists have a letter more than we, or we one letter for another; yet we may hold together in the *radix*'.[111] Gilbert Ironside commented how 'the true Church of Christ, ever was, and will be a mixt congregation; in this, like *Nebuchadnezars* Image, which had mixed feet of clay and Iron'.[112] And Thomas Bedford, through the haunting image of real-life, stillborn conjoined twins (depicted in Figure 12), argued:

156 Staging the old faith

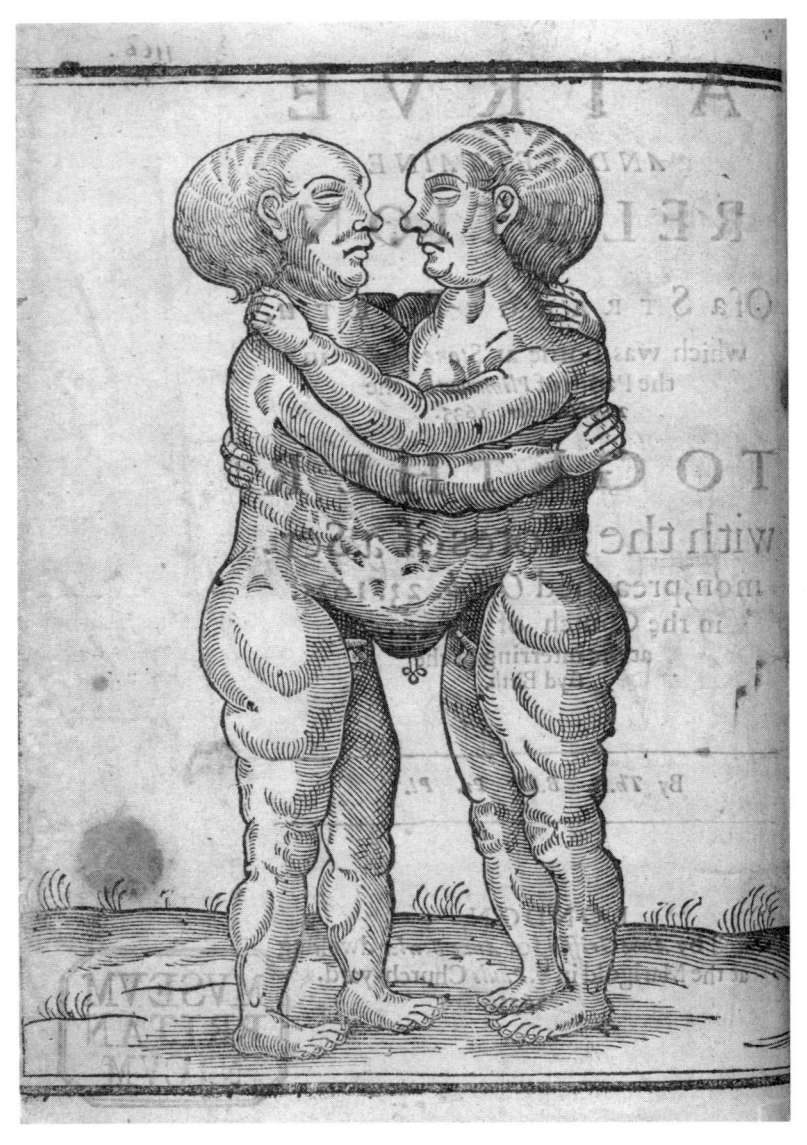

12 Frontispiece to Thomas Bedford, *A True and Certaine Relation of a Strange-Birth* (London: 1635).

These two were one body; Christians are one spirit: though severall bodies and soules, yet one and the same spirit diffused into all, to enlive and quicken all. Nor would it have beene more prodigious for these Twinnes (suppose they had lived to bee men) to have quarrelled and contested one against another: than it is for Christians to quarrell and contend, specially to live in the minde of irreconciliation?[113]

Such Christian charity was conspicuously reflected in recusant reports concerning King Charles's own beliefs. Southcot recounted a conversation between the King and Dr Fludd, where King Charles stated that 'he neither hated the Papists nor their Religion'.[114] In June 1636 King Charles refused to restore the Protestant College established by his father to dispute Roman Catholic polemics, commenting: 'too much time is spent on controversies which displease me. I would rather study were devoted to reunion.' As the Queen's confessor, Father Phillip, ecstatically declared: 'Does not this show the King's goodwill'?[115] By November 1636 King Charles had produced his own revised version of a possible Oath of Allegiance, and by May 1637 he told George Con, the papal agent, that 'at the price of my life I want us to be in agreement'.[116]

In some ways it is unsurprising that in May 1636 a Roman Catholic evaluation of the *Present State of the Protestant Church of England* concluded that:

> it seemeth to bee evident, that an union or reconciliation with the Church of Rome is not only desired, but alsoe aymed at by them; [they] would have it generally believed ... that there are noe fundamentall or essentiall differences in religion betweene the Church of Rome, & them. Whereupon as they doe not hould themselves guilty of schisme or heresy, but true members of the Catholique Church, condemning their predecessors, the first Protestantes of England, whome they confesse ingenuously to have gon too farr in their pretended reformacion of the English Church.[117]

With a thaw in Pope Urban VIII's demeanour towards the English court (reflected in his much vaunted affection for King Charles and his non-committal response to Davenport's controversial text), the celebrated image of 'Carlo Maria' seemed on the cusp of being firmly underpinned by a spiritual buttress. George Wither was not alone in his hope that the religious charity expressed by the royal pair might 'shew, that, *Swords*, *Flames*, *Threats*, and *Furie*, make no true *Accords*'.[118] Freed from the masquing constraints of showcasing Henrietta Maria's proselytising role of Indamora, William Davenant incisively probes this debate on the commercial stage. Davenant's *Love and Honour* is a nuanced exploration of compromise and conciliation, a tempered ideal which is itself surprisingly politically destabilising.

Love and Honour: William Davenant's staging of a tempered Catholicism

Arthur Nethercot once critiqued *Love and Honour*, licensed on 20 November 1634, as the work of 'a docile and brilliant pupil of the queen', commenting how 'only the denizens of a nunnery could have found anything offensive in this elevated production'.[119] Yet as theatre records make clear, this play was originally produced not for the ultra-elite glitterati of Whitehall but the more searching audience of the Blackfriars theatre. Sir Humphrey Mildmay noted his attendance at this 'play of Love & Honour' in December 1634 with 'the :2: Southlandes'.[120] Indeed, it was not until 'New-years night' of 1637 that the play is known to have been performed before the King and Queen at the Whitehall Cockpit.[121] This possibility of commercial theatre acting as a vibrant conduit of ideas between the court and the town complicates traditional understanding of Caroline drama. Undoubtedly, *Love and Honour* was influenced by Henrietta Maria's theatrical preferences, but this by no means emasculates the drama. Davenant was not just a 'spokesman' for the court.[122] He was fully alive to the complex subtleties of his day and, in the politically alert atmosphere of the Blackfriars theatre, *Love and Honour* explores that charged issue of the moment, religious union.[123] The play itself centres on the capture of Evandra, Princess of Milan, by the military hero Prospero for the state of Savoy. The vengeful Duke of Savoy seeks her death, whilst his son, Prince Alvaro, endangers his own life in granting her sanctuary. The plot hinges around the complicated attempts of Evandra and her companion Melora to rescue their princely benefactor. Both women defiantly face a public execution only to be saved by a series of timely revelations. So tragedy is neatly averted in this tragicomedy which Davenant's contemporary, Thomas May, observed to be the most fitting genre for the Caroline stage.[124]

Evandra, the focus of Davenant's text, is a heroine deeply rooted in the neoplatonic ideals which held 'much swaye' in the fashionable society of mid-1630s London. Like Indamora in *The Temple of Love*, Evandra is associated with images of light. Alvaro compares her to 'the first fair light' which breaks through 'thick / And silent darkness' (II.i.168–9) and rhapsodises how flowers 'sprung up / invited by her eyebeames from their cold roots' (I.i.319–20). Most noticeably Evandra is consistently praised as 'a great example of a female fortitude' (3.i.740). Calladine marvels at her steely determination to face death, asking: 'can such a virtuous courage dwell in your sex?' (IV.i.285). Such actions clearly place Evandra within the neoplatonic 'femme forte' tradition, promoted by French thinkers like Jacques du Bosc, and popularised in 1630s London through Walter Montagu's translation of Du Bosc's *L'Honneste Femme* some two years prior to Davenant's staging.[125] Notably Du Bosc specifically praises such valorous women: 'les histoires sont pleines de leurs actions genereuse pour la conservation de leur pais, pour l'amour de leurs marys et pour la Religion de leurs ancestres' [histories are full of their generous actions for the conservation of the peace, for the love of their husbands, and for the Religion of their ancestors].[126] Moreover, as Ian Maclean exposes in his exploration of feminism in French literature, this heroic female figure was closely related to, and inspired by, that 'most exceptional of all women', the Virgin Mary, to whom Henrietta Maria was renowned for her special devotion.[127] *Love and Honour* positively resonates with this ideal of the ultimate 'femme forte'. Melora greets Evandra, deemed by Alvaro 'the pride of Italy' (I.i.272), in evocatively Marian terms: 'Hail! the most beauteous virtue of the world' (III.i.81). The transforming power of Evandra's incomparable virtue is manifest from her redeeming influence upon the errant Prospero. As Prospero recalls, at first 'a mist / of fury hung between us' (II.i.351–2), but overcome by Evandra's beauty and nobility of spirit, he capitulates into a 'penetential Enemy', who comes 'to weep away [his] trespass at [her] feet' (II.i.168–9), braving torture and even death to ensure her safety.

Not content with one heroine cast in the *à la mode* mould of the femme forte, so favourable to his queen, Davenant reinforces this model with a fascinating stage double. Evandra's companion in captivity, Melora, is similarly renowned for her beauty and virtue. Furthermore, her very name links her to Du Bosc's writings. In particular the frontispiece to *L'Honneste Femme*, illustrated in Figure 13, displays four hands embossed with the key virtues of

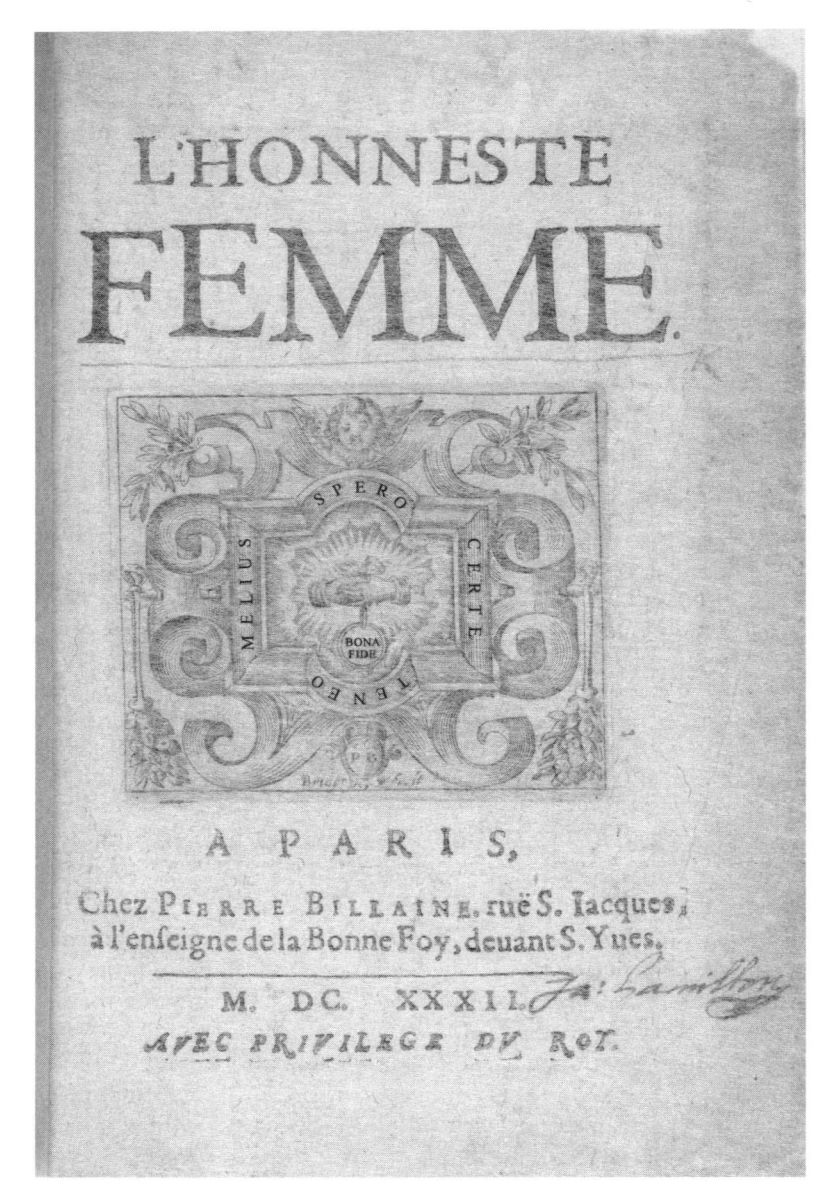

13 Frontispiece to Jacques Du Bosc, *L'Honneste Femme* (Paris: 1632).

'spero', 'certe', 'teneo' and 'melius', clasping a medal emblazoned with the slogan 'bona fide' [good faith]. Stemming from the maxim 'melius' meaning 'better', Melora's own courageous magnanimity is unquestioned. Calladine is astonished by Melora's 'beauty so o'ercoming and exact' (IV.i.14), and, on learning of her 'valiant piety' in attempting to save the lives of Evandra and Alvero, he declares 'her mind more noble than her shape' (4.1.36–7). When later confronted by the equally stunning vision of Evandra, the overwhelmed Calladine tightens the focus on the women's interdependence:

> I did not think the stock of nature could,
> In this her colder age, be rich enough
> To store the world with two such beauties that
> Together take their growth, and flourishing. (IV.i.266–9)

In the cultural moment of the 1630s, such an affinity between these 'femmes fortes', Melora and Evandra, evokes the politically charged mutuality of Henrietta Maria and the Virgin Mary, those two female figures so widely debated in topical pamphlet literature. As Danielle Clarke has argued, 'the Queen's devotion to the Virgin Mary exemplified a widespread fear about female agency, and about Henrietta Maria's power to influence religious and political policy'.[128] With Evandra loosely associated with the celestial Mary, so the narrative of Melora's romance specifically draws on the myth of Henrietta Maria's betrothal. Despite Evandra's undoubted preeminence, Melora marries Alvaro, reminding him of their engagement, some 'five years since' when 'disguis'd you stole to see a triumph' (V.i.464–5). Similarly, in the official version of the Carlo-Maria fable, the young Prince Charles had first fallen for Henrietta Maria on his incognito travels to Spain to woo the Infanta. Breaking his journey in France, Charles had secretly watched Henrietta Maria dance, and left his heart at the French court. Significantly, these women, rooted in the explicit ideals of devout humanism which Henrietta Maria herself both practised and staged, are unflinching in their determination both to save Prince Alvaro and to achieve eternal glory. As Evandra asks:

> Why should these mighty spirits lay so vast
> An obligation on our sex, and leave
> Eternal blushes on our souls. (III.i.670–2)

Yet, where on the elite stage, in masques from *The Temple of Love* to *Luminalia*, Davenant celebrates such ambition, repeatedly *Love and Honour* firmly curbs such heroic female aspirations. Both women are ultimately denied the opportunity to erase these 'eternal blushes' from their souls. Evandra is visibly upset when Leonell is able to deny her execution with his own death, accusing him of 'quite undo[ing] our glorious strife' (V.i.352). And when, in turn, her father offers his life, again Evandra asks why he has destroyed her 'noble fame' so 'virtuously pursu'd' (V.i.392).

Prince Alvero complements such an unflinching pursuit of glory: a figure who like William Strode's King in *The Passions Calm'd* conspicuously engages with the religio-political problems surrounding Charles I's own kingship, Alvero is the ultimate appeaser. Like Indamora's 'Royal Lover' in *The Temple of Love*, Alvaro is a hero who has no need to undergo the purifying process so integral to neoplatonism. Evandra praises him as a 'Prince renown'd and precious for / your faith and courtesy' (II.i.243–4), whilst Melora perceives him as the 'noblest and the best of men' (III.i.516). Most notable are his repeated attempts to heal the volatile divisions between Leonell (Evandra's original champion) and Prospero (her captor turned defender). In *Love and Honour*, Alvaro counsels against such discord in terms which reverberate with the besetting problems of the fragmenting religious landscape of Caroline England. Entreating both men to sheathe their swords, Alvaro shrewdly comments how 'heaven affects plurality / Of worshippers t'adore and serve' (IV.i.641–2).[129]

Such engagement with the controversial religious issues of the day is intensified through Alvaro's attempts to rein in his tyrannical father the Duke of Savoy. The Duke is the only figure in the play who is impervious to the beauty of Evandra and Melora. On the point of sacrificing both women to appease his sense of vengeance, the Duke's bitterness smacks of the popular caricature of the puritan, that 'great friend' to 'all seeds of discord' (*Temple of Love*, Argument). In *Love and Honour* such vitriolic anger markedly destabilises the state. The Duke secretly plans to disinherit the conciliatory Alvaro, whilst the people are so outraged by the prospect of these sacrificial executions that they have a 'mind' to 'rebel' (IV.i.458). Furthermore, Leonell's and Prospero's discord over Evandra, a figure who palpably alludes to the Catholic Church, evokes the damaging disagreements which were visibly erupting amongst the Roman Catholic clergy in the mid-1630s. The split between the Regulars and the Jesuits was so deep and public (as the packed volumes of letters in the Westminster Cathedral Archive bear witness) that Thomas Williams writing to William Laud observed how 'the Priests and Jesuits be in such hatred and contradictions among themselves, that they employ their best wits and endeavours to supplant each other'.[130] Indeed, at the very moment *Love and Honour* was licensed, Cardinal Panzani was setting out from Rome with his papal mission to finally resolve these priestly disputes. For, disturbingly, these clerical arguments had filtered through to the recusant laity. One official report for Rome noted a 'coldnesse' in 'their wonted brotherly Charitable correspondence' which directly stemmed from 'the divisions and distractions amongst the priests'.[131] Fr Leyburn's distress at such conflict is apparent from his anxiety that, as 'our king is a most vertuous and just prince . . . I beseech God that the Catholiques of this country may be made worthie of him'.[132]

Yet despite his elevated status, Alvaro is not without criticism. Undoubtedly Alvaro is the epitome of a platonic lover, intuitively recognising Evandra's exceptional qualities. Yet he is so in awe of Evandra that he becomes lost in a reverential inertia. On learning of the imminent death of both Evandra and Melora, he quite literally lies down to contemplate such generosity of spirit, an apathy which he himself later questions: 'Why . . . didst thou undo my soul / With so so strange courtesy?' (V.i.175–6). In a court furiously debating the potential of a union with Rome, *Love and Honour* signals Davenant's own position on religious union: encouraging Alvero into action, whilst curbing the heroic ambitions of his female protagonists, who are clearly rooted in current debates surrounding Henrietta Maria's religious and political agency. As contemporary pamphlet literature spotlights, those figures actively seeking a mutual compromise between the established and Catholic Churches stimulated great political unease. Davenant engages with this debate in *Love and Honour* through his shaping vision of rapprochement. As the arch-mediator Alvaro counsels, in matters of love, or religious worship, men should be like 'Strange rivers that to the same ocean trace', and, like the image of Bedford's stillborn twins, 'when their torrents meet, curl and embrace' (IV.i.629–30). This conciliatory attitude is reinforced through the fate of Prospero. Throughout the text he is associated with a jarring militancy: curiously there is no room for such a figure in Savoy's unified state, as Prospero realises when he undergoes voluntary exile: 'I'll to the war! / And fight to win you a perpetual peace' (V.i.512–13).

The realpolitik of a religio-political rapprochement

The ideal which Davenant urges in *Love and Honour* of a mutual religious settlement, encouraging peace and concord, with discord willingly exiled from the state has an undeniable political charge. In the climate of mid-1630s England even the faintest possibility of Davenant's staged expression of 'a blessed UNION, a blessed CONCORD' reaching fruition actually deepened fissures within the state.[133] Indeed such an appeasing hero as Alvaro would be provocative in his very conciliation. Unlike Davenant's stage characters of Savoy, hardened recusants (whether puritan or Catholic) did not all disappear to distant realms. The subversive power of Davenant's drama is manifest from the fate of moderate Catholic reformers such as Leander Jones and Christopher Davenport. The Vatican completely dismissed Leander's attempts to create a more compassionate version of the oath of allegiance, because the words of the reformulation were 'so pregnant of an ungrateful sense to them'.[134] Likewise it was said that if Christopher Davenport had been in Rome when his tract *Deus, Natura Gratia* was published he would have been 'mew'd up between two stone walls, and his book burn[t] under his nose'.[135] Turning to Protestant circles, the puritan faction, alarmed by even the whiff of conciliation, retreated further into oppositional entrenchment. T. S. even saw the virulent plague of 1636 as God's vengeance against those 'men of two religions . . . that say with their tongues, *Vivat Rex* and wish in their hearts, *Pravaleat Papa*'.[136] Ironically, this very ideal of concord which Davenant boldly voiced in *Love and Honour* resulted in Laud advising Charles to issue further edicts against the recusant community.[137] As his comment concerning George Con underscores, Laud's own vision for the established Church had been fundamentally misunderstood: 'we have here Signor Coneo. If he is Ambassador, Agent or Spy I know not, nor do I wish to know; but I do know he is destroying what I am building up with so much trouble.'[138]

Increasingly the fulcrum of these surmounting tensions was rooted in that ultimate femme forte of the Caroline court, Queen

Henrietta Maria. Quite simply, the puritans deemed the Queen's influence upon her husband to be of 'destructive perswasions'.[139] Such suspicions of the Queen were compounded by the alleged malign pressure exerted upon her by the manipulative forces of Roman Catholic Europe. These rumours are encapsulated in Thomas Williams's report to Archbishop Laud that Henrietta Maria's Capuchin monks were in fact 'creatures' of Cardinal Richelieu. According to Williams, in the event of the King's death they were 'to labour with her, that the Princes their children should be brought up Papists . . . and Popery be brought in'.[140] Curiously such misgivings about the Capuchin order were shared by at least part of the English recusant community. Fr Leyburn commented in a letter to Fitton, 'I am certayne that [the Capuchins] complye with the Jesuits, and never did any one good office for us'.[141] Despite concerted efforts to understand Henrietta Maria's French Catholicism, the recusant community continued at a grassroots level to distrust the baroque splendours of the Counter-Reformation. Leyburn, on receiving a letter 'full of comfort and good hopes' for English Catholics decided with Fr Phillip, her confessor, that he would only 'acquainte her Majesty with as much as concerneth her'.[142] Henrietta Maria's own awareness of this seemingly unbridgeable cultural chasm was illuminated by her wry comment that English Catholics 'would think little of Heaven itself, unless they got it at the hands of Spain'.[143]

Within a matter of four months Davenant had staged two provocative visions of a symbolic religious union. In *The Temple of Love*, through the triumphant zeal of his Roman Catholic Queen, he explored the possibility of Charles I's own apostasy and the re-establishment of England's old faith. Yet in *Love and Honour*, Davenant proffered the more moderate vision of a negotiated and mutual compromise between the Roman Catholic and established Churches. Ultimately both dramatic models were seriously undermined: macrocosmically in the realpolitik of a splintered Caroline state, and microcosmically by a recusant community which refused a wholehearted allegiance to Henrietta Maria as their champion and figurehead. Yet even if these visualisations were ultimately unsuccessful by repositioning *Love and Honour* within contemporary debates, Caroline commercial theatre is opened up to the modern reader as a site which energetically discussed the sensitive issues of the moment. Likewise, through the liberating space of commercial theatre, Davenant frees himself from charges of subservience to Whitehall. Undoubtedly his heroines stem from the Queen's theatrical and religious preferences. Yet the ideal which Davenant creates, of a religious peace secured by negotiated compromise, strongly critiques the increasingly strident Catholicism practised by his key patroness, the Queen. In April 1635 the imprisoned priest Fr William Courtenay was so disillusioned with the state of English Catholicism that he observed: 'it is apparent, that the rents, which the weak hands of childish policy amongst Catholicks daily make in the garment of Christ, must be sewed with prayers, and not with pens, which are nields to wound, but not to amend such tearings'.[144] William Davenant, however, continued to engage audaciously with such concerns. As we explore in Chapter 5, in *The Fair Favourite* (1638) he proffers a refashioned vision of a tempered Roman Catholicism which once more urges the monarchs, in George Wither's words, to demonstrate 'how, all the *Daughters*, of the SPOUSE *Divine* / Might Reconciled be'.[145]

Notes

1 George Wither, *A Collection of Emblemes, Ancient and Moderne* (London: 1635), sig. *4v.
2 Howell, *Ho-Elianae*, p. 203.
3 See Chapter 3, note 120.
4 The Earl of Dorset's religious inclinations foxed his contemporaries: see David L. Smith, 'Catholic, Anglican or Puritan? Edward Sackville, Fourth Earl of Dorset and the Ambiguities of Religion in Early Stuart England', *Transactions of the Royal Historical Society*, 6th series, 2 (1992), 105–24.
5 That this was a matter of contemporary amusement is evident from poems such as 'Upon the Authors writing his name (as in the title of his book) Davenant' which satirize: 'Thus *Will* intending *D'Avenant* to grace / Has made a Notch in's name like that in's face' in George Villiers, the first Duke of Buckingham, and Sir John Denham, *Verses Written by Severall of the Authors Friends, to be Re-printed With the Second Edition of Gondibert* (London: 1653).
6 Albert J. Loomie (ed.), *Ceremonies of Charles I: The Notebooks of John Finet, 1628–1641* (New York: Fordham University Press, 1987), p. 196.
7 Rev. Joseph Mead to Sir Martin Stuteville, 24 April 1630, within Birch, *Court and Times*, vol. 2, p. 77.

8. James Shirley, *The Grateful Servant* (London: 1630), sig. A1v; see also supporting verse from John Fox and Philip Massinger, sigs A1v, A4v.
9. Alan J. Fletcher, *Drama, Performance, and Polity in Pre-Cromwellian Ireland* (Toronto: University of Toronto Press, 2000), p. 269.
10. Alfred Harbage, *Cavalier Drama: An Historical and Critical Supplement to the Study of the Elizabethan and Restoration Stage* (New York: Russell and Russell, 1936), p. 21.
11. William Cartwright, *Comedies, Tragi-Comedies, With Other Poems* (London: 1651), 'The Siege: Or Loves Convert', IV.vii.26–7.
12. Cited in Charles L. Squier, *Sir John Suckling* (Boston: Twayne Publishers, 1978), p. 63. William Habington's *Cleodora* was also staged at Blackfriars. See Frederick C. Fleay, *A Chronicle History of the London Stage, 1559–1642* (London: Reeves and Turner, 1890), p. 351.
13. Keith Sturgess, *Jacobean Private Theatre* (London: Routledge and Kegan Paul, 1987), p. 57.
14. *Ibid.*, p. 19.
15. Harbage, *Cavalier Drama*, p. 165; Fleay, *London Stage*, p. 312.
16. Butler, *Theatre and Crisis*, pp. 100–40, 282, 306.
17. Julie Sanders, 'Caroline Salon Culture and Female Agency: The Countess of Carlisle, Henrietta Maria, and Public Theatre', *Theatre Journal*, 52 (2000), 449–64, p. 463.
18. In pamphlet literature the persuasive powers of Catholic doctors and apothecaries to persuade vulnerable Protestants to convert to Rome on their deathbeds was notorious; see for example the appendix 'A Catalogue of such Popish Physicians in and *about the City of London*' within Gee, *Foot Out of the Snare*, sigs X1–X2.
19. Mary Edmond, *Rare Sir William Davenant. Poet Laureate, Playwright, Civil War General, Restoration Theatre Manager* (Manchester: Manchester University Press, 1987), pp. 45–6; Gervase Huxley, *Endymion Porter: Life of a Courtier 1587–1649* (London: Chatto and Windus, 1959).
20. Edmond, *Rare Sir William*, p. 88.
21. Arthur Nethercot, *Sir William D'Avenant* (Chicago: University of Chicago Press, 1938), pp. 235–6.
22. *Ibid.*, p. 259.
23. *Ibid.*, p. 260.
24. Wither, *Emblemes*, sig. *4v.
25. Cyprien of Gamache, 'Memoirs of the Mission', p. 311.
26. *Ibid.*, p. 311.
27. Cited by Diane Purkiss, *The English Civil War: Papists, Gentlewomen, Soldiers and Witchfinders in the Birth of Modern Britain* (Boulder, Colo.: Basic Books, 2006), p. 31.

28 Cyprien of Gamache, 'Memoirs of the Mission', pp. 311–12.
29 *Ibid.*, p. 313.
30 *Ibid.*
31 *Ibid.*, pp. 313–14.
32 *Ibid.*
33 *Ibid.*, p. 314.
34 Henrietta Maria to the French ambassador, 25 April 1633, AAW/A27, p. 127.
35 Draft of Memorial by Fitton to the French ambassador, 26 April 1633, *ibid.*, p. 129.
36 George Leyburn to Richard Smith, 14 January 1634, *ibid.*, p. 401.
37 For heated discussions regarding the need for an English Roman Catholic bishop see AAW/A27, pp. 402–9.
38 Albion, *Court of Rome*, p. 152. Albion's translations of source material housed in Italy have been invaluable.
39 *Ibid.*, p. 159.
40 Heather Wolfe (ed.), *Life and Letters, Elizabeth Cary, Lady Falkland* (Cambridge: RTM, 2001); Thomas Longueville, *The Life of Sir Kenelm Digby* (London: 1896), and for the extraordinary proselytising fervour of Olivia Porter see Albion, *Court of Rome*, pp. 208–13.
41 Cyprien of Gamache, 'Memoirs of the Mission', p. 302.
42 *Ibid.*, p. 330.
43 Petition from St Giles-in-the-Fields, Middlesex, to the Council, March 1637. *CSP Dom, 1636–1637*, p. 499.
44 Albion, *Court of Rome*, pp. 186–7.
45 AAW/A28, Short Instructions, p. 25.
46 *Ibid.*
47 William Morgan [Case] to an [English Secular Priest], 4 February 1634, AAW/A27, pp. 408–9.
48 Havran, *Catholics in Caroline England*, p. 83.
49 George Leyburn to the Bishop, 8 April 1634, AAW/A27, p. 427.
50 William Davenant, *The Temple of Love* (London: 1635), included in Stephen Orgel and Roy Strong (eds), *Inigo Jones: The Theatre of the Stuart Court*, 2 vols (Berkeley: University of California Press, 1973), vol. 2, pp. 598–629. All subsequent references are to this edition and are in the text.
51 Angelo Correr, Venetian ambassador, to the Doge and Senate, 13 February 1635, quoted in *ibid.*, p. 599.
52 Graham Parry, *The Golden Age Restor'd: The Culture of the Stuart Court, 1603–1642* (Manchester: Manchester University Press, 1981), p. 196.
53 Stephen Orgel, 'Plato, the Magi and Caroline Politics: A Reading of *The Temple of Love*', *Word and Image*, 4 (1998), 663–77.

54 Veevers, *Images of Love*, pp. 133–42.
55 The word 'Temple' is used in *Royales Ceremonies*, p. 11; Cyprien of Gamache, 'Memoirs of the Mission', p. 313.
56 Daniel J. Steible, 'A Critical Edition of Sir William Davenant's *The Temple of Love* and *The Platonic Lovers*' (Ph.D. dissertation, University of Cincinnati, 1939), p. lv.
57 J. B. Fletcher, 'Précieuses at the Court of Charles I', *Journal of Comparative Literature*, 1 (1903), 120–53, p. 128; and E. Marchant, *Sir William Davenant* (Oxford: Davenant Society: 1936), p. 16.
58 The Earl of Newport was himself illegitimate and known to have had an affair with the Queen's Maid of Honour, Eleanor Villiers. Turning to the female masquers, Lady Anne Carre would have reminded the spectator of her mother's inauspicious union with Robert Carre, Earl of Somerset (indeed Anne was born in the Tower of London); and Lady Marquess Hamilton was publicly estranged from her husband.
59 Cyprien of Gamache, 'Memoirs of the Mission', p. 316.
60 *Ibid*.
61 Hawkins, *Partheneia Sacra*, pp. 1–2, 107, 114.
62 Veevers, *Images of Love*, pp. 124, 127, 133.
63 'N. N.', *Maria Triumphans; Being a Discourse, Wherin By Way of Dialogue the B. Virgin Mary Mother of God is Defended* (St Omer: 1635). Regarding possible details of authorship see Erica Veevers, 'The Authorship of *Maria Triumphans*', *N&Q*, 34 (1987), 313–14.
64 Such language infuses Davenant's poems 'To the Queene, Entertain'd At Night By the Countesse of Anglesey', and 'To the Queene, Presented With a Suit, in the Behalfe of F. S. Directed, From Orpheus Prince of Poets, to the Queene of Light', in A. M. Gibbs (ed.) *William Davenant: The Shorter Poems, and Songs From the Plays and Masques* (Oxford: Clarendon Press, 1972), pp. 28, 32.
65 Sarah Cohen, *Art, Dance and the Body in French Culture of the Ancien Régime* (Cambridge: Cambridge University Press, 2000), p. 10.
66 Veevers, *Images of Love*, p. 141.
67 Shirley, *The Cardinal*, IV.i.35; See also Charles Forker, 'Archbishop Laud and Shirley's *The Cardinal*', *Transactions of the Winconsin Academy of Sciences*, 47 (1958), 242–8.
68 Joseph Mede, *The Name Altar, or Θυσιαστηριον, Anciently Given to the Holy Table* (London: 1637).
69 Fitton to unrecorded, 8 March 1636, p. 365, AAW/A28, p. 365.
70 *The Great Eclipse of the Sun, Or, Charles His Waine Over-Clouded, by the Evill Influences of the Moon, . . . Otherwise, Great Charles, Our Gracious King, Eclipsed by the Destructive Perswasions of His Queen, by the Pernicious Aspects of His Cabbinet Counsell and, by the Subtill Insinuations of the Popish Faction* (London: 1644), p. 3.

71 Barberini to Panzani, December 1635, in Joseph Berington (ed.), *The Memoirs of Gregorio Panzani, Giving an Account of His Agency in England, in the Years 1634, 1635, 1636* (Birmingham: Swinney and Walker, 1793), p. 203.
72 William Sanderson, *A Compleat History of the Life and Raigne of King Charles From His Cradle to His Grave* (London: 1658), p. 141.
73 See also Frances Dolan, *Whores of Babylon, Catholicism, Gender and Seventeenth-Century Print Culture* (Notre Dame: University of Notre Dame Press, 2005 reprint), p. 136.
74 Albion, *Court of Rome*, p. 148.
75 William Laud, *A Speech Delivered in the Starr-Chamber On Wednesday, the XIVth of June, 1637. At the Censure of J. Bastwick, H. Burton, & W. Prinn; Concerning Pretended Innovations in the Church* (London: 1637), p. 4.
76 Robert Skinner, *A Sermon Preached Before the King at White-Hall, the Third of December* (London: 1634), p. 29. This is strongly reiterated in Alexander Read, *Sermon Preached April 8th 1635, At a Visitation At Brentwood in Essex* (London: 1636), which includes a seventeen-page list of 'things indecent' within the sanctity of a church.
77 John Prideaux, *The Patronage of Angels: A Sermon Preached at the Court* (Oxford: 1636), especially, pp. 22–3; see also Anthony Stafford, *The Female Glory; Or, the Life and Death of Our Blessed Lady, the Holy Virgin Mary* (London: 1635).
78 Henry Valentine, *Private Devotions, Digested into Six Letanies* (London: 1640), p. 190. See also William Austin, *Devotionis Augustinianae Flamma* (London: 1635).
79 John Pocklington, *Sunday No Sabbath. A Sermon Preached Before the Lord Bishop of Lincolne At His Lordships Visitation At Ampthill in the County of Bedford, August 17th 1635* (London: 1636), p. 40. This fiery denunciation is echoed in Robert Powell, *The Life of Alfred, or Albred . . . Together With a Parallel of Our Soveraigne Lord King Charles* (London: 1634), especially pp. 150–1.
80 Pocklingon, *Sunday No Sabbath*, p. 40.
81 Francis White, *A Treatise of the Sabbath-Day. Containing, a Defence of the Orthodoxall Doctrine of the Church of England, Against Sabbatarian-Novelty* (London: 1635), sig. ***4r.
82 Peter Hausted, *Ten Sermons, Preached Upon Severall Sundayes and Saints Dayes* (London: 1636), p. 222. See also John Browning, *Concerning Publike-Prayer, and the Fasts of the Church* (London: 1636), especially pp. 41–2.
83 William Quelch, *Church-Customes Vindicated in Two Sermons Preached At Kingstone Upon Thames* (London: 1636), pp. 14–15.

84 Thomas Taylor, *A Mappe of Rome, Lively Exhibiting Her Mercilesse Meeknesse and Cruell Meries to the Church of God: Preached in Five Sermons, On Occasion of the Gunpowder Treason* (London: 1619, 1634), sig. A2r.
85 Ephraim Pagitt, *Christianographie; Or, the Description of the Multitude and Sundry Sorts of Christians in the World Not Subject to the Pope* (London: 1635), sig. a3v.
86 Thomas Becon, *The Displaying of the Popish Masse: Wherein Thou Shalt See, What a Wicked Idoll the Masse Is* (London: 1588, 1637), p. 330.
87 John Rhodes, *The Countrie Mans Comfort: Or Religious Recreations Fitte For All Well Disposed Persons* (London: 1588, 1637).
88 Jane Dudley, *The Life, Death, and Actions of the Most Chaste, Learned and Religious Lady, the Lady Jane Grey* (London: 1636), p. 4.
89 John Bastwick, *The Answer of John Bastwick . . . to the Exceptions Made Against His Letany . . . This Is to Follow The Letany as a Second Part Thereof* (London: 1637), p. 19.
90 William Prynne, *Certaine Quaeres Propounded to the Bowers At the Name of Jesus* (London: 1636), p. 20. Prynne's vehemence is matched in Scotland. See David Calderwood, *A Re-Examination of the Five Articles Enacted at Perth* (Edinburgh: 1636), especially the preface; George Gillespie, *A Dispute Against the English-Popish Ceremonies Obtruded Upon the Church of Scotland* (Edinburgh: 1637).
91 William Prynne, *A Quench-Coale: Or, a Briefe Disquistion and Inquirie, in What Place of the Church or Chancell the Lords-Table Ought to Be Situated* (London: 1637), p. 36.
92 Thomas Odell, *A Briefe and Short Treatise Called the Christians Pilgrimage to His Fatherland* (Amsterdam: 1635), sig. A2r. See also Henry Burton, *An Apology of an Appeale* (London: 1636); William Prynne, *Newes from Ipswich* (Ipswich: 1636), p. 4.
93 William Prynne, *A Looking-Glasse For All Lordly Prelates, Wherein They May Cleerely Behold the True Divine Originall and Laudable Pedigree, Whence They Are Descended* (London: 1636), pp. 45–6.
94 *Ibid.*, p. 44.
95 Lueas Wadding, *The History of the Angelicall Virgin Glorious S. Clare*, trans. Sr Magdalen Augustine (Douai: 1635), sig. A4r. See also John Falconer, *The Life of St Catherine* (St Omer: 1634); Thomas Buckland, aka Edmund Thomas Hill, *A Plaine Path-Way to Heaven: Meditations, or Spirituall Discourses Upon the Ghospells of All the Sondayes in the Yeare* (St Omer: 1637), p. 219.
96 Owen, *Antidote Against Purgatory*, sig. *2v.

97 F. E., aka Lechmere, aka Edmund Stratford, *A Reflection of Certaine Authors That Are Pretended to Disavow the Churches Infallabilitie in Her Generall Decrees of Faith* (Douai: 1635), sig. *3r.
98 B. C., Αδελφομαχια, *Or The Warrs of Protestancy; Being a Treatise, Wherein Are Layd Open the . . . Dissentions of the Protestants Among Themselves* (St Omer: 1637), pp. 7–8.
99 Matthew Wilson, *A Direction to be Observed by N. N. If Hee Meane to Proceede in Answering the Booke Intitled Mercy and Truth* (printed secretly in England: 1636), pp. 22–3.
100 *Ibid.*, p. 26.
101 Thomas Doughty, *Of the Visible Sacrifice of the Church of God. The First Part* (Brussels: 1637), p. 26.
102 For a complete list see 'Account of the Anglican Bishops', within Albion, *Court of Rome*, Appendix V, pp. 412–14.
103 Information Touching the Present State of the Catholic Church in England, 1636, AAW/A28, pp. 411–12.
104 Gerard Sitwell, 'Leander Jones' Mission to England 1634–5', *RH*, 5 (1959), 132–82.
105 Leander Jones to the Vatican, 'Instructions relating to the reconciliation of moderate Papists and Protestants', March 1634, *CSP*, vol. 1, p. 209.
106 Leander Jones to Windebank, August 1634, *ibid.*, vol. 1, pp. 128–9.
107 John Berchmans Dockery, *Christopher Davenport: Friar and Diplomat* (London: Burns and Oates, 1960), p. 84.
108 Mr Wilford to Fr Leander Jones, May 1635, *CSP*, vol. 1, p. 272.
109 Albion, *Court of Rome*, pp. 254–5.
110 AAW/A28, p. 411.
111 Robert Shelford, *Five Pious and Learned Discourses* (Cambridge: 1635), p. 239. See also Richard Crashaw's commendatory poem, sig. A1.
112 Gilbert Ironside, *Seven Questions of the Sabbath Briefly Disputed, After the Manner of the Schooles* (Oxford: 1637), sigs A5r–A6v.
113 Thomas Bedford, *A True and Certaine Relation of a Strange-Birth, Which Was Borne At Stone-House in the Parish of Plimmouth, the 20 of October, 1635; Together With the Notes of a Sermon, Preached Octob. 23. 1635. In the Church of Plimmouth, At the Interring of the Sayd Birth* (London: 1635), p. 21.
114 AAW/A29, p. 157.
115 Albion, *Court of Rome*, p. 187.
116 Con to Barberini, 5 May 1637, *Ibid.*, p. 247.
117 Instruction Concerning the Present State of the Protestant Church of England, May 1636, AAW/A28, pp. 413–14.
118 Wither, *Emblemes*, sig. *4v.
119 Nethercot, *Sir William D'Avenant*, p. 121.

120 Gerald E. Bentley, 'The Diary of a Caroline Theatregoer', *MP*, 35 (1938), 61–72, p. 66.
121 Bawcutt, *Records of Sir Henry Herbert*, p. 200.
122 Philip Bordinat and Sophia Blaydes, *Sir William Davenant* (Boston: Twayne Publishers, 1981), p. 154.
123 William Davenant, *Love and Honour*, in *The Dramatic Works of Sir William Davenant*, 5 vols (Edinburgh: William Paterson, 1873), vol. 3, pp. 91–192. All subsequent references are to this edition and are in the text.
124 Thomas May, *The Tragedy of Antigone, the Theban Princesse* (London: 1631), sigs A4v–A5r.
125 Walter Montagu, *The Accomplished Woman* (London: 1656). See also Sanders, 'Caroline Salon Culture', p. 453.
126 Jacques du Bosc, *L'Honneste Femme* (Paris: 1632), p. 128. Pierre Le Moyne evocatively sums up this spiritual force of compassion, beauty and courageous piety in *La Gallerie des Femmes Fortes* (Paris: 1647): 'Ce n'est pas la hauteur de la taille, ny la force du corps qui fait les Heros: c'est la grandeur et l'élévation de l'Ame: c'est la vigueur & la fermeté de l'Esprit: Et il peut y avoir des Ames fort élevées & de premiere grandeur en de petits Corps; il peut y avoir un Esprit extremement ferme, et d'une extréme vigueur, dans une chair fort infirme. De ce costé là donc il n'y a rien qui puisse diminuer le droit des Femmes' [It is neither the height of the figure nor the power of the body which makes Heroes; it is the magnitude and the elevation of the soul; it is the vigour and the resolution of the spirit. One can have a strong soul which is exalted and of the first magnitude in a small body; one can have a spirit of an extreme steadiness and of an extreme vigour in a flesh which is greatly infirm. Therefore there is nothing which can diminish the right of Women], p. 311.
127 Ian Maclean, *Woman Triumphant: Feminism in French Literature, 1610–1652* (Oxford: Clarendon Press, 1977), p. 64.
128 Danielle Clarke, 'The Iconography of the Blush: Marian Literature of the 1630s', in Kate Chedgzoy, Melanie Hansen and Suzanne Trill (eds), *Voicing Women: Gender and Sexuality in Early Modern Writing* (Edinburgh: Edinburgh University Press, 1998), pp. 111–28, p. 111.
129 This quotation differs slightly in the Folio version. James Tupper suggests that this was because this text was taken down from memory from an actual performance. It is suggestive that this fragment reverberates even further with contemporary religious issues: 'Does not the best / Of objects, Heaven, affect plurality / Of worshippers, and would be rather by / Consent of many, than by one ador'd?' (IV.i.640–4). See J. W. Tupper (ed.), *Love and Honour and the Siege of Rhodes by Sir William D'Avenant* (Boston: D.C. Heath & Co., 1909).

130 Thomas Williams to the Lord Archbishop of Canterbury, August 1634, *CSP*, vol. 1, p. 139.
131 AAW/A28, p. 411.
132 George Leyburn to Richard Smith, April 8 1635, AAW/A27, p. 427.
133 Wither, *Emblemes*, sig. *4v.
134 Mr Wilford to Fr Leander Jones, May 1635, *CSP*, vol. 1, p. 272.
135 Dockery, *Christopher Davenport*, p. 91.
136 T. S., *Sermons, Meditations, and Prayers, Upon the Plague, 1636* (London: 1637), p. 13.
137 Such as *A Proclamation Restraining the Withdrawing His Majesties Subjects From the Church of England and Giving Scandal in Resorting to Masse* (London: 1637).
138 Albion, *Court of Rome*, p. 230. Laud's position is supported by Peter Heylyn's official answer to Henry Burton in *A Briefe and Moderate Answer to the Seditious and Scandalous Challenge of Henry Burton, Late of Friday-Street* (London: 1637).
139 Anon., *Eclipse of the Sun*, title page.
140 Thomas Williams's story regarding the French Capuchins' refusal to include native English friars within their mission, 'lest their natural love and loyalty to their King and country, should cause them to reveal any plots' is corroborated by a letter from the Benedictine Leander Jones to Secretary Windebank. Thomas Williams to the Lord Archbishop of Canterbury, August 1634, *CSP*, vol. 1, pp. 141, 143; Leander Jones to Secretary Windebank, *CSP*, vol. 1, pp. 167–8.
141 George Leyburn to Fitton, 5 July 1633, AAW/A27, p. 187.
142 George Leyburn to Fitton, 1 March 1633, AAW/A27, p. 53.
143 Con to Barberini, March 1637, Albion, *Court of Rome*, p. 164.
144 The Humble Remonstrance of Edward Courtenay, Prisoner, to Sir Francis Windebank, April 1635, *CSP*, vol. 1, p. 262.
145 Wither, *Emblemes*, sig. *4v.

5

'This broken time': the tempering of an international Catholicism, 1637–1640[1]

By the late 1630s William Davenant had firmly entrenched himself at the core of Queen Henrietta Maria's circle of patronage. Having successfully displaced James Shirley as early as 1634 from his theatrical niche, Davenant's goal, by 1638, was the coveted position of Poet Laureate, a sinecure made available in 1637 by the widely lamented death of Ben Jonson. The contest for the Laureateship was very much a topic of the moment. Indeed John Suckling's satirical verse 'The Wits, or The Session of the Poets' nominated twenty-two possible contenders, mockingly discarding Davenant as 'in all their Records either in Verse or Prose, / There was not one Laureat without a nose'.[2] Nudging aside rivals from Richard Brome to Francis Lenton and Thomas Killigrew, Davenant was awarded the 'Laurel of Bay' and granted a yearly annuity of £100.[3] Reflecting this elevated poetical status, 1638 witnessed the publication of Davenant's *Madagascar*, a volume of poems dedicated not only to his constant champion Endymion Porter but to Henry Jermyn, the Queen's most trusted adviser.[4] By 1639 further evidence of Davenant's powerful court connections emerged when he secured a royal patent granting him the exciting prospect of establishing his own theatrical premises: to set up a 'Theatre or Playhouse, with necessary tireing and retiring Rooms and other places convenient . . . to exercise Action, musical Presentments, Scenes, Dancing and the like'.[5] Immediate ripples of consternation suggest the impact such an impresario would have made on the map of commercial theatre. As a professional playwright, with an enviable court network, Davenant was perfectly poised to feed the increased appetite amongst Caroline audiences for the spectacular scenery and elaborate costumes inherent to elite court productions. Unhappily for Davenant this patent was rescinded.[6] Yet, by June 1640, he swiftly seized upon an unlooked-for opportunity to put his innovative ideas into practice. On the imprisonment of William Beeston, manager of the Cockpit theatre, an official letter from the Lord Chamberlain empowered Davenant 'to take into his Government and care' Beeston's players, who were instructed to 'obey the sayd Mr Davenant and follow his Orders and dirrecions as they will answere the contrary'.[7] Impending war prevented Davenant from exploiting this enviable possibility. That summer Davenant was engaged in Scotland serving King Charles in the Second Bishops' War. By September 1642 Parliament had ordered the closure of the theatres, deciding that 'while these sad Causes and set times of Humiliation doe continue, publike-Stage-playes shall cease, and be forborne'.[8]

As this chapter establishes, the court of Queen Henrietta Maria into which Davenant was so strategically embedding himself was increasingly associated with a fervent brand of international Catholicism. The combined visible presence of the Vatican's papal agent, George Con, together with the arrival of the Queen's *devôt* mother, Marie de Médicis, strengthened Henrietta Maria's own Counter-Reformation resolve. Barely three years after licensing, Davenant's staged ideal in *Love and Honour* of a negotiated religious union was becoming increasingly ephemeral. The possible ramifications aroused by such a burgeoning court Catholicism alarmed both puritans and Laudians alike. Notably Henrietta Maria emerged in late 1630s Protestant polemic as an overly powerful consort whose religion posed a direct threat to Charles I, and menaced the well-being of the English nation.

Anxiety over this potent combination of the seeming influence of Henrietta Maria, together with the ambition of Catholic Europe, was not confined to members of the established Church. One would expect Davenant, a dramatist so closely associated with Henrietta Maria, and so frequently charged with sycophancy, to freely celebrate the Queen's success. Indeed, he does this with great aplomb in the masque *Luminalia* (1638) which stunningly showcased Henrietta Maria's Catholic triumphs to the Western world. However, *The Fair Favourite* (licensed 1638, printed 1673) signals a remarkable imaginative distance from *Luminalia*'s dazzle. Performed amid mounting unease regarding both the increasingly restless Scottish Calvinists and Henrietta Maria's deliberate intriguing to maintain her controversial Catholic revival, *The Fair Favourite* actively promotes a model of queenship which selflessly mediates between the King and all his peoples. Such a creative shift suggests that, in his plays at least, Davenant refused to be circumscribed by his court position and boldly questioned Henrietta Maria's obdurate and potentially alienating stance. Most surprising, however, for a playwright who had so deliberately edged his way into the Queen's court coterie is that, by 1640, Davenant's disquiet even crept into that most elite of dramatic genres, the court masque. As Poet Laureate, Davenant composed the verse for *Salmacida Spolia* (1640), a masque epitomised by Henrietta Maria's startling appearance as an Amazon in military armour, poised to defend both Charles I and the Catholic community. Significantly, Davenant's celebration of Henrietta Maria's bellicose image is decidedly awkward. This fundamental structural antithesis between Inigo Jones's 'speaking pictures' and Davenant's libretto further questions the once notorious paradigm of Caroline theatre as the shimmering, unquestioning reflection of a court which blithely danced whilst the fires of civil war ignited.[9]

Luminalia: spotlighting a flourishing Catholic revival?

In a probably apocryphal reported moment, on 8 December 1638, the Feast of the Immaculate Conception of the Virgin Mary, Henrietta Maria was astounded by the considerable attendance at the papal agent's chapel. When she asked if the Pope had hoped for such success, George Con's uncompromising reply, that Urban VIII anticipated 'the conversion of England', prompted Henrietta Maria to vow, 'we must act then and not talk'.[10] Such queenly bravado indicates the serious nature of Henrietta Maria's ambitions in the late 1630s, a confidence spurred on by the Vatican legate's own religious zeal. The political potential of Con's unique position (as the Queen's servant, yet her spiritual adviser with unparalleled access to the King) was recognised internationally. Purportedly, Con's mandate was to facilitate easy access between Henrietta Maria and the Pope. But, as his correspondence with Cardinal Barberini makes clear, Con's ultimate (if tantalisingly unlikely) goal was the conversion of Charles I to Rome.[11] In the meantime he worked tirelessly with Charles towards a version of the Oath of Allegiance which would prove acceptable to the courts of both

Rome and England. As the Worcesters, a leading recusant family, remarked, this would have been 'the greatest boon the Catholics could have hoped for'.[12] Reflecting Henrietta Maria's satisfaction with her papal adviser, the Queen repeatedly urged the Curia to elevate Con to the Cardinalate, arguing that such a move would simultaneously lift the spirits of English Catholics and draw England closer to Rome. However, encapsulating the Vatican's vacillating approach to the incredible renaissance of Catholicism within the very heart of Whitehall, Urban VIII insisted that 'great caution was to be used in Mr Conn's case, lest other queens should expect the same favour'.[13] The Curia's insinuation that 'Mr Conn ought first to do some signal service for the church, under her majesty's influence and protection' infuriated Henrietta Maria who, with some cause, perceived such procrastination as a slight to her own Counter-Reformation efforts in England.[14]

From his arrival in 1636 George Con had effected a successful entrance into court life, receiving a raft of invitations which ranged from the Earl of Northumberland to go hunting and the Marquis of Hamilton to tour the Bodleian Library.[15] Building from this platform Con initiated an insidious circumvention of the barriers which continued to afflict the practising of Roman Catholicism. By March 1637 Con had erected a papal chapel in his London home (complete with the Barberini arms) which provided a notorious centre for the ever more fashionable court practising of Roman Catholicism (Figure 14). Notably, in July 1637, the marriage of Francis Browne, Viscount Montagu to the Earl of Worcester's daughter, Elizabeth, was celebrated here, whilst, in March 1638 the Countess of Arundel conducted the Earl of Bath and other Protestant friends on a private tour of the chapel's Good Friday Sepulchre.[16] Con's apparent influence with Charles I, twinned with Henrietta Maria's undoubted sway, was a winning combination, apparent from their encouragement of the King to order the retrieval of confiscated Mass vestments, to remit a Jesuit from the death sentence and even to intervene in the patrimony of a priest.[17] By May 1638 the real potential of the persuasive powers of Con and Henrietta Maria was revealed with the selection of a known recusant to the key position of Secretary to the Queen. As Caroline Hibbard points out, in an astonishing departure from government policy which specifically excluded Roman Catholics from public office, John Winter was appointed; a man 'never thought of',

'This broken time'

14 'Altar of Repose in George Con's Chapel, 1637', from a pen and ink sketch found among Con's dispatches in the Barberini Library, Vatican.

nephew of the Earl of Worcester, 'related to one of the infamous Gunpowder Plotters', and 'closely associated with the Jesuits'.[18]

This powerfully Catholic atmosphere which infiltrated England from within the Queen's court was intensified by a flurry of exiles from the French court of Louis XIII. In May 1638 the Duchesse de Chevreuse visited Henrietta Maria. Setting up her own household in London, this known Hispanophile openly cultivated George Con, took the Princess Mary to Mass and, most significantly, urged the Queen to invite her mother, Marie de Médicis, to take refuge in England.[19] Accordingly, in October 1638, the Queen Mother 'said to be ominous, where ere she came', settled in St James's Palace.[20] Lady Brilliana Harley remarked how, overwhelmed after fourteen years of separation, 'the Quene mother was so transported with joy, as they say, at the sight of the quene, that shee was in a trance'.[21] Once recovered from this 'trance', Marie de Médicis opened yet another Roman Catholic chapel to be served by her Jesuit confessor. This reinforced her daughter's religious zeal and provided a further explicit symbol of a tangible Roman Catholicism within London.[22] In 1635 Montague, the Bishop of Chichester, had remarked to Gregorio Panzani: 'had you been acquainted with this nation ten years ago, you might have observed such an alteration in the language and inclinations of the people, that it would not only put you in hopes of an union, but you would conclude it was near at hand'.[23] By 1638, with pursuivants themselves now pursued in the Star Chamber for their harsh treatment of recusants, and the Spanish ambassador, Õnate, openly processing through the London streets, on Maundy Thursday, with priests and recusants brandishing crucifixes, it would seem that this moment had arrived.[24] Remarkably the central image from Thomas Heywood's pageant *Porta Pietatis* (1638) plainly depicted the Virgin Mary enthroned, and '*next* Religion *crown'd*', on the very Gate to Piety which symbolised 'the doore by which all zealous and devout' Londoners would 'enter into the fruition of their long hoped for hapinesse'.[25] Even government reprisals, in the form of proclamations which threatened the severest penalties against English Catholics hearing Mass in the Queen's chapel, and forbade proselytisation by Roman Catholic priests and laymen, left Henrietta Maria and her confederates undaunted.[26] Indeed, only three days after such a proclamation in December 1637, in a public show of defiance, Henrietta Maria audaciously opened her chapel to the crowds who flocked for Midnight Mass. With a congregation which provocatively included prominent court ladies renowned for their recent apostasies, like Lady Newport, George Con openly marvelled how 'such a concourse had seldom been seen'.[27]

Once more Henrietta Maria turned to the stage to effectively project her latest, and most potent, achievement in her self-professed role as champion of English Catholicism. Collaborated upon by Inigo Jones and William Davenant, the Queen's direct input into *Luminalia* is evident from the fascinating comment that the invention was 'suddenly done and showed her majesty' before staging.[28] Having received the Queen's approval, on 'Shrovetide night', 6 February 1638, Henrietta Maria presented *Luminalia* before the King, a shimmering paean which powerfully blazed Henrietta Maria's Counter-Reformation successes to Whitehall and the wider courts of Europe.[29] The play opens on a scene of darkness, with tales of 'prophetic priests' 'constrained' to obscure themselves and 'live in disguises' (20–1): the references to the practices which had been (and to some extent continued to be) so integral to the survival of

England's old faith are more than evocative. As the missionary martyr Robert Persons commented in August 1581, to avoid discovery it had become even 'the custom of the Catholics themselves to take to the woods and thickets, to ditches and holes even for concealment'.[30] Some fifty years later Catholic priests remained in disguise, but as John Floyd had prophesied in the mid-1620s, the mists which had shrouded the fortunes of English recusants certainly seemed to be lifting, by 1638, to reveal 'the presage of a fayre day'.[31] In *Luminalia* Aurora descends to the masquing stage of Whitehall to tell of the advent of a 'terrestr'al beauty', the role played by Henrietta Maria, who would enlighten the darkness of 'this hemisphere' (278–9). Suggestively, those same priests who had been forced to 'hide their heads in caves' (21–2) invoke the dawn of this 'earthly star' (282), insinuating, as with the central architectural conceit in *The Temple of Love*, a fusion between the traditions of England's old faith and the vibrancy of the Queen's French Catholicism.

Visually, the arrival of 'this goddess of brightness' (29–30) after the initial gloom of the antimasque of Night, quite literally would have dazzled the expectant courtiers. As Barbara Ravelhoeffer argues, even from the lines of Inigo Jones's sketch for Queen Henrietta Maria's costume (displayed in Figure 15) the desired effect for an overwhelming brilliance is unmistakable, with the myriad rays of shooting light, cut in 'star–like beams of white . . . tacked together with twists of gold' (360–2).[32] But, on the eve of the masquing occasion itself, when encasing this 'queen of brightness' (357), the sparkle from the fabric's glinting panels of silver and aurora would have been intensified by Jones's ingenious 'glory with rayes' (356), which surrounded 'the Queen's majesty's seat' (356) to express directly Henrietta Maria's deific role. Encircled in turn by her gloriously apparelled female cohort, this stunning vision simultaneously served to strengthen the powerful focus on Henrietta Maria herself: for 'those beauties neare her' were quite simply 'made up of beams / They gathered from her useless scattered light' (343–4). As Erica Veevers first argued, *Luminalia* is the apotheosis of the light and beauty so central to the Queen's masques. This scintillating apparition of Henrietta Maria in a dazzle of Counter Reformation glory – 'the chief in souls' (391) – would have had, as John Peacock perceptively observes, 'the impact of a baroque religious painting in which the Catholic Queen figures as her namesake, the Virgin Mary'.[33]

15 Inigo Jones's sketch for the costume of *Henrietta Maria or a Lady Masquer* from *Luminalia*, 1638.

Enflaming contemporary debates: 'the party of the queen grows very strong'

Luminalia's intense display of Henrietta Maria's role as a champion of Counter-Reformation Catholicism completely eclipsed the hope, dramatised by Davenant in *Love and Honour* (1634), of a rapprochement between the Churches of Rome and England. The cumulatively destabilising, and ultimately alienating, power of such a dangerously international Catholic force deeply disturbed all factions within the established Church. William Laud was distinctly alarmed at the consequences of this determined Roman Catholic resurgence upon his own programme of a return to a primitive Catholicism. Writing to the Earl of Strafford in November 1637, Laud commented, 'I conceive it most true that the party of the queen grows very strong. And, I fear some consequences of it very much.'[34] At Laud's instigation, King Charles attempted to quell this upsurge. William Sanderson relates how 'the Arch Bishop publiquely complained to the King, and Councell Table: telling his *Majesty* that the Insolencies of others took advantage from such audacious behaviour, as Mr *Walter Montague*, Sir *Toby Mathews*, all the *Queens* Officers, and others of the *Kings* Court, a rol of whom he there presented'.[35] Determined to defend and redefine his own vision of the Church of England, Laud republished his *Relation of the Conference between Laud and Fisher* (1639). Dedicating the tract to Charles I, he bemoaned the '*hard Condition*' of the Church of England and boldly laid the underlying responsibility for the country's protection upon his King, warning '*unlesse* Your Majesty *looke to it, to Whose Trust Shee is* committed, *Shee'll be grownd* to powder'.[36]

Such a public identification of Rome as a force which ultimately opposed Laud's vision of the established Church of England was widely supported. Noticeably, by 1638, the Laudian party had retreated from a more diplomatic treatment of recusant adversaries. Daniel Featley in his preface to *Stricturae in Lyndomastigem* pronounced that if

> there were any hope to gaine by mildnesse, and win by yeelding unto [recusants] *as much as might be, without prejudice to the Truth; I should then persuade all that write against them, to temper their Inke rather with Rose-water than Vinegar. But in all my conflicts with them, at home and abroad, I find them like nettles*, which sting if they be gently touched, but hurt not at all if they be roughly handled.[37]

With some truculence Thomas Fuller remarked that conciliation between the Churches of England and Rome was ultimately unlikely:

> Our reconciliation with *Rome* is clogged with the same impossibilities: She may be *gone* to, but will never be *met with*, such her *Pride* or as *Peevishness*, not to stir a step to obviate any of a different Religion. *Rome* will never so farr *un-pope* it self, as to part with her pretended *Supremacy* and *Infallibility*, which cuts off all possibility of Protestants Treaty with her.[38]

Yet this Laudian response to the mounting pressure of international Catholicism also reveals the impossibility of the fractured Church of England uniting to jointly combat her common enemy. Repeatedly Laudian commentators drew parallels between the puritan and Recusant communities. Richard Gardiner argued: 'We Preach, and Print *Noe Peace with Rome*, and yet by our owne confession *Rome* doth but *indirectly* undermine Christs Person, and Offices. How then can they then expect *faire Quarter*, who *directly* renounce the Godhead of his *Person* and the Office of his *Mediatorship*?'[39] George Downame dramatically depicted how

> those golden dayes are past, and now are dog-dayes come, everyone biting and barking at his Neighbour, not like Christians, not like Brethren, not like Saints, but like Beares and Tygers, wee teare one another, like *Scythians* and Canibals we eat up one another, as void of all naturall affection. Oh my beloved, is this Christianity?[40]

The puritan response was equally as vehement. John Lilburne directed his invective upon England's 'idolatrous' Prelates, urging his non-conformist readers to maintain 'couragious resolutions like valiant souldiers of *Jesus Christ*, and fight manfullie in this his spirituall battell'.[41] Godly anxieties focused on those Laudian ministers whom they worried were communicating spiritually 'with *Antichrist* and his adherents'.[42] Thus the Scottish Catholic apostate Thomas Abernethie actually maintained how he would rather have entered the Scottish Kirk because it was 'furthest from Popish idolatrie, and neerest to Apostolicall puritie', asking: 'what madnesse . . . were it in a Mariner, for to come out of a sunken ship, to enter into another which is sinking, and may have a tight one?'[43] Capitalising upon this dissent within the Church of England, recusant writers continued to seek to widen the breach between the

Laudian and Nonconformist factions. John Floyd in *The Church Conquerent Over Humane Wit* even redefined the terms '*Protestants*' and '*Protesters*':

> though with you, *Protestants* and *Protesters* be the same, yet it is not so according to the acception of the word *Protestant* commonly receaved . . . in *England* (as all men know) by the name of *Protestants* we properly understand, that part of the pretended English *Reformation*, which is con-distinct from *Puritans*, and opposite against them. Hence *Protestants* with us be not the whole multitude of Protesting Biblists, or of the pretended reformed Churches, but, only one branch of them, the most moderate of all, & that which doth least exorbitate from the *Doctrine* and *Discipline* of the *Roman* Church.[44]

In contrast to such internal fracturing, Thomas Doughty's *Of the Visible Sacrifice in the Church of God* (1638) provided an enviable image of Roman Catholic unity where 'all offer one, and the same *Sacrifice*, and communicate of one, and the same substantiall body, and bloud of Christ . . . And therefore all who worthily communicate in the Catholick Church, are all one.'[45]

By the late 1630s the significant swell of unrest provoked by the Queen Consort's forthright practising of Roman Catholicism was threatening to engulf the Scottish recusant community. As early as December 1637 the Venetian ambassador reported how the Queen's papal agent was alleged to have 'had a hand' in the Scottish prayer-book crisis. George Con was rumoured to have

> encouraged the efforts of the archbishop, hoping that either the people will yield to his ordinances, which approach closely to those of the Roman church, or by opposing them they will bring about civil war between the Protestants with considerable advantage to the Catholic party, to whom the archbishop would have to approach more and more nearly in order to suppress the other.[46]

Rather unsurprisingly, the eruption of puritan outrage at what Fr Andrew Leslie described as King Charles's attempt 'to introduce the Anglican ritual into the Scottish synagogue' was felt most keenly by Scottish recusants.[47] In August 1638 Fr James Macbreck, writing to his Jesuit Father General, reported how 'the madness and hatred of the Puritans against the Catholics grow fiercer every day, and many whole families of Catholics have been compelled to seek a refuge in England'.[48] Firmly embedded within this heated conflict was the hardening and deepening of factions in response to the proselytising Catholic fervour at the core of the Queen's household. Increasingly, Protestant communities located their anxiety as deriving directly from Henrietta Maria, reflecting alarm at her unparalleled position as 'darling of the King's breast' and her progressively interventionist Roman Catholic stance.[49]

Whilst Puritan pamphlets focused on duplicitous Biblical women, Laudian tracts strongly advocated the need for husbands to govern their wives. George Ballard in *The History of Susanna* vociferously commended Joachim on his decision to 'marry one / Of *Judahs* Tribe, and not of *Babylon*', provocatively suggesting how '*He, that from* Babylon, *a good wife takes,* / *Snatcheth an Eeele out of a Bag of Snakes*'.[50] Similarly John Canne critiqued the 'unlawfull love' which Samson held for 'his *deare Delilah*' with the inflammatory question, 'Did not that wicked woman occasion trobles in Israel, by seekinge to put downe their right kinge, & set up her selfe?'[51] By 1638 such vehement censure of the royal marriage crept into more moderate Protestant polemic. In an anonymous tract one author entreated 'all men (especially of reason and religion) ... to show themselves to be men, and to take the staffe againe into their owne hands; considering that the husband is the wives head; unto whom she ought to be in subjection in all things'.[52] Building on this Pauline philosophy, John Preston reminded his reader in *The Golden Scepter* that the 'wedding affection, is such an affection, as when one prefers her husband before all others', a directive plainly illuminated in the text's frontispiece.[53] In this series of marital vignettes, the obedient wife humbles herself before her husband. The omnipotent King raises his Queen as his equal only when assured of his wife's submission, a union suggested in the mutuality of glance and handshake (Figure 16). This royal pair bears a striking resemblance to Preston's own monarchs, and the sketches appear to draw from and suggestively refashion Van Dyck's iconic 1632 portrait, itself a reworking of Daniel Mytens's 1630 portrait (Figure 17). Preston in *The Golden Scepter* can be seen to be presenting a godly reorientation of Van Dyck's luminous painting, where King Charles (turning his back on the crown and orb of state) devoutly gazes at a heavily pregnant Henrietta Maria, who in turn boldly stares at the viewer, rather than at her kingly husband. Francis Rous definitively glosses this popular debate, in his neat elision of Charles's combined roles of King of England, head of the established Church and husband to Henrietta Maria:

16 Frontispiece to John Preston, *The Golden Scepter Held Forth to the Humble. With the Churches Dignitie by Her Marriage and the Churches Dutie in Her Carriage. In Three Treatises* (London: 1638).

188 Staging the old faith

17 Daniel Mytens, with additions by Anthony Van Dyck, *Charles I and Henrietta Maria*, 1630–1632.

will not this husband, who is light it selfe and love it selfe, teach his
owne wife by this most perfect light, and from this most perfect love?
Yea, certainly, in the bed of love he will not onely tell her the words
of his counsels; but by a sacred unction (being one spirit with her)
hee will make her to see the counsells of his words.[54]

In *The Fair Favourite* William Davenant engages with this divisive issue which so engrossed his contemporaries. Like Rous, he advocates a model of good queenship which directly opposed Henrietta Maria's own increasingly adamant, and ultimately divisive, militant stance. However, Davenant inverts Preston's humbling of the female monarch. Notably, this Queen of *The Fair Favourite* leads her husband to wisdom, and selflessly mediates between opposing factions. Such an image negates Protestant anxiety, as voiced by George Ballard, that *'the man, that wives, with an Idolatresse, / Marries temptation'*.[55] Yet, crucially, such an ideal also signalled an alternative to the uncompromising Roman Catholicism urged upon Henrietta Maria by Rome. From Davenant's perspective, this textual model of female conciliation implied a timely return to the ethos of religious accommodation so sensitively explored in *Love and Honour*.

The Fair Favourite: a daring strategy of conciliatory queenship?

Licensed on 17 November 1638, *The Fair Favourite* is known to have been staged twice at the Whitehall Cockpit before the King and Queen.[56] The play focuses on the fracture of court and kingdom when the King's rightful affection for his Queen is usurped by an ungoverned passion for his favourite, Eumena. Arthur Nethercot dismisses *The Fair Favourite* as 'weak', whilst Philip Bordinat and Sophia Blaydes condemn Davenant's ready 'idealisation of women of the court' as 'a reflection' of the playwright's own compromised position as Poet Laureate.[57] Yet *The Fair Favourite* has an undeniable political edge. An immediate intellectual distance from the increasingly sectarian mindset of England's own queen is signalled from the play's source material. *The Fair Favourite* draws on the popular writings of Nicolas Caussin. This French Catholic thinker, whose ideals Henrietta Maria had herself espoused, encouraged proselytisation by compassion rather then contention. In this play known to have been performed before his royal patroness Davenant promotes the passive zeal which had been so essential to Henrietta

Maria's earlier religious success, rather than the disfiguring spectre of religious oppression and subsequent disaffection which, in 1638, stigmatised the Queen and her court.

In contrast to *Love and Honour* where Davenant explores the possibility of religious union through textual doubling, *The Fair Favourite* is a play marked by a series of textual dislocations. Crucially the root of such division is embedded within the heart of the monarchy. From the opening scene, returning triumphant from war, the King publicly rejects his Queen's eager protestations of love. Deeming their marriage to be one of 'provinces' rather than hearts, instead the King seeks solace from his favourite, Eumena (I.i.83). Ominously this monarchical rift is a blight which infects the whole court and ruptures both familial and fraternal bonds. Eumena's brother Oramont, maddened by 'suspicions' about his sister's honour (II.i.121), vows to extinguish 'the taper' of her life (II.i.180). The friendship between Oramont and Amadore, deemed to be 'more lasting than ourselves' (II.i.166) is abruptly crushed when Amadore, determined to prove Eumena's innocence, challenges Oramont to a duel. These schisms are mirrored in the barely disguised estrangements of court factions. As the courtiers Saladine and Thorello comment, the great noblemen 'hug, and consent before / The public face, as they were twins' yet 'hate each other with / As true devout a heart, as over-zealous fools / That differ in their faiths' (III.i.114–17). Again responsibility for such discord is laid upon the King. As Aleran remarks, 'Twere good the King would reconcile / These civil factions in his Court' (III.i.118–19).

Such fundamental disruption within the state is conspicuously healed by the mediatory power of the Queen, an embodiment of neoplatonic wonder, who is hailed throughout the court as 'a great / Example of fair virtue' (II.i.304–5). Although aware that her own 'calamities stand in / Continual use of pity and redress' (II.i.252–3), the Queen of *The Fair Favourite* is marked by her concern for her subjects. She refuses to condemn Eumena, rebukes Oramont for his 'injurious' (II.i.313) slander against his sister's honour, and even succeeds in engineering a reunion between Oramont and the recently resurrected Amadore. As Oramont marvels, in language redolent of the praise lavished upon Henrietta Maria's own masquing personas,

Her vertue is as restless as the sun,
Still moving, and yet never tir'd; and like
His purer beams, it comforts every thing. (V.i.214–16)

The ameliorating effect on the court of such selfless appeasement is immediately evident from Eumena's reaction to this Queen, 'whose goodness works in such extremes' (II.i.349). Empowered by the Queen's integrity, Eumena denies the King's sexual advances; otherwise, as she states to the King, she 'could not easily refrain / From wishing' she might 'meet' his love 'with / Equal flame' (II.i.420–1). This powerfully suggestive ideal of queenship which implodes conflict and heals dissent vividly engages with Henrietta Maria's own stage roles. Most noticeably, in an echo of Henrietta Maria's performance in the title role of *L'Artenice*, the Queen offers the ultimate erosion of the self, planning to leave the court and join 'a little convent' (III.i.266).

Such a distinct parallel with Queen Henrietta Maria's own stage performances intensifies through the figure of the 'Fair Favorite' (II.i.176), Eumena. Like the harassed Fidamira from *The Shepherds' Paradise*, Eumena is also moulded from Queen Henrietta Maria's preferred neoplatonic cast of radiant integrity. Amadore deems her 'pure, as first / Created light' (IV.i.43–4), the King hails her as a 'vertuous maid' (I.i.170) and even Oramont, by the end of the play, admits 'thy causeless suff'rings have rais'd / Thee to the dignity of Saints' (V.i.370–1). Such praise is supported from Eumena's unequivocal response to the Queen's generosity, chiding the King for his cruel treatment of his wife and refuting 'forged whispers' (I.i.225) that in the King's absence the Queen has behaved with jealousy. Whilst her ladies are blithely 'laughing and shrieking' (II.i.334) with 'cavaliers / That start upon [them] in the dark' (II.i.335–6), Eumena sits alone with her books, causing her companion to tease her that she will 'grow as grave as an old abbess' (II.i.341). And, when the King insists on bestowing his regal powers upon her, she grants only the just petitions, and refuses a 'loud return of thanks' (III.i.168). Portentously, such 'innocently sweet' (IV.i.46) actions are transformed by the imagination of the wider populace into the bewitching menaces of a malicious siren. Oramont warns Gartha how his sister has become 'the peoples secret scorn' (I.i.305), whilst Eumena herself laments her powerlessness to prevent the 'discolouring' of 'the beauty of my Fame / Till she turn black' (II.i.380–1). The dangers of such vicious misconceptions are only too apparent, as Oramont's deliverance of his bloody sword to Eumena makes spectacularly clear. Oramont blames Amadore's apparent death on Eumena's 'bewitching beauty' which 'with strange charms / Had conquer'd and destroyed him' (IV.i.354–5).

Significantly, the uxorious actions of the King are at the heart of these disorders. Unlike the discerning Prince Alvaro in Davenant's *Love and Honour*, the King of *The Fair Favourite* emerges as a monarch who is enslaved by his passions. The destructive obsession of the King leads him both to despise his own kingship as too circumscribed, and encourages the mistreatment of his virtuous Queen and his chaste subject, Eumena. In the opening scene the very ideal of kingship is questioned when the King, alone with his counsellors, (shockingly) asks Radegond not only to 'unarm' him, but adds 'would thou couldst un-King me too' (I.i.127–8).[58] The King's own disaffection for the cares of his crown, rooted in the denial of his consuming infatuation with Eumena (whom his counsellors had tricked him from marrying some years earlier) spreads throughout the court. Oramont boldly probes the King's 'dark prerogative' (II.i.138), judging it 'most fear'd, because / It least is understood' (II.i.139–40). Conspicuously, both the Queen and Eumena distrust the rigours of the King's laws. When Oramont's life is endangered, the Queen pleads: 'dare you derive / Your attributes from Heaven, yet mercy want' (IV.i.498–9). Moved by the women's entreaties, the King relents, but the distance between his earthly crown and divine kingship is hideously revealed when in return for such 'justice' the King demands that Eumena should repay sexually his 'fervent passions that / So long have courted your slow love' (IV.i.585–6).

Notably these ramifications surrounding the dangers of such unguarded kingly passion deepen when examined against what I have identified as the direct source of Davenant's text, the widely read fourth book of Nicolas Caussin's *The Holy Court*.[59] Translated from the French in 1638, this is the final instalment of a Roman Catholic tract whose first volume, Caussin informs us, had '*its first life breathed into it by the animating spirit of her sacred Majesties Royall acceptance*', Queen Henrietta Maria herself.[60] As the letters of Lady Brilliana Harley reveal, this treatise was eagerly sought after. Writing to her son Ned, in November 1638, Lady Brilliana remarked how she would 'willingly have the French booke you rwite me word of'; finally receiving a copy in February 1639, 'this day Hall brought me "the Holy Court" from Worster'.[61] The title page plainly sets out the aim of *The Holy Court* as to urge the 'command of reason over the passions'. To illustrate this point, Caussin relates the history of the Emperor Lotharius, a tale which provides striking parallels with Davenant's plot for *The Fair Favourite*. In his youth Lotharius was in love with the beautiful Valdrada, but time and reason made him marry Theutbergue, a 'beawtifull, and vertuous Princesse'.[62] Like the King of *The Fair Favourite*, Lotharius returned to his old love, was 'seldome personally' with his wife, and 'perpetually in mind, and affection' with Valdrada.[63] Again, as with Davenant's text, Lotharius's counsellors suggest a divorce by 'falsly imputing adultery, and barrenesse' to Theutbergue.[64] Moreover, having restored her honour, Theutbergue, like the Queen of *The Fair Favourite*, prepares to become a nun. The plots then diverge as Lotharius refuses to reform, takes the sacraments with a false conscience and dies on a return voyage from Rome. For Caussin, the crux of this tale was the opportunity to emphasise the importance of a virtuous love. As he observed, if love 'be good it rayseth a City of peace, wherein chast amityes sway, and with them, Trueth, Faith, Honour, Vertues, contentments, delights. If it be bad, It makes a Babylon full of confusion, where cares, feares, grieffs, warre, enmityes, impurities, adulteries, incests, sacriledges, bloud, murther, and poison enhabit.'[65]

Such a depiction of the danger inherent to 'bad' love does not simply apply to the court of *The Fair Favourite*. When read against the polemical tracts spewing from the English printing presses in the late 1630s, Caussin's commentary also appraises the Caroline court and the fear that the King's uxorious love for his queen was corrupting the English nation. This 'Babylon of confusion' is accentuated in *The Fair Favourite* by Eumena's seemingly subversive power which the people perceive as perverting first the King and then his courtiers. As the enraged Oramont warns Amadore:

> ... Now thou hast
> Seen her, all the power of human art cannot
> Redeem thee from her charms. She hath
> Bewitch'd thee to a doating love, and told thee
> Tales as void of truth, as those which Syrens sing
> When list'ning seamen perish in the flood
> For what they foolishly believ'd. (IV.i.53–9)

Such snares in *The Fair Favourite* are revealed to be phantasmagoric. In reality, Eumena, consistently, in the face of the King's 'passionate excess', 'forbear[s] to usurp [the Queen's] interest' (V.i.481–2). The King alone has to temper his ungoverned passions, a conquest which he achieves, in true neoplatonic fashion, through the love radiating from the Queen's court, a spiritual journey which restores integrity and unity to the nation. The central implication of this concept of self-mastery is further signalled by the attempts of Amadore and Oramont to govern their individual obsessions. Again such enlightenment is achieved through the mediation of the Queen.

In the distant lands of *The Fair Favourite*, Davenant directly engages with the religio-political concerns of late 1630s Caroline England. In *The Heavenlie Academie* Francis Rous implied that stability could be restored to the court and nation only if the King bestowed upon his wife an 'inward and spirituall eye, to see the inward riches and realities of his counsells'.[66] *The Fair Favourite* inverts this Protestant thinking. Davenant draws on the neoplatonic writings of Caussin, so that the Queen brings the King to right conduct. In this 'miracle of love' (V.i.439) the King commands his courtiers to:

> Do homage to your Queen!
> Not as she shares the Prerogatives of my crown,
> But the Prerogatives of love, whose
> Everlasting throne is in my breast. (V.i.448–51)

As Bordinat and Blaydes suggest, Davenant celebrates the vision of a united monarchy through a depiction of womanhood which would be particularly appealing to Henrietta Maria. However, Davenant's is a dramatic model which in turn critiques the dangerously divisive Catholicism emerging from within Henrietta Maria's own court. Surprisingly, for a dramatist so closely identified with Henrietta Maria's household, the Queen of *The Fair Favourite* is one who selflessly mediates between a prince and all his peoples, and is herself empowered as an intrinsic force of well-being to the nation. *The Fair Favourite*, as with *Love and Honour*, ends on a note of war. Oramont willingly exiles himself to military action as 'a long hard penance' to 'expiate' his 'sins of jealousy' against Eumena and to redeem himself before the Queen (V.i.500–1). With preparations for the First Bishops' War already apace, can Davenant be seen to be indulging in some literary wishful thinking? Hoping that Henrietta Maria's critics and faithful servants alike might similarly prove their loyalty in the fields of Britain's most northern Kingdom?

Salmacida Spolia: showcasing a Counter-Reformation Amazon, Henrietta Maria's final masquing vision

By 1640 the pattern of a conciliatory queenship so audaciously staged in *The Fair Favourite* was increasingly under pressure. Contemporary writings emphasise how anxiety surrounding the Queen's progressive practising of Catholicism was enflamed by King Charles's catastrophic attempt to regulate Protestant worship throughout his three kingdoms. Ironically, the Scottish prayer book crisis of 1637, the prelude to the Bishops' Wars of 1639–40, was both a product of widespread concern regarding the threat of Popery and a key factor in the Queen's increasingly confrontational, Roman Catholic stance. As early as 1637 Henrietta Maria's court had been accused of inciting the troubles in Scotland. By 1639, from Scottish Catholics' own testimonies, the recusant community was greatly imperilled by what Sir Kenelm Digby deemed this 'broken time'.[67] One Scottish Jesuit commented how 'our fortunes fluctuate like the waves of the sea'.[68] Barely eighteen months later Fr James Macbreck bemoaned how the Scottish Calvinists were 'resolved to stamp out the last sparks of true religion, and leave neither name nor trace of Catholic in any part of this accursed land'.[69] With these 'common reports of the discontentments in Scotland', the Dean of England's secular clergy, Anthony Champney, believed it to be 'expedient' for English Catholics to offer their service to King Charles. As he gravely warned, 'the business importeth them chieflie, for if the faction of those rebellious spiritts should prevaile (which God forbid) the Catholickes doubtlesse will feele the ill effects of it more than others'.[70]

Queen Henrietta Maria was directly 'acquainted' with this recusant decision. As Champney elucidates, not only did the Queen 'aproove it' but she 'earnestlie' desired 'that it may bee . . . sett forward'.[71] Remarkably, by June 1639, the collection from English Roman Catholics to assist Charles financially in his Scottish wars amounted to some £10,000. As John Dauncey recorded: 'almost as great a sum was gathered from them, as from the more numerous

Protestants, many of them proportioning their affections beyond their abilities'.[72] Additionally the Queen urged the Catholic community to pray and fast for the King's victory at Berwick and even asked the Catholic ladies of the country to donate their jewels to the cause. Such indefatigable canvassing amongst the English and the wider European communities typified the Queen's actions in the prelude to Civil War. In addition to this national campaign amongst her recusant subjects, Henrietta Maria schemed with the papal agent to attempt to secure financial aid from Roman Catholic Europe. Essentially, as Caroline Hibbard succinctly argues, both Cardinal Barberini and George Con perceived the Scottish war in terms of a personal crusade against Calvinism. With some inevitability, by 1640, Henrietta Maria had increasingly adopted a campaign-like mentality to Scottish affairs, fostering an aggressive form of queenship which was directly at odds with the mollifying figure urged on Henrietta Maria in *The Fair Favourite*.

Rumours quickly began to circulate of a popish 'fifth column-type' intrigue. These fears were fuelled by a second Roman Catholic levy, collected by documented militant recusants such as Thomas Shirley.[73] Growing anti-papist anxiety was exacerbated by Charles I's appointment of the Earl of Arundel to command his troops against the Scottish rebels. Although nominally a Protestant, Arundel was widely suspected as having Roman Catholic sympathies. Robert Baillie identified him as a 'known papist, and the head of the Spanish and Popish faction in England'.[74] Godly concern was further aggravated when Catholic priests were seen to be loitering around the royal camp at York.[75] With Arundel's administration of a new army oath – which was widely perceived to be more anti-protestant than anti-Catholic – by September 1639 misgivings concerning the motives of the Spanish fleet which lurked off the Downs were being embellished into reports of an imminent second Armada.[76] To the wider Protestant imagination it seemed that the recusant community was defiantly stripping off an always-suspect veneer of allegiance to the English nation, to reveal the oppositional Roman Catholic force of Protestant nightmare. Such a horror was even voiced by the moderate Sir Edmund Verney, bearer of the King's standard. Writing to his son Ralph, from the royal army camp itself, Verney remarked how 'the catholiks' use 'all the means and wayes they can to sett uss by the ears, and I thinck they will not fail of theyr plott'.[77]

Barely eight months after a humiliating truce at Berwick, and with Whitehall actively attempting to raise moneys for a second Scottish campaign, Queen Henrietta Maria jointly presented with King Charles I what turned out to be the last masque of the Caroline reign, *Salmacida Spolia*.[78] Rehearsals had begun in early December 1639. The Earl of Northumberland rather incredulously remarked to his sister how, despite the difficult circumstances, 'their majesties are not less busy now than formerly you have seen them at the like exercise'.[79] T. B. Edwards has described *Salmacida Spolia*, staged at Whitehall on Tuesday 21 January 1640, as a performance 'almost in defiance of the political storm which was beginning to break'.[80] Yet, as contemporary reports suggest, this particular 'storm' was already very much aroused and this masque, entirely rooted in its occasion, exposes a translucent moment of heightened political and religious crisis. In this very month James Howell, writing to Sir Kenelm Digby, gloomily foreboded that 'Unlesse God be pleas'd to make up these ruptures' twixt us and *Scotland*, we are likely to have ill days'.[81] The godly Lady Brilliana Harley had prophesied as early as April 1639 that this would be the 'yeare in which maney are of the opinion that [the] Antichrist must begine to falle'.[82] And an anonymous recusant letter from 1640 warned how 'many things are sett on foote against' Catholics.[83] In a key analysis of King Charles's masquing role of Philogenes or Lover of his People (Figure 18), Martin Butler focuses on *Salmacida Spolia* as a creation of the King's court.[84] Yet this masque, performed as Karen Britland first highlighted in honour of Marie de Médicis, is in fact centred more precisely on Henrietta Maria.[85] Moreover, the Queen's own role of 'Chief Heroine' (18) and her spectacular entrance as an Esther in Amazon costume completely overshadowed King Charles's more passive grandeur. Stemming directly from a decisive moment of religio-political crisis, *Salmacida Spolia* can more properly be seen as the final remodelling of those Counter-Reformation ambitions which Henrietta Maria had so boldly staged in elite performances ranging from *L'Artenice* to *Luminalia*.

Characterised by Furie as an 'over-lucky, too-much-happy isle' (134), a thread of awkward unease twists throughout *Salmciada Spolia*. Where Divine Poesy in *The Temple of Love* lavishly praises Charles 'as beloved in heaven' (121), Concord in *Salmacida Spolia* decrees how it is Philogenes' 'fate to rule in adverse times' (190). This prophecy is repeated by the Good Genius of Great Britain,

18 Inigo Jones's sketch for the costume of *The King* in *Salmacida Spolia*, 1640.

and together they lament 'O who but he could thus endure / To live and govern in a sullen age' (196–7). Such difficulties are visually reinforced by the 'craggy rocks' and 'inaccessible mountains' (293–4) which 'heroes' (299) like Philogenes must negotiate in order to ascend the Throne of Honour. Even the song in direct tribute to Philogenes opens with a questioning and equivocal 'if':

> *If* it be kingly patience to outlast
> Those storms the people's giddy fury raise
> Till like fantastic winds themselves they waste,
> The wisdom of that patience is thy praise. (my emphasis, 360–3)

The possibility of doubt entrenched within this qualification somewhat undercuts the opulent tableau of Philogenes enthroned in his seat of gold, surrounded by his noble masquers and with captives passively bound at his feet (342–53). As Davenant's detailed argument of the masque informs us, Philogenes' 'reward' for such kingly 'prudence' is the heavenly gift from the God Pallas of 'the Queen personating the Chief Heroine, with her martial ladies' (18–21). Mark Franko has skilfully argued how in court ballets, the bodies of the court masquers were themselves a means of cultural expression 'designed to aggrandize the monarch'.[86] In *Salmacida Spolia* the vivid staging of the strangely quiescent Philogenes, against the bold militance of his Chief Heroine, palpably articulates a political statement of female empowerment which repeatedly skews the audience's gaze away from the kingly hero.

Even before the Chief Heroine's spectacular martial arrival, her advent is trumpeted, and her status magnified, by the Chorus of the Beloved People's address to Marie de Médicis, the masque's principle spectator. Emphasising the links between mother and daughter, the group revere Marie de Médicis because she 'bred' Henrietta Maria, 'the stream from whence our blessings flow' (318). Such adulation was in itself potentially problematic for, to most observers, Marie de Médicis would have been perceived as the ultimate symbol of political conspiracy.[87] Indeed, by August 1640, Marie de Médicis was to emerge as the mastermind behind the Hussey affair, an alleged Irish-Catholic plot to overcome the English nation. As Elizabeth of Bohemia wryly commented to Sir Thomas Roe: 'it is certaine the Queen Mother hath strange people about her that are able to undertake or doe anie impertinence'.[88] With rumours of intrigue swirling around Henrietta Maria's own scheming in the outbreak of the Scottish troubles, the Queen of England would seem to be very much her mother's daughter.

This combination of both direct and unspoken parallels between mother and daughter intensifies the orientation of *Salmacida Spolia* as a masque which stems from the Queen's court. Yet it also enables this masque to be read as the final fashioning of Henrietta Maria's projection of herself as the champion of Catholicism within England. For the song addressed to the Queen Mother identifies a further embedded analogy between the two queens: that of the status of their royal husbands, both of whom governed nations split by two religions.[89] The Beloved People recall how it was on Marie de Médicis's 'bosom' that Henri IV 'laid his weary head / When he rewarded victories with rest' (320–1); her Médicis 'beauty kept his valour's flame alive' (322) and (insinuatingly) her 'Tuscan wisdom taught it how to thrive' (323). Notoriously Henri IV had decided to convert to Roman Catholicism for political reasons, most specifically the alleged security of the French nation. In *Salmacida Spolia*, Henrietta Maria's own proselytising love for her husband and subjects, so brilliantly projected through her role as Chief Heroine, gestures towards a similar resolution for Philogenes, the 'Lover of his People'.

Although heavily pregnant with the future Henry, Duke of Gloucester, Henrietta Maria made her final intrepid stage appearance from the heavens themselves (Figure 19). Gradually emerging into sight from within a 'huge cloud of various colours' (381) such 'as the Gods are feigned to descend in' (383–4), the dazzling impact of the Chief Heroine's entrance would have been both enthralling and provocatively suggestive. As Erica Veevers has commented, if in the role of Philogenes 'there is the suggestion of the forgiving Christ, there is in the role of the Queen the suggestion of the Militant Virgin'.[90] Such a parallel is intensified by the rays of light which, as in *Luminalia*, surrounded the Queen's seat of glory. In a song from *Salmacida Spolia* to be printed but not sung, the elite audience amuse themselves through one particularly tricky scene change by pondering upon that 'uncertain path which leads to heaven' (333). From the 'speaking pictures' which Inigo Jones created, it would seem that the Chief Heroine was by no means beset by such anxieties. Indeed, Inigo Jones's unsurpassed ability to translate Henrietta Maria's ideals on to the stage transforms *Salmacida Spolia* into a powerful visualisation of the international

'This broken time'

19 Inigo Jones's sketch *The Queen Descends from a Great Cloud* in *Salmacida Spolia*, 1640.

and militant Roman Catholicism which was so central to the Queen's court.

This powerfully nuanced vision is first conceptualised and promoted to the Caroline court through the 'strangeness' of the 'Amazonian habits' of Henrietta Maria and her ladies (Figure 20). As Davenant relates, 'the Queen's majesty and her ladies were in Amazonian habits of carnation, embroidered with silver, with plumed helms, baldrics with antique swords hanging by their sides, all as rich as might be; but the strangeness of the habits was most admired' (392–6). In donning such a martial costume Henrietta Maria immediately provided an optical reference to the masquing career of her own mother-in-law, Anna of Denmark. In Samuel Daniel's *Vision of the Twelve Goddesses* (1604) Queen Anna had appeared as Pallas Athene in a mantle embroidered with 'weapons of engines of war', whilst in Ben Jonson's *Masque of Queenes* (1609) she had performed the role of Penthesileia, the renowned Queen of the Amazons.[91] Kathryn Schwarz has argued that, in these Jacobean masques, such bellicose iconography provides a 'direct challenge to the terms of male sovereignty itself', in particular the 'notorious peace–keeping of James I'.[92] In her examination of Ben Jonson's notes to the *Masque of Queenes*, Schwarz determines that the 'final step in the construction of [the] Amazon is the death of the husband; of the King'.[93] The threatening implication of Henrietta Maria's own appropriation of such a martial costume is immediately redolent from the gossip of 1639 which scornfully denounced the King's Whitehall palace as 'an *Amazonian Castle*'.[94] Yet, in *Salmacida Spolia*, Henrietta Maria's adoption of this Amazon costume refigures suggestions of marital emasculation and regicide. Rather this military garb should more properly be read as a projection of the Queen's ultimate practising of a specifically Roman Catholic female virtue, advocated within the French devotional writings of Jean Pierre Camus, and precisely located within his *Admirable Events* (1639).

Camus's popular volume *Admirable Events*, dedicated by the translator S. du Verger to Queen Henrietta Maria, aimed (like the English martyr Robert Southwell) to combat the 'trash' of romance writings, which he compared 'to dainty garden knots & borders which have Serpents hidden under their flowers'.[95] Significantly, within his own selection of moral tales, Camus recounted two paradigms of Amazonian virtue, 'The Generous Poverty' and 'The

20 Inigo Jones's sketch *Henrietta Maria or a Lady Masquer in Amazonian Habit* in *Salmacida Spolia*, 1640.

Amazon'. In 'The Generous Poverty' the courageous Rosana dies in battle to save both her husband and her king. Camus suggests how

> In this Event all men may plainely see, that vertues strive to enter in ranke into the Elegie of this generous Amazon, purity, magnanimity, constancy, valour, courtesie, resolution, courage, but above all that makes it most illustrious who can but admire to see love, and honour, with honesty to bee so straightly conjoyned in her spirits?[96]

Similarly in the 'Tale of the Amazon' Camus praises the virtuous Yoland who dons 'mans aparel' to follow her Lover', and who 'tooke such delight in all the exercises of armes, that she became an Amazon'.[97] Camus draws from this tale the signification that this 'love which gave her courage, raised her strength beyond the vigour not only of her sex, but of men'.[98] Drawing on Camus's devotional writings, through her stunning appearance in military dress, Henrietta Maria's own martial manifestation in *Salmacida Spolia* can be seen as a profoundly visible sign of her deep religious faith and, through this, as an overt symbol of her heroic love for Charles I.

The mnemonic effect of Henrietta Maria's self-presentation as an Amazonian whose love 'raiseth the courage of the weakest sex' is reinforced by a second symbol within *Salmacida Spolia*, that of the bridge in the penultimate scene.[99] C. V. Wedgwood identified Inigo Jones's preferred model for this masque as a newly constructed bridge in Rome, the city still proscribed in English law from visits by English subjects.[100] More precisely John Peacock has painstakingly argued how 'Jones's bridge is an idealised reworking of the Ponte Rotto, with features from the Ponte Cestio and Ponte Fabricio; and the "suburbs" seen through it are the cluster of buildings on the right bank of the Tiber beyond the Ponte Fabricio' (Figures 21 and 22).[101] Peacock sees this bridge as an allusion to the 'grandiose projects for the great city which was Charles's capital...and the replacement of the damaged medieval fabric of London Bridge with a new bridge in antique Roman style'.[102] Undoubtedly this scene is in alignment with the Augustan views of Charles I. Yet Peacock, like Martin Butler, forgets the crucial fact that this masque is a joint production by the English monarchs. For Queen Henrietta Maria, the connotations bursting from Jones's reference to Rome as the location for the designs of his 'Suburbs

21 Inigo Jones's sketch of a *Design for the Bridge* in *Salmacida Spolia*, 1640.

22 Inigo Jones's sketch of *The Suburbs of a Great City* in *Salmacida Spolia*, 1640.

of a Great City' cannot be underestimated. Rome was both the seat in militant Protestant tradition of the Whore of Babylon and the living centre of Henrietta Maria's own faith. Extraordinarily it is over this architectural scene that 'a heaven opened full of deities' (462). Martin Butler might argue that this masque, observed from the King's standpoint, is a 'gesture of royal willingness to build bridges to moderate opinion'.[103] Viewed from the perspective of the Queen's court however, this particular bridge can be seen as a visual pathway to Henrietta Maria's ambition of, at the very least maintaining her establishment of court Roman Catholicism, if not restoring England to the Roman Catholic faith. *Salmacida Spolia* concludes with a scene visually representing a direct link to Rome, where the royal couple are told to

> Live still, the pleasure of our sight,
> Both our examples and delight;
>
> So long, until you find *the good success*
> *Of all your virtues in one happiness.* (475–8, my emphasis)

For Henrietta Maria, a devout Catholic princess who was repeatedly urged to convert her own husband, this 'one happiness' could ultimately be found only in a marriage, not merely of hearts but of united religious belief.

Such a reading gives an added resonance to the song addressed to the Queen Mother. From this perspective, the 'Chorus of the Beloved People' emerges as an idealised version of the English recusant community. It has been well documented how Marie de Médicis specifically urged her daughter to act as defender and champion of the troubled English Catholics. In the upheaval of 1640s Caroline England, this community would have had especial reason to 'grieve' that their 'blessings' were 'too great to last' (307), to acknowledge that it was because of Henrietta Maria that their 'hopes are longer lived' (311) and to laud Marie de Médicis as 'the stream from whence our blessings flow' (318). Indeed the close cultural tie signalling this complex bond between Henrietta Maria and her Catholic subjects is palpably evident from a letter dated April 1639. Written in the hand of John Winter, and circulated under Henrietta Maria's signature, the Queen expressly stated her 'good' belief in 'the loyalty and affection of his Majestyes Catholicke subjects'. Urging them to 'freely and cheerfully' pledge 'som considerable summe of money', Henrietta Maria promised 'so we shall be very sensible of it as a particular respect to our selves, and will endeavour in the most efficacious manner we can to improve the merit of it'.[104] Moreover, the impact of Henrietta Maria's staging as a Counter-Reformation Amazon would have sent a powerful message to the wider, European, Roman Catholic community. It was only with some diffidence that the Vatican recognised either the Queen's difficulties or her courage in continuing to protect and further the cause of English recusants. In April 1637, in a letter to Cardinal Barberini, Con had reported how the Queen had asked 'if the Pope knew of all they were doing for the Catholics in England and if he would know how to exploit such an unhoped for beginning'.[105] By 1640 in *Salamacida Spolia* such queenly pique had been transformed into a defiant statement. In the masquing hall of Whitehall, the Chief Heroine boldly stood both as a living symbol of the vital presence of Catholicism in England and as a challenge to the Curia itself to champion this increasingly imperilled Catholic revival.

Thus there is a sense in *Salmacida Spolia* that, although the monarchs present this masque together, and are in agreement that Fury must be quelled, they are dancing to different agendas. Whereas Charles in his entrance embodies a curious antithesis of passive dominance, Henrietta Maria's self-presentation is of an active and defiant virtue.[106] Immediately prior to the antimasque, Concord and the Good Genius of Great Britain remark how in this 'sullen age', it is 'harder far to cure / The people's folly than resist their rage' (197–9). With this regal double act, there is the suggestion that both options are covered. If the 'giddy' (360) people fail to bow to Charles's wisdom, then Henrietta Maria is armed and ready to fight in a battle which the papal agent (at the very least) perceived in crusade-like terms. Tellingly, religion is specifically named as the people's 'vice' (152). Such a juxtaposition of royal agendas seriously questions Butler's analysis of *Salmacida Spolia* as a masque whereby the King endeavoured to reach out to moderate opinion. For Inigo Jones's powerful staging of Henrietta Maria's radical Roman Catholicism ultimately compromises Charles I's own quiescent appearance as Philogenes, lover of the people.

Indeed, the extreme frisson of this sensitive political moment assaults the masque form itself, crystallised in the tension which vibrates between Inigo Jones's visual and William Davenant's verbal media. Jarring undercurrents swirl around these dazzling visions, so stunningly contrived by Inigo Jones, to unhinge the delicate balance of the masque's form. In the 1640 printed edition of the masque, in noticeably smaller typography than the announcement of Inigo Jones as the originator of *Salmacida Spolia*'s 'Invention, Ornament, Sceans and Apparitions', William Davenant's name appears, stating his creative responsibility for 'what was spoken or sung'.[107] Inigo Jones's vivid translation of the Catholic Amazons of Camus's cautionary tales into a Chief Heroine, valiantly sheathed in military armour, complete with sword and helmet, is an overwhelming imaginative leap from the mediatory queenly figure of Davenant's *The Fair Favourite*. Undoubtedly, this provocative spectacle was one which the Surveyor of the King's Works, Inigo Jones, found easier to stage than the Poet Laureate, William Davenant. Such dissension between the visual and spoken medium of the masque was by no means new. Ben Jonson famously feuded with Inigo Jones during their masquing collaborations for *Love's Triumph* and *Chloridia*. Frustrated by what he deemed the 'trappings' of the masque replacing its 'soul', Jonson freely mocked the 'politic eyes' needed to 'pierce into the mysteries / Of many colours, read them and reveal / Mythology there painted on slit deal!'[108] However, in *Salmacida Spolia* this conflict between the verbal and visual was more pronounced for, by 1640, as the masque's title page proudly proclaims, Jones was quite literally the 'dominus-do-all'. Such a fundamental creative tension undercuts and intrudes upon the blinding dazzle of Jones's spectacle to further entrench *Salmacida Spolia* within the heightened political anxieties of 1640 Caroline England.

D'Aveanant's unease at Henrietta Maria's militantly Catholic vision subtly permeates throughout his libretto. On close reading, the Chorus of the Beloved People who so lavishly praise both the Queen and Marie de Médicis are revealed to have 'instructed eyes' (306). This sense of enforced praise somewhat qualifies their extravagant eulogy and is redolent with the more equivocal support for the Scottish Wars which emanated from some Catholic quarters. One anonymous contemporary document amongst the Herbert of Cherbury papers (with some wisdom) specifically urged Catholics 'that they bee not to forward' in offering either money or men for the Northern Expedition, for fear of 'making themselves rather weaker Pillars of the Kingdome than they were before'.[109] Moreover, despite Roman Catholic support within the court for financial aid for the Scottish Wars, contributions in the regions were rather more reluctant. In an influential essay Keith Lindley has explored the extent of Catholic neutralism during the Civil War, although Michael Questier suggests this is somewhat overstated.[110] Building on this equivocation, doubt even creeps into the elaborate praise which celebrates the mesmerising arrival of the Chief Heroine herself. Despite her neoplatonic, goddess-like powers, apparently there were those sceptics who could 'her virtue doubt' (416), although these unbelievers were swiftly corrected 'for through the casements of her eyes / Her soul is ever looking out' (418–19). This creative conflict between Jones and Davenant reaches a climax in the masque's final scene, causing an integral dissonance to the spherical tuning up of the visually striking 'celestiall prospect' (463). As Martin Butler has commented, Davenant's syntax in the final song casts a shadow of ingrained anxiety over the King and Queen sitting in state:

> All that are harsh, all that are rude,
> Are by your harmony subdued;
> Yet so into obedience wrought,
> *As if* not forced to it, but taught. (471–4, Butler's emphasis)

Unquestionably, Butler is correct in his succinct observation that Davenant's grammar highlights the subversion contained within Charles's offer of appeasement, tellingly revealing 'the need to reassert the King's inviolable authority'.[111] Yet, once again, for the song to be entirely understood it must be recognised that this song addresses both monarchs. Any concern here is equally (if not more directly) a result of Davenant's ultimate disquiet with the strident warrior image so daringly enacted by his patroness, Queen Henrietta Maria, and so distant from Davenant's ideal model of queenship. As Davenant manifestly reveals in a contemporary poem to the Queen, the Poet Laureate believed Henrietta Maria's proper role was to 'become (which doth augment your state) / the Judges Judge, and Peoples Advocate'.[112] Such 'Triumphs' – both 'just and mercifully good' – were far removed from the uncompromising martial image of an Esther in Amazon clothing which Davenant so awkwardly celebrated in *Salmacida Spolia*.[113]

In *The Holy Court*, a work established as a source for Davenant's *The Fair Favorite*, Caussin glorifies St Lewis as 'an Example to all Princes, in as much as may concerne the continency of the maryed'.[114] In this tale St Lewis and his Queen are magnified as a paradigm of virtuous love: 'both of them lived, and conversed with so much integrity, sweetnesse, and admiration, that one would have thought them a payre of Angells on Earth'.[115] Such praise was integral to the celebration of Henrietta Maria and Charles I in the Caroline masques. However, in Davenant's *The Fair Favorite* this bliss is achieved only by the selfless mediation of a Queen whose determined attempts at a loving conciliation succeed in unifying the kingdom. The boldness of Davenant's dramatic ideal, emerging from within Queen Henrietta Maria's household, is starkly apparent when read against Henrietta Maria's own visual self-projection in *Salmacida Spolia*. At a moment of acute cultural and political collapse, Inigo Jones's powerful staging of this queenly Amazon, itself undercut by Davenant's inherent anxiety at this potentially alienating vision, seriously questions any promotion of *Salmacida Spolia* as a masque attempting rapprochement between court factions. Rather, through such identification with the pronounced militancy of Henrietta Maria's uncompromising ideals, the King's party was, quite naturally, pushed towards a more oppositional position, further fracturing the Caroline court. Again, Caussin's St Lewis serves as a tantalising gloss both on Philogenes' frozen tableau of passivity and on King Charles's own royal conduct. Evocatively, the love which Caussin's St Lewis held for his wife, like Charles I's for Queen Henrietta Maria, was

> accompanyed with so much respect, and confidence, that he dispatched not any busynesse, without communicating it with her: In such sort that when he was to conclude the conditions of his deliverance, with the Sarazins, he freely told them, he could not signe them without the advise of the Queene his wife, who was not farre off. At which these Barbarians were much amazed, but he answered them, it onely belonged to them to account their wives for slaves, and that his, was his Lady, and Mistresse.[116]

Notes

1 Sir Kenelm Digby to the Bishop of Chalcedon, 7 February 1639, AAW/A29, p. 253.
2 John Suckling, 'The Wits' or 'A Session of the Poets', in Thomas Clayton (ed.), *The Works of Sir John Suckling*, 2 vols (Oxford: Clarendon Press, 1971), vol. 1, pp. 71–6, ll. 47–8.
3 Edmond, *Rare Sir William*, p. 73.
4 William Davenant, *Madagascar: With Other Poems* (London: 1638).
5 Edmond, *Rare Sir William*, p. 75.

'This broken time' 211

6 Alfred Harbage, *Sir William Davenant, Poet, Venturer, 1606–1688* (Philadelphia: University of Pennsylvania Press, 1935), p. 68.
7 *Ibid.*, p. 72; Nethercot, *Sir William Davenant*, pp. 180–1.
8 Harbage, *Cavalier Drama*, p. 177.
9 For a typical expression of such a paradigm see Robert Ashton, *The English Civil War: Conservatism and Revolution, 1603–1649* (London: Weidenfeld and Nicolson, 1978), pp. 30–3.
10 Con to Barberini, December 1636, within Albion, *Court of Rome*, p. 163.
11 For letters detailing a variety of conversations regarding Charles I's possible conversion see Albion, *Court of Rome*, pp. 235, 247–8.
12 *Ibid.*, p. 270.
13 Berington, *Memoirs of Gregorio Panzani*, p. 256.
14 *Ibid.* This episode shows Henrietta Maria's diplomatic skills, as the Queen still gave Panzani a 'diamond ring of great value'.
15 Albion, *Court of Rome*, pp. 161–2.
16 *Ibid.*, pp. 163, 203.
17 *Ibid.*, pp. 164–5, 245.
18 Hibbard, *Popish Plot*, pp. 62–3.
19 *Ibid.*, pp. 85–7.
20 William Sanderson records Marie de Médicis's arrival as being incited 'hither by our *Queen* her Daughter, at the beginning of our Ingagement into all the misery that succeeded', *A Compleat History*, p. 247.
21 Lady Brilliana Harley to Edward Harley, 17 November 1638, Lewis, *Letters of the Lady Brilliana Harley*, p. 10.
22 This continental form of Roman Catholicism had become increasingly popular at court, reflected in contemporary recusant tracts *The Second Book of the Dialogues of St. Gregory*, trans. C. F. (Douai: 1638), and *The Mistical Crowne of the Most Glorious Virgin Marie*, trans. R. H. (Douai: 1638).
23 Berington, *Memoirs of Gregorio Panzani*, p. 248.
24 Albion, *Court of Rome*, p. 165. For details of this procession which progressed from the Queen's chapel via Con's chapel and concluded at the Spanish ambassador's residence see Hibbard, *Popish Plot*, p. 57.
25 Thomas Heywood, *Porta Pietatis: Or, the Port or Harbour of Piety* (London: 1638), sigs B4r–C2v.
26 Havran, *Catholics in Caroline England*, p. 149.
27 Dorothea Townshend, *Life and Letters of Mr Endymion Porter: Sometime Gentleman of the Bedchamber to King Charles the First* (London: T. F. Unwin, 1897), p. 166.

28 William Davenant, *Luminalia: The Queen's Festival of Light* (London: 1638), included in Orgel and Strong (eds), *Inigo Jones: The Theatre of the Stuart Court*, vol. 2, pp. 704–23, ll. 9–10. All subsequent references are to this edition and are in the text.
29 For further criticism on this masque see Britland, *Drama at the Courts*, pp. 168–76; Ravelhofer, *The Stuart Masque*, pp. 180–1; Veevers, *Images of Love*, pp. 142–9.
30 Robert Persons to Alfonso Agazzari, August 1581, within *Letters and Memorials of Father Robert Persons, SJ*, ed. L. Hicks (London: John Whitehead and Son, 1942), p. 86.
31 See Chapter 1, note 31.
32 Ravelhofer, *The Stuart Masque*, p. 181.
33 John Peacock, *The Stage Designs of Inigo Jones: The European Context* (Cambridge: Cambridge University Press, 1995), p. 327.
34 William Laud, *Works*, ed. William Scott, 7 vols (Oxford: 1847), vol. 7, pp. 334, 380.
35 Sanderson, *Compleat History*, p. 220.
36 William Laud, *A Relation of the Conference Betweene William Laud, Then, Lord Bishop of St. Davids; Now Lord Arch-Bishop of Canterbury: And Mr Fisher the Jesuite. By the Command of King James* (London: 1639), sig. *1v.
37 Daniel Featley, *Stricturæ in Lyndomastigem: Or, An Answere By Way of Supplement to the Chapters Remaining in the Booke Intituled, A Case For the Spectacles* (London: 1638), sig. A3v. See also Peter Taylor, *A Sermon Preached in St. Maries Oxford on the Anniversary of the Gunpowder Plot* (Oxford: 1638), especially p. 25.
38 Thomas Fuller, *The Church History of Britain: From the Birth of Jesus Christ Until the Year MDCXLVIII* (London: 1655), Book XI, sig. Eeee3v.
39 Richard Gardiner, *A Sermon Preach'd in the Cathedrall Church of Christ in Oxford on Christmas Day; Wherein Is Defended the Catholique Doctrine That Christ Is True God, Truely Incarnate* (Oxford: 1638), pp. 26–7. See also Foulke Robartes, *Gods Holy House and Service* (London: 1639), p. 98; William Parks, *The Rose and the Lily* (London: 1638), p. 33; John Cooper, *The Foolish Prophets Displayed* (London: 1638).
40 George Downame, *An Apostolicall Injunction for Unity and Peace* (London: 1639), p. 34.
41 John Lilburne, *A Worke of the Beast: Or a Relation of a Most Unchristian Censure, Executed Upon J. Lilburne* (London: 1638), p. 18. See also Nathaniel Wickins, *Wood Street-Compters Plea for Its Prisoner* (London: 1638).

42 John Canne, *A Stay Against Straying: Or an Answer to a Treatise, Intituled: The Lawfulnes of Hearing the Ministers of the Church of England by John Robinson* (Amsterdam: 1639), p. 141.
43 Thomas Abernethie, *Abjuration of Poperie* (Edinburgh: 1638), p. 37. See also William Guild, *An Antidote agaynist Poperie: Fit (God Willing) to Preserve and Arme Everie One Agaynst the Seduction Thereof. Most Necessarie For All, in This Back-Slyding Age* (Aberdeen: 1639), sig. ¶9v.
44 John Floyd, *The Church Conquerant Over Humane Wit* (St Omer: 1639), pp. 133–4.
45 Thomas Doughty, *Of the Visible Sacrifice in the Church of God, the Second Part* (Brussels: 1637–8), p. 70. See also Matthew Wilson, *Christianity Maintained: Or a Discovery of Sundry Doctrines Tending to the Overthrowe of Christian Religion* (St Omer: 1638), pp. 3–4.
46 Correr to the Doge and Senate, September 1637. *CSP Ven 1636–9*, p. 273.
47 Fr Andrew Leslie to Fr General, 2 October 1635, within William Forbes Leith, *Memoirs of Scottish Catholics During the XVIIth and XVIIIth Centuries*, 2 vols (London: Longmans, Green and Co., 1909), vol. 1, p. 172.
48 Fr James Macbreck to Fr General, 14 August 1638, *ibid.*, p. 189.
49 Davenant, *Temple of Love*, l. 512.
50 George Ballard, *The History of Susanna. Compiled According to the Prophet Daniel, Amplified With Convenient Meditations* (London: 1638), sig. B2r.
51 Canne, *A Stay Against Straying*, p. 6.
52 Anon., *An Exposition upon the Apostle's Creed* (London: 1638), p. 8.
53 John Preston, *The Golden Scepter Held Forth to the Humble. With the Churches Dignitie By Her Marriage, and the Churches Dutie in Her Carriage. In Three Treatises*, 3 vols (London: 1638), vol. 2, p. 21.
54 Francis Rous, *The Heavenlie Acadamie* (London: 1638), pp. 122–3.
55 Ballard, *History of Susanna*, sig. B3v.
56 Steele, *Plays and Masques at Court*, pp. 272–3; Bawcutt, *Records of Sir Henry Herbert*, p. 204; Edmond, *Rare Sir William*, p. 68. In this discussion of *The Fair Favourite*, I am referring to *Works*, vol. 4, pp. 201–80. All subsequent references are in the text.
57 Nethercot, *Sir William D'Avenant*, p. 165; Bordinat and Blaydes, *Davenant*, p. 57.
58 Such Richard II-like sentiments were later endorsed by Henry King, *A Sermon Preached at St. Pauls, March 27 1640. Being the Anniversary of His Majesties Happy Inauguration to His Crowne* (London:

1640): 'They that onely looke upon the glittering matter of a Diadem, and the Lustre of the Jewels set in it, may apprehend somewhat to delight the eye: but could they understand how many cares are lodged and concentred within the Pale and Circle of that Crowne . . . they scarce would take it for the wearing, though it lay in their way', p. 30.
59 Nicolas Caussin, *The Holy Court Fourth Tome: The Command of Reason Over the Passions* (Rouen: 1638). For a sensitive discussion of Caussin's complete works see Veevers, *Images of Love*, pp. 76–82.
60 Caussin, *Holy Court IV*, sig. ã2v.
61 Lady Brilliana Harley to Edward Harley, 30 November 1638 and 1 February 1639, within Lewis, *Letters of Lady Brilliana Harley*, pp. 13, 27.
62 Caussin, *Holy Court IV*, p. 291.
63 *Ibid*.
64 *Ibid*.
65 *Ibid*., p. 10.
66 Rous, *Heavenlie Acadamie*, p. 123.
67 See note 1.
68 Fr Rob to Fr General, 30 November 1639, within Leith, *Scottish Catholics*, p. 195.
69 Fr James Macbreck to Fr General, 13 June 1641, *ibid*., p. 215.
70 Circular Letter from A. Champney, to exhort Catholics to offer their service to King Charles I, 2 January 1638, AAW/A29, p. 145.
71 *Ibid*.
72 Dauncey, *Henrietta Maria de Bourbon*, p. 59. See also Magee, *English Recusants*, pp. 73–5.
73 See Chapter 2, note 30.
74 D. Laing (ed.), *The Letters and Journals of Robert Baillie*, 3 vols (Edinburgh: 1841–2), vol. 1, p. 216.
75 Andrew Hopper, '"The Popish Army of the North": Anti-Catholicism and Parliamentarian Allegiance in Civil War Yorkshire, 1642–46', *RH*, 25 (2000), 12–28, p. 13.
76 For the background to this new Oath of Allegiance see Hibbard, *Popish Plot*, pp. 117–20.
77 John Bruce (ed.), *Letters and Papers of the Verney Family Down to the End of the Year 1639* (London: John Bowyer Nichols, 1853), p. 228.
78 David Scott, *Politics and War in the Three Stuart Kingdoms, 1637–49* (Basingstoke: Palgrave Macmillan, 2004), pp. 20–5.
79 *Historical Manuscript Commission*, 3rd Report (London: 1874), p. 79.

80 William Davenant, *Salmacida Spolia*, in Orgel and Strong (eds), *Inigo Jones: The Theatre of the Stuart Court*, vol. 2, pp. 728–85. T. B. Edwards, *A Book of Masques in Honour of Allardyce Nicoll* (Cambridge: Cambridge University Press, 1967), p. 339. Details of a second performance of *Salmacida Spolia* on 18 February 1640 are given by Wayne H. Phelps, 'The Second Night of Davenant's *Salmacida Spolia*', *N&Q*, 26 (1979), 512–13.
81 Letter to Sir Kenelm Digby, undated, within Howell, *Ho-Elianae*, section 6, p. 67.
82 Lady Brilliana Harley to Edward Harley, 6 April 1639, within Lewis, *Letters of the Lady Brilliana Harley*, p. 41.
83 Part of a letter containing political news apparently before the Civil War broke out, AAW/A29, p. 429.
84 Butler, 'Politics and the Masque', 59–74.
85 Karen Britland, 'An Under-Stated Mother-in-Law: Marie de Médicis and the Last Caroline Court Masque', in McManus (ed.), *Women and Culture*, pp. 204–23.
86 Franco, *Dance as Text*, p. 5.
87 The Queen Mother openly disavowed her supposed intriguing, see *A Declaration of the Queen, Mother of the Most Christian King* (London: 1639).
88 Lily M. Baker (ed.), *The Letters of Elizabeth Queen of Bohemia* (London: Bodley Head, 1953), p. 137.
89 The contemporary polemicist Richard Brathwaite specifically translated this tract by Philippe de Commynes which argued that Henri IV was murdered 'because the King tolerated two Religions in his Kingdome', *An Epitome of All the Lives of the Kings of France From Pharamond the First, to the Now Most Christian King Lewis the Thirteenth* (London: 1639), pp. 342–3.
90 Veevers, *Images of Love*, p. 203.
91 Orgel and Strong, *Inigo Jones: The Theatre of the Stuart Court*, vol. 1, pp. 130–54.
92 Kathryn Schwarz, 'Amazon Reflections in the Jacobean Queen's Masque', *SEL*, 35 (1995), 293–319, p. 296.
93 *Ibid.*, p. 310.
94 D. L., *The Scots Scouts Discoveries By Their London Intelligencer, And Presented to the Lords of the Covenant of Scotland, 1639* (London: 1642), p. 25.
95 Jean Pierre Camus, *Admirable Events: Selected Out of Foure Bookes, Written in French by the Right Reverend John Peter Camus, Bishop of Belley. Together With Morall Relations, Written by the Same Author. And Translated into English by S. Du Verger* (London: 1639), sig. a4v.

96 *Ibid.*, p. 26.
97 *Ibid.*, p. 346.
98 *Ibid.*, p. 348.
99 *Ibid.*, p. 349.
100 C. V. Wedgwood, *Truth and Opinion, Historical Essays* (London: Collins, 1960), p. 153.
101 Peacock, *Stage Designs*, p. 106.
102 *Ibid.*, p. 108.
103 Butler, 'Politics and the Masque', p. 66.
104 The Queen's Invitation to the Catholics to show their loyalty to the King, 17 April 1639, AAW/A29, p. 257; see also Havran, *Catholics in Caroline England*, p. 153.
105 Con to Ferragalli, April 1637, within Albion, *Court of Rome*, p. 273.
106 Butler, 'Politics and the Masque', pp. 67–9.
107 William Davenant, *Salmacida Spolia, A Masque Presented by the King and Queene's Majesties, at White–hall, on Tuesday the 21 Day of January 1639* (London: 1640).
108 Ben Jonson, 'An Expostulation with Inigo Jones', CXVIII, ll. 45–8, in *Ben Jonson, The Complete Poems*, ed. George Parfitt (New Haven: Yale University Press, 1996), pp. 345–7.
109 Add MSS 37,157, Herbert of Cherbury Papers, 17–18, No. 33.
110 Keith Lindley, 'The Lay Catholics of England', p. 220.
111 Butler, 'Politics and the Masque', p. 70. See also Butler, *Theatre and Crisis*, pp. 58–9.
112 William Davenant, 'To the Queen' (c.1640–1641), in Gibbs (ed.) *Shorter Poems*, pp. 139–40, ll. 45–6.
113 *Ibid.*, ll. 48–9.
114 Caussin, *Holy Court IV*, p. 296.
115 *Ibid.*
116 *Ibid.*, pp. 296–7.

Conclusion

The analysis in this book confirms that staging the concerns of the wider Roman Catholic community formed a significant dynamic within Caroline drama. In the largely secular society of twenty-first century England it is only too easy to dismiss both the early modern Protestant's fear of the menacing spectre of Popery, and the Catholic's equally staunch determination that the old faith should adapt and survive. Henrietta Maria's arrival as a self-styled second Esther to the English recusant community sharpened and intensified this vigorous religio-political debate. The Queen's audacious performance in pastorals and court masques has been rightly hailed as a progressive breaching of the boundaries of accepted English theatrical practice. Together with Queen Anna's feminocentric entertainments, these dramatic advances undoubtedly encouraged the appearance of the female actress in Restoration commercial theatre. Yet, for a daughter of France, where there was a precedent for such royal performances, stagings such as *L'Artenice* and *The Shepherds' Paradise* equally and, perhaps more acutely, allowed Henrietta Maria to project her vision of her role as Queen Consort and, within that, her championing of Catholicism in England. As the vitality of the superbly crafted stump-work hanging in Fenton House testifies, the ramifications of such a queenly display could not be confined to those nobles and diplomats invited to assemble on these royal occasions. Rather, the continuing significance of England's old faith and the Queen's position as 'defender and deliverer' of English Catholics was deftly probed on the commercial stage. In a highly charged atmosphere, before a politically alert audience, James Shirley explored the concerns of the more militant recusant. Reflecting the nuances within the Catholic faction, William Davenant promoted a model of a negotiated and mutual compromise between the Roman Catholic and established Churches. Undoubtedly, both dramatists created plays which would have especially appealed to the Queen, employing the genres of tragicomedy, romance and pastoral to highlight the redeeming agency of female virtue. Yet far from being vapid or sycophantic, once contextualised within the stimulus of contemporary polemical debates, these works can be seen to engage energetically with the vibrant political issues of the cultural moment.

Ultimately, however, the potency of this drama produced under the auspices of the Queen's household can be measured by discussion outside Whitehall. Notably, some of the most devastating attacks on Henrietta Maria were achieved by boldly harnessing, and grotesquely inverting, those dramatic genres and tropes so closely associated with the Queen's staged expression of her ideals. This is brilliantly spotlighted in Nathanael Richards's *Messallina: History of the Roman Empresse*.[1] Licensed around 1635, possibly acted in the more popular environs of London's Fortune Theatre and printed in 1640, the play focuses on what Sophie Tomlinson has termed 'the rampant libertanism' of Messallina, a 'lustful and degenerative symbol of ancient Rome'.[2] Yet, in the volatile political climate of 1640s England, the publication of a play showcasing the malign influence of a dangerously powerful consort, with strong links to Rome (and an insatiable and controversial passion for the theatre) resonated with a Queen alarmingly closer to home, Henrietta Maria. Such a reading is positively encouraged from the commendatory verse which accompanied the printed text. Fellow playwright Thomas Rawlins marvelled how the stage could bring to life the multi-faceted and alarming image of '*Romes* mightie Whore' (165), applauding '*that happy wit whose veines can stirre / Religious thoughts, though in a* Theator' (173–4).[3]

Messallina's court is repeatedly identified with that epitome of militant Protestant anxiety, the Popish court of the Roman Whore of Babylon.[4] The sage Annaeus Mela counsels the upright Montanus to 'fly *Rome*' if he wishes to 'contemplate Heaven', for 'the impious maladies' which Messallina 'breeds / Experience tells, are *hookes to catch at soules*' (III.ii.1597–8, my emphasis). Significantly, these '*hookes*' employed by Messallina in Ancient Rome find a direct parallel in Caroline England through the shimmering tropes specifically associated with the Queen's staging of her Counter-Reformation triumphs. From her earliest performance in *L'Artenice* the Queen's eyes had been celebrated as transforming conduits of virtue.[5] Strikingly, in *Messallina*, Silvius also praises the 'attractive force' of the Empress's 'amazing eyes, those glorious lights / Fixt in the Firmament of your sweet face' (II.i.923–5). Yet Richards inverts this symbol of queenly integrity to one of ultimate corruption. In Messallina such 'bewitching lampes' are false, 'fed with the oyle of whorish / Fortitude' (V.1.2033–5) which 'blinds devotion' (I.i.464) and leads her enslaved captives to destruction.

Richards intensifies such dramatic mirroring between the courts of Messallina and Henrietta Maria through his suggestive manipulation of images of light. In the elite realm of the Caroline court masques Henrietta Maria was consistently identified with a heavenly radiance. Most prominently, as we have explored in *Luminalia*, she literally appeared as an 'earthly star' (282) with blatantly Catholic overtones. Similarly Messallina is repeatedly associated with brilliance. Veneria, the Bawd, prays that the Empress may 'ever glister like the Sunne' (I.i.515), the Emperor Claudius deems her his 'starre on earth' (I.i.532), Saufellus encourages her to 'burne high bright glorious wonder of thy Sex' (I.i.565), whilst Messallina herself vows to 'live in pleasure' though she 'burne in fire' (I.i.585–6). Where Henrietta Maria's glowing luminosity purifies and revitalises, Messallina's glaring light scorches and blinds so that 'all virtues lose their light' (I.i.672–3). Through this twinned inversion of the symbols of light and vision which were so integral to Henrietta Maria's dazzling performances, Richards forcefully reminds his audience of the perceived insidious dangers inherent in the Queen's own Roman Catholic household.

Such an open assault, launched on Henrietta Maria and the Roman Catholic faith through the Queen's own dramatic ideals, highlights the overarching cultural agency of the Queen's drama, and indicates the importance of playwrights such as Shirley and Davenant who were publicly identified as "her Majesties Servants". However, that Nathanael Richards's vicious attack was so well received hints at the astonishing reversal(s) of fortunes suffered by the recusant community. In the 1630s, with the erection of the Queen's purpose-built Roman Catholic chapel and open (if idle) talk of the King's imminent conversion, triumph or (at the very least) tolerance seemed within the recusant community's grasp. Yet by autumn 1640 Giustinian, the Venetian ambassador, recorded alarm within Catholic circles, how some were 'hurriedly selling their goods with the intention of going to live quietly in some other country until the present ill feeling has softened and the troubled state of this kingdom has altered'.[6] Such a complete volte-face bears remarkable testimony to the central tenet of this book, that the English Reformation was by no means experienced as an inexorable process. Moderate Protestants, like John Taylor the Water Poet, might ultimately have believed that the recusant, in his curious phrase, marginally 'barrell's better herring' than the puritan.[7] But Father Cyprien of Gamache recorded with heartfelt bias, how

> at that time you heard nothing talked of in London but the ruin and desolation of the Catholics. They had no longer any divine service; the Queen's chapel was shut up. They durst not now go, as formerly, to the ambassador's: the vehement animosity of the Puritans inflamed the people against them. Their house was plundered, their goods were carried off; plots, designs, enterprises, criminal correspondence, which they had never thought of, were attributed to them.[8]

Indeed, by the eve of the Long Parliament, Giustinian prophesied complete annihilation, observing how this new session 'will mean the total desolation of the Catholic Faith in this country'.[9]

Such anxiety regarding the increasing peril of English Catholics was well founded. In January 1641 all priests were ordered under pain of death to leave the country. By October 1641 the uprising of the Irish Catholics and lurid tales of the terrible massacres of the Irish Protestants crystallised the nation's worst fears. Thomas Stockdale, secretary to General Fairfax, commented how the daily arrival of 'the distressed Protestants of Ireland who come hither driven from their habitations by the Papists, do animate the people here against the Popish party . . . which is one good effect of many evils'.[10] What becomes increasingly apparent is that, by 1642, the treacherous spectre of the recusant community as a malevolent nemesis of the godly Englishman was firmly re-entrenched within Protestant thinking.[11] The early 1640s are marked by a rash of alarmist Puritan tracts exposing multiple, alleged, and utterly hare-brained, popish conspiracies.[12] As Andrew Hopper has argued, some sixty years later the grip on the national consciousness of this Catholic force of Protestant nightmare is apparent from Joseph Lister's solemn reminiscences, 'What sad and strange conjectures, or rather conclusions, will surprise and fear make! Methinks I shall never forget this time.'[13] With Pym suggesting that Catholics should be forced to wear 'distinctive and recognizable dress', and a marked increase in the execution of discovered priests, it was little wonder that as the Carmelite Fr Gervasius noted 'many Catholics are emigrating to America, especially Virginia'.[14]

With religion 'being daily discussed', one furiously debated topic was that of Henrietta Maria and her self-adopted Counter Reformation mission of succouring and fostering Catholicism within England.[15] From the godly viewpoint the Queen threatened a dangerous and over-reaching success. The moment the Short Parliament sat in April 1640, Sir Francis Rous of Truro implacably asssserted how 'the root of all our grievances' was 'an intended union betwixt us and Rome'.[16] This widespread popular belief was fomented through incendiary tracts such as the anonymous *Englands Complaint*, which brazenly harangued: 'Doth not all the world know, that She is a Papist, and by the meanes of her example, *Chappels*, *Priests*, *Friars*, are not many thousands both in *Court* and *City*, and other places, brought into that Snare?'[17] With the closure of the Short Parliament, in May 1640, troops were ordered to guard Somerset House indicating the inherent threat to the Queen's person. By May 1641 Giustinian, reported that '*disgraceful pasquinades*' against the Queen were openly posted in the streets of London.[18] Indeed, the fundamental distrust of Henrietta Maria as a Roman Catholic canker at the heart of Caroline government was starkly scratched in threatening graffiti on to the very window of the King's antechamber: 'God save the King. God confound the Queen with all her offspring. God grant the Palatine to reign in this realm.'[19] By 1642, with the ominous and painful reminder of the execution of the King's first minister Strafford, Henrietta Maria's own position seemed increasingly perilous. Amongst the swirl of rumours, Dauncey recorded the 'strange report' of 'the Parliaments intentions to draw up Articles of High Treason' against the Queen 'upon a fond conceit that the Queen had so much power with the King, as to misadvise him'.[20]

As the Queen's confessor, Fr Phillip observed, Henrietta Maria was 'much afflicted' by this precarious political atmosphere where 'the *Puritans*, if they durst, would pull the good Queen in pieces'.[21] One Catholic commentator, in January 1641, remarked how 'our Queene whether in earnest or in jest sayd the other daye she was so ill . . . that shee must goo to France for a time'.[22] This singular combination of withdrawal and challenge stamped Henrietta

Maria's actions in these tumultuous years. The motif of retreat frequently re-emerged in her correspondence with Charles I during their enforced separation. In particular she threatened to find sanctuary in the haven of a convent, a topos first hinted at in her performance of *L'Artenice* and fulfilled in 1651 when she became the benefactor of a Visitandine convent in Chaillot, Paris.[23] More consistently, she adopted the Amazonian image signalled in *Salmacida Spolia*, writing to the King: 'my intentions are to serve you as long as I can, and to suffer with you all sorts of hazards, in order by some means to try to merit your affection'.[24] The Queen's efforts in The Hague to raise finances for the Royalist cause are well documented.[25] She was closely associated (as were Shirley and Davenant) with what became known as the Popish Army under the command of the Duke of Newcastle.[26] And, on her brief return to England in 1643 she was, quite literally, deemed the '*Generalissima*'. Dauncey records with some bias how she marched 'with an undaunted and more than Womanlike resolution in the head of her Army'.[27] Despite the systematic destruction of her achievements for the Roman Catholic faith in England, visually enacted by armed men desecrating her chapel at Somerset House, the Queen behaved with '*Amazonian courage*'.[28] Nor did she forget her Catholic subjects, tenaciously requesting Charles to 'above all, have a care not to abandon those who have served you, as well the bishops as the poor Catholics'.[29] Such resolution is encouraged in early 1640s recusant tracts. For as Fr Gervasius privately observed in July 1641, with 'the persecution against Catholics ... making headway ... many Catholics take the oath acknowledging the Royal supremacy, and conform to the Protestant Church in order to avoid punishment'.[30] Notably, renewed resolution was strongly encouraged in early 1640s recusant tracts. Lawrence Anderton urged his reader to 'imitate then a skilfull Generall in the warres, who laboureth not only to hinder his Enemies attempts and approaches, but withall seeketh to assault his Enemyes'.[31] Likewise John Wilson compiled his *English Martyrologe* as a 'comfort & consolation' for the Roman Catholics of Great Britain 'whose hartes & mindes are firmely fixed in the honour and veneration of so glorious and elected Wightes, and for the imbracing whereof you daily suffer so great and many Pressures'.[32]

In response to Roman Catholic Europe who, in 1625, had urged this mission upon the teenage princess, Henrietta Maria was adamant that her endeavours for the English recusant community would remain firmly etched on the cumulative Roman Catholic memory. By 1645, her almoner, Fr Phillip, specifically reminded her countrymen how this daughter of France – like St Bertha and St Clothilda – was a 'princess' who had 'set up the altars, and the true worship of God in England', and 'caused the Catholic religion again to grow and triumph there, with all the splendour and glory imaginable'.[33] Indeed Fr Phillip directly pinpointed the Queen's estrangement from the English nation, and her reduced circumstances in Paris, because she 'is a Catholic, and re-established, and made to flourish again the Catholic religion in England'.[34] In English recusant circles this secular misery was transformed into a symbol of the Queen's spiritual success. Projecting forwards to the heady days of the Restoration, Fr George Leyburn was to imply that Henrietta Maria had even overreached Queen Esther herself, being 'as glorious a Queen in the sight of God, as was Queen Hester, whom not onely you have equal'd as to professing of the true faith, but surpassed, as to the many sufferings your Majestie hath endured patiently unto gaining a crown of Martirdome'.[35] As this book establishes, such a mutable 'Esther' ideal stimulated debate on both the elite and commercial stage. The flourishing Counter-Reformation revival within the Queen's household was at the heart of Henrietta Maria's own transgressive performances and was a fundamental dynamic within the plays of James Shirley and William Davenant. This spirited discourse which spanned the Queen's reign is central to any understanding either of the Queen and her court or of the shaping of the old faith in Caroline England. For these stagings vividly expose the potency within the wider cultural imagination, of the embedded and much debated image of Henrietta Maria as a

> Queen of England, who by . . . sweet steps, walked fairly on towards the conversion of that kingdome . . . A princess, who . . . [gave] a confidence to the poor English Catholics, to come forth from their retirements, where they remained shut up in obscurity, and to appear in the light, with their faces erected, to profess and exercise their religion with all assurance.[36]

Notes

1 Nathanael Richards, *The Tragedy of Messallina, the Roman Emperesse*, ed. A. R. Skemp (London: David Nutt, 1910). All subsequent

references are to this edition and are in the text. This is Richards's only extant play but he wrote two volumes of poetry: *The Celestiall Publican* (London: 1630), and *Poems Sacred and Satyricall* (London: 1641).
2 Tomlinson, *Women on Stage*, p. 123.
3 Thomas Rawlins's commendatory poem is published with *Messallina*, p. 16, l. 165.
4 Butler, *Theatre and Crisis*, pp. 192–3.
5 Poems which draw upon the conceit of Henrietta Maria's eyes include 'To the Queene, upon a New-yeares day', and 'To the Queen, returning to London after a long absence', in William Davenant, *Madagascar* (London: 1638), pp. 74, 106–7. See Gibbs (ed.), *Davenant's Shorter Poems*, pp. 47, 67–8.
6 Giustinian to the Doge and Senate, November 1640, *CSP Ven, 1640–42*, p. 93.
7 John Taylor, *A Swarme of Sectaries and Schismatiques* (London: 1641), p. 18.
8 Cyprien of Gamache, 'Memoirs of the Mission', p. 354.
9 Giustinian to the Doge and Senate, September 1640, *CSP Ven, 1640–42*, p. 79.
10 Cited by Hopper, 'The Popish Army of the North', p. 15.
11 For a scholarly historical examination of this phenomenon see Robin Clifton, 'Popular Fear of Catholics in England during the English Revolution', *P&P*, 52 (1971), 23–55.
12 *A True Coppy of a Bold and Most Peremptory Letter Sent to the Hon. Earle of Salisbury by ABC to Mitigate his Persecuting of Recusants* (London: 1641); *Treason Discovered From Holland: Or a Discoverie of a Most Damnable and Divellish Attempt of Two Jesuites and Three Other Catholiques Against the Life and Person of the Ladie Elizabeth at the Hague* (London: 1641); *A Great Conspiracy of the Papists Against the Worthy Members of Both Houses of Parliament* (London: 1641).
13 Cited by Hopper, 'The Popish Army', p. 16.
14 Purkiss, *Civil War*, p. 106; Albion, *Court of Rome*, p. 369; AAW/A30, pp. 47, 123; Benedictus-Maria Zimmerman, *Carmel in England: A History of the English Mission of the Discalced Carmelites, 1615 to 1849* (London: Burns and Oates, 1899), p. 139.
15 Fr Gervasius of the Blessed Sacrament [Walter Luddington], May 1641, within Zimmerman, *Carmel in England*, p. 140.
16 Hibbard, *Popish Plot*, p. 149.
17 Anon., *England's Complaint to Jesus Christ, Against the Bishops' Canons of the Late Sinfull Synod* (London: 1640), sig. B4r. See also Robert Baillie, *Ladensium Autokatakrisis, The Canterburians Self-Conviction* (Amsterdam: 1640).

18 Giustinian to the Doge and Senate, May 1641, *CSP Ven, 1640–42*, pp. 151–2.
19 Albion, *Court of Rome*, p. 339.
20 Dauncey, *Henrietta Maria de Bourbon*, pp. 69–70.
21 Robert Philips, *The Coppy of a Letter of Father Philips, the Queenes Confessor, Which Was Thought to Be Sent Into France, to Mr Montague* (London: 1641), p. 1.
22 AAW/A30, p. 1.
23 See also Britland, *Drama at the Courts*, pp. 192–215.
24 Green, *Queen's Letters*, p. 106; see also pp. 55–9.
25 *Ibid.*, pp. 64–5.
26 William Cavendish, *A Declaration Made by the Earl of New-Castle... For His Resolution of Marching into Yorkshire. As Also a Just Vindication of Himself From That... Aspersion Laid Upon Him, For Entertaining Some Popish Recusants in His Forces* (London: 1643).
27 Dauncey, *Henrietta Maria de Bourbon*, p. 99.
28 *Ibid.*, p. 95.
29 Green, *Queen's Letters*, p. 283.
30 Zimmerman, *Carmel in England*, pp. 140–1.
31 Lawrence Anderton, *Miscellenia: Or a Treatise Contayning Two Hundred Controversiall Animadversions Conducing to the Study of English Controversies in Fayth, and Religion* (St Omer: 1640; Menston: Scolar Press, 1973), p. 380. Anderton emphasises that this will not be in any 'tumultuous or undutiful manner' as we, 'need to beare all reverence to the State, and Loyalty to his *Majesty*... who is full of commiseration and pitty', p. 389.
32 John Wilson, *The English Martyrologe Conteyning a Summary of the Most Renowned and Illustrious Saints of the Three Kingdomes England, Ireland and Scotland* (St Omer: 1642), sig. *2r.
33 Green, *Queen's Letters*, p. 292.
34 *Ibid.*, p. 295.
35 George Leyburn, *To Her Most Excellent Majestie Henrietta Maria, Queen of Great Britaign: Dr. Leyburn's Apologie* (Douai: 1660), p. 9.
36 Green, *Queen's Letters*, p. 293.

Bibliography

Manuscripts

Archive at Westminster Cathedral, London, Series A, vols 20–30.
British Library, Add MSS 37, 157, Herbert of Cherbury Papers.
British Library, Kings Mss, 135.
HMC Rutland I.
HMC Salisbury XXII.

Works published before 1850

Abernethie, Thomas, *Abjuration of Poperie* (Edinburgh: 1638).
Adams, Thomas, *A Commentary: Or, Exposition Upon the Divine Second Epistle Generall, Written by the Blessed Apostle St. Peter* (London: 1633).
Anderton, Lawrence, *The Progenie of Catholicks and Protestants. Wherby On the One Side Is Proved the-Lineal Descent of Catholicks For the Roman Faith and Religion, From the Holie Fathers of the Primitive Church Even From Christs Verie Time Until These Our Dayes: And On the Other the Never-Being of Protestants* (Rouen: 1633).
Anderton, Lawrence, *Miscellania: Or a Treatise Contayning Two Hundred Controversiall Animadversions Conducing to the Study of English Controversies in Fayth, and Religion* (St Omer: 1640).
Anderton, Lawrence, *The Non-Entity of Protestancy. Or, a Discourse, Wherein is Demonstrated, That Protestancy Is Not Any Reall Thing, But in Itselfe a Platonicall Idea; a Wast of All Positive Fayth and a Meere Nothing* (St Omer: 1653).
Anon., *The Interpreter: Wherin Three Principall Termes of State Much Mistaken by the Vulgar Are Clearly Unfolded* (Edinburgh: 1622).
Anon., *Something Written by Occasion of That Fatall and Memorable Accident in the Blacke Frier* (London: 1623).

Anon., *Les Royales Ceremonies Faites en l'Edification d'une Chapelle de Capucins à Londres en Angleterre, dans le Palais de la Royne* (Rheims: 1633).

Anon, *A Proclamation Restraining the Withdrawing His Majesties Subjects From the Church of England and Giving Scandal in Resorting to Masse* (London: 1637).

Anon., *An Exposition upon the Apostle's Creed* (London: 1638).

Anon., *England's Complaint to Jesus Christ, Against the Bishops' Canons of the Late Sinfull Synod* (London: 1640).

Anon., *A Declaration of the Daily Grievances of the Catholique Recusants of England. With Protestations to the Same for Their Loyaltie and Truth to Their King and Countrey* (London: 1641).

Anon., *A Great Conspiracy of the Papists Against the Worthy Members of Both Houses of Parliament* (London: 1641).

Anon., *The Voice of the Lord in the Temple* (London: 1641).

Anon., *Treason Discovered From Holland: Or a Discoverie of a Most Damnable and Divellish Attempt of Two Jesuites and Three Other Catholiques Against the Life and Person of the Ladie Elizabeth at the Hague* (London: 1641).

Anon., *A Copy of Generall Lesleys Letter to Sir John Suckling. With Sir John Sucklings Answer to His Letter* (London: 1641/2).

Anon., *The Kingdoms Weekly Intelligencer Sent Abroad to Prevent Misinformation*, Number 6 (London: 31 January to 6 February 1642).

Anon., *The Scots Scouts Discoveries By Their London Intelligencer, And Presented to the Lords of the Covenant of Scotland, 1639* (London: 1642).

Anon., *Treason Discovered From Holland: Or a Discoverie of a Most Damnable and Divellish Attempt of Two Jesuites and Three Other Catholiques Against the Life and Person of the Ladie Elizabeth At the Hague* (London: 1642).

Anon., *The Game at Chesse: A Metaphoricall Discourse Shewing the Present Estate of this Kingdome* (London: 1643).

Anon., *The Great Eclipse of the Sun, Or, Charles His Waine Overclouded, by the Evill Influences of the Moon ... Otherwise, Great Charles, Our Gracious King, Eclipsed by the Destructive Perswasions of His Queen, by the Pernicious Aspects of His Cabbinet Counsell, and, by the Subtill Insinuations of the Popish Faction* (London: 1644).

Anon., 'The Dramatic Works and Poems of James Shirley, Now First Collected', *American Quaterly Review*, 16 (1834), 103–66.

Arias, Francisco, *A Treatise of Benignitie*, trans. Tobias Matthew (St Omer: 1630).

Austin, William, *Devotionis Augustinianae Flamma: Or Certaine Devout, Godly and Learned Meditations* (London: 1635).

B., A., aka Matthew Wilson, *A Defence of Nicholas Smith Against a Reply to His Discussion of Some Pointes Taught by Mr. Doctour Kellison in His Treatise of the Ecclesiasticall Hierarchy* (Rouen: 1630).

B., L., *The Answere of a Catholike Lay Gentleman, to the Judgement of a Devine, Upon the Letter of the Lay Catholikes to the Sayd Lord Bishop of Chalcedon* (Brussels: 1631).

B., W., aka Lawrence Anderton, *One God, One Fayth: Or a Discourse Against Those Lukewarme-Christians, Who Extend Salvation to All Kinds of Fayth and Religion* (St Omer: 1625).

Baillie, James, *Spiritual Marriage: Or the Union Betweene Christ and His Church* (London: 1627).

Baillie, Robert, *Ladensium Autokatakrisis: The Canterburians Self-Conviction* (Amsterdam: 1640).

Ballard, George, *The History of Susanna: Compiled According to the Prophet Daniel, Amplified With Convenient Meditations* (London: 1638).

Bastwick, John, *The Answer of John Bastwick . . . to the Exceptions Made Against His Letany . . . This Is to Follow the Letany as a second Part Thereof* (London: 1637).

Bastwick, John, *The Second Part of the Lateny of John Bastwick, Doctour of Phisick* (London: 1637).

Beaumont, Francis, and John Fletcher, *Cupids Revenge* (London: 1615).

Becon, Thomas, *The Displaying of the Popish Masse: Wherein Thou Shalt See, What a Wicked Idoll the Masse Is* (London: 1588, 1637).

Bedell, William, *The Copies of Certaine Letters Which Have Passed Between Spaine and England in Matter of Religion, Concerning the Generall Motives to the Romane Obedience. Betweene J. W. and W. Bedell* (London: 1624).

Bedell, William, *An Examination of Certaine Motives to Recusancie* (London: 1628).

Bedford, Thomas, *A True and Certaine Relation of a Strange-Birth, Which Was Borne At Stone-House in the Parish of Plimmouth, the 20 of October, 1635; Together With the Notes of a Sermon, Preached Octob. 23 1635. In the Church of Plimmouth, At the Interring of the Sayd Birth* (London: 1635).

Berington, Joseph (ed.), *The Memoirs of Gregorio Panzani, Giving an Account of His Agency in England, in the Years 1634, 1635, 1636* (Birmingham: Swinney and Walker, 1793).

Bernard of Clairvaux, St, *A Hive of Sacred Honie-Combes*, trans. Antonie Batt (Douai: 1631).

Bernard, Richard, *Good Christian, Looke to Thy Creede* (London: 1630).

Birch, Thomas (ed.), *The Court and Times of Charles the First*, 2 vols (London: Henry Colburn, 1848).

Bishop, William, *Maister Perkins Reformed Catholique. Together with Maister Robert Abbots Defence Thereof Largely Refuted* (Douai: 1625).
Bolton, Robert, *Some Generall Directions For a Comfortable Walking with God* (London: 1625).
Bosc, Jacques du, *L'Honneste Femme* (Paris: 1632).
Brathwaite, Richard, *Whimzies: Or, a New Cast of Characters* (London: 1631).
Brerely, John, aka Lawrence Anderton, *The Liturgie of the Masse: Wherein Are Treated Three Principal Points of Faith* (Rouen: 1620).
Brerely, John, aka Lawrence Anderton, *Virginalia. Or Spirituall Sonnets in Prayse of the Most Glorious Virgin Marie, Upon Everie Severall Title of Her Litanies of Loreto* (Rouen: 1632).
Brewer, Thomas, *The Weeping Lady: Or London Like Ninivie in Sack-Cloth. Describing the Mappe of Her Own Miseries, in This Time of Her Heavy Visitation; With Her Hearty Prayers, Admonition, and Pious Meditations* (London: 1625).
Brome, Richard, *The Court Beggar* (London: 1653).
Broughton, Richard, *The Judgement of the Apostles* (Douai: 1632).
Browning, John, *Concerning Publike-Prayer, and the Fasts of the Church* (London: 1636).
Buckland, Thomas, aka Edmund Thomas Hill, *A Plaine Path-Way to Heaven: Mediatations, or Spirituall Discourses Upon the Ghospells of All the Sondayes in the Year* (St Omer: 1637).
Burton, Henry, *A Tryall of Private Devotions: Or a Diall For the Houres of Prayer* (London: 1627).
Burton, Henry, *The Baiting of the Popes Bull: Or An Unmasking of the Mystery of Iniquity* (London: 1627).
Burton, Henry, *Conflicts and Comforts of Conscience* (London: 1628).
Burton, Henry, *Israels Fast: Or a Meditation Upon the Seventh Chapter of Joshuah: A Faire Precedent For These Times* (London: 1628).
Burton, Henry, *Babel No Bethel: That Is the Church of Rome No True Visible Church of Christ* (London: 1629).
Burton, Henry, *Truth's Triumph Over Trent: Or the Great Gulfe Betweene Sion and Babylon* (London: 1629).
Burton, Henry, *An Apology of an Appeale* (London: 1636).
Butterfield, Robert, *Maschil: Or, a Treatise to Give Instruction, Touching the State of the Church of Rome Since the Councell of Trent, Whether Shee Be Yet a True Christian Church* (London: 1629).
C., B., *Puritanisme the Mother, Sinne the Daughter* (St Omer: 1633).
C., B., *Αδελφομαχια: Or The Warrs of Protestancy; Being a Treatise, Wherin Are Layd Open the ... Dissentions of the Protestants Among Themselves* (St Omer: 1637).

C., I., *Saint Marie Magdalens Conversion* (secretly printed in England: 1603).
C., I. B., *A Looking Glasse For New Reformers. Answering Paul Rainalds, Scotishmans Letter Perswading His Brother to Forsake the True Ancient Catholike and Roman Religion* ('Lion': false imprint, probably Bordeaux, not before 1625).
C., W., *The Fatall Vesper: Or a True and Punctuall Relation of That Lamentable and Fearefull Accident, Hapning on Sunday in the Afternoone, Being the 26. of October Last, by the Fall of a Roome in the Black-Friers* (London: 1623).
Cade, Anthony, *A Justification of the Church of England: Demonstrating It to Be a True Church of God, Affording All Sufficient Meanes to Salvation*, 2 vols (London: 1630).
Cade, Anthony, *A Sermon of the Nature of Conscience* (London: 1639).
Calderwood, David, *A Re-Examination of the Five Articles Enacted at Perth Anno 1618* (Edinburgh: 1636).
Cameron, John, *An Examination of Those Plausible Appearances Which Seeme Most to Commend the Romish Church, And to Prejudice the Reformed* (London: 1626).
Camus, Jean Pierre, *Admirable Events: Selected Out of Foure Bookes*, trans. S. du Verger (London: 1639).
Canne, John, *A Necessitie of Separation From the Church of England, Proved by the Nonconformists Principles* (Amsterdam: 1634).
Canne, John, *A Stay against Straying: Or an Answer to a Treatise, Intituled: The Lawfulnes of Hearing the Ministers of the Church of England by John Robinson* (Amsterdam: 1639).
Carlell, Lodowick, *The Deserving Favourite* (London: 1629).
Carlell, Lodowick, *Arviragus and Philicia* (London: 1639).
Cartwright, William, *Comedies, Tragi-Comedies with Other Poems* (London: 1651).
Caussin, Nicolas, *The Holy Court. Or, the Christian Institution of Men of Quality: With Example of Those Who in Court Have Flourished in Sanctity*, trans. Thomas Hawkins, 2 vols (Paris [St Omer]: 1626).
Caussin, Nicolas, *The Holy Court, Fourth Tome. The Commaund of Reason, Over the Passions*, trans. Thomas Hawkins (Rouen: 1638).
Cavendish, William, *A Declaration Made by the Earl of New-Castle . . . For His Resolution of Marching Into Yorkshire. As Also a Just Vindication of Himself From That . . . Aspersion Laid Upon Him, For Entertaining Some Popish Recusants in His Forces* (London: 1643).
Charles I, *By the King: A Proclamation For the Better Confining of Popish Recusants* (London: 1626).
Charles I, *A Proclamation Concerning the Execution of the Lawes Against Recusants* (London: 1627).

Charles I, *A Proclamation Declaring His Majesties Royall Pleasure and Command For Putting the Lawes and Statutes Made Against the Jesuites, Priestes and Popish Recusants in Due Execution* (London: 1628).

Charles I, *A Proclamation Restraining the Withdrawing His Majesties Subjects From the Church of England and Giving Scandal in Resorting to Masse* (London: 1637).

Chassanion, Jean, *The Merchandizes of Popish Priests: Or A Discovery of the Jesuites Trumpery Newly Packed in England* (London: 1629).

Cholmley, Hugh, *The State of the Now-Romane Church* (London: 1629).

Cibber, Theophilus, *The Lives of the Poets of Great Britain and Ireland* (London: Griffiths, 1753).

Clarke, John, *Holy Incense for the Censers of the Saints: Or a Method of Prayer, With Matter, and Formes in Selected Sentences of Sacred Scripture* (London: 1634).

Commynes, Philippe de, *An Epitome of All the Lives of the Kings of France From Pharamond the First, to the Now Most Chrisitan King Lewis the Thirteenth*, trans. Richard Brathwaite (London: 1639).

Cooper, John, *The Foolish Prophets Displayed* (London: 1638).

Copinger, John, *The Theatre of Catholique and Protestant Religion* (St Omer, 1620).

Cosin, John, *A Collection of Private Devotions: In the Practice of the Ancient Church Called the Houres of Prayer* (London: 1627).

Crashaw, William, *The Jesuites Gospel: Written by Themselves* (London: 1621).

Crashaw, William, *Englands Lamentable Complaint to Her God* (London: 1629).

Darcie, Abraham, *Genealogie et Alliance de l'Ancienne et Renommee Maison de la Trimoville* (London: 1626).

Dauncey, John, *The History of the Thrice Illustrious Princess Henrietta Maria de Bourbon, Queen of England* (London: 1660).

D'Avenant, William, *Love and Honour* (London: 1635).

D'Avenant, William, *The Temple of Love: A Masque Presented by the Queens Majesty, and Her Ladies At Whitehall, On Shrove Tuesday, 1634* (London: 1635).

D'Avenant, William, *The Platonic Lovers* (London: 1636).

D'Avenant, William, *The Witts* (London: 1636).

D'Avenant, William, *Luminalia: The Queen's Festival of Light* (London: 1638).

D'Avenant, William, *Madagascar: With Other Poems* (London: 1638).

D'Avenant, William, *Salmacida Spolia. A Masque* (London: 1639).

D'Avenant, William, *The Unfortunate Lovers* (London: 1643).

D'Avenant, William, *Gondibert: An Heroic poem* (London: 1651).

Davenport, Christopher, *Deus, Natura, Gratia* (Langduni: 1634).
Donne, John, *The First Sermon Preached to King Charles At St. James, 3 April 1625* (London: 1625).
Donne, John, *Devotions Upon Emergent Occasions* (London: 1626).
Donne, John, *Sermon Upon Easter Day* (London: 1626).
Donne, John, *Sermon Upon the Nativity* (London: 1626).
Doughty, Thomas, *Of the Visible Sacrifice of the Church of God*, 2 vols (Brussels: 1637).
Downame, George, *An Apostolicall Injunction for Unity and Peace* (London: 1639).
Drayton, Michael, *The Battle of Agincourt* (London: 1627).
Dudley, Jane, *The Life, Death and Actions of the Most Chaste, Learned and Religious Lady, the Lady Jane Grey, Daughter to the Duke of Suffolke* (London: 1636).
Fage, Mary, *Fames Roule: Or the Names of Our Dread Soveraigne Lord King Charles, His Royall Queen Mary, and His Most Hopefull Posterity: Together with, the Names of the Dukes . . . of England, Scotland and Ireland: Annarammatiz'd and Expressed by Acrosticke Lines on Their Names* (London: 1637).
Falconer, John, *The Mirrour of Created Perfection: Or the Life of the Most Blessed Virgin Mary, Mother of God* (St Omer: 1632).
Falconer, John, *The Life of St. Catherine* (St Omer: 1634).
Faret, Nicolas, *The Honest Man; Or the Art to Please in Court*, trans. Edward Grimstone (London: 1632).
Featley, Daniel, *Stricturae in Lyndomastigem: Or, An Answere By Way of Supplement to the Chapters Remaining in the Book Intituled, A Case For the Spectacles* (London: 1638).
Ferdinand II, *A Relation of a New League* (London: 1626).
Fisher, Ambrose, *A Defence of the Liturgie of the Church of England* (London: 1630).
Fitz-Herbert, Thomas, *The Reply of T. F. in Defence of the First Two Chapters of His Supplement to the Discussion* (St Omer: 1614).
Fletcher, Phineas, *The Locusts: Or Apollyonists* (Cambridge: 1627).
Floyd, John, *A Word of Comfort: Or A Discourse Concerning the Late Lamentable Accident of the Fall of a Roome, At A Catholike Sermon, in the Black-friars At London* (St Omer: 1623).
Floyd, John, *The Church Conquerant Over Humane Wit* (St Omer: 1639).
Ford, John, *Tis Pitty Shee's a Whore* (London: 1633).
Fosbroke, Thomas, *Berkelely Manuscripts: Abstracts and Extracts of Smyth's Lives of the Berkeleys* (London: John Nichols and Son, 1821).
Freake, William, *The Doctrines and Practices of the Society of Jesuites* (London: 1630).

Fuller, Thomas, *The Church-History of Britain: From the Birth of Jesus Christ, Until the Year MDCXLVIII* (London: 1655).

Gardiner, Richard, *A Sermon Preach'd in the Cathedrall Church of Christ in Oxford on Christmas Day: Wherein Is Defended the Catholique Doctrine That Christ Is True God, Truely Incarnate* (Oxford: 1638).

Gataker, Thomas, *An Anniversarie Memoriall of Englands Delivery from the Spanish Invasion* (London: 1626).

Gee, John, *The Foot Out of the Snare: With a Detection of Sundry Late Practises and Impostures of the Priests and Jesuites in England* (London: 1624).

Gee, John, *New Shreds of the Old Snare* (London: 1624).

Gillespie, George, *A Dispute Against the English-Popish Ceremonies Obtruded Upon the Church of Scotland* (Edinburgh: 1637).

Goad, Thomas, *The Dolefull Even-Song: Or a True, Particular and Impartiall Narration of That Fearefull and Sudden Calamity, Which Befell the Preacher, Mr. Drury* (London: 1623).

Gosselin, Peter, *State Mysteries of the Jesuites: By Way of Question and Answers* (London: 1623).

Gregory, St, *The Second Book of the Dialogues of St. Gregorie the Great*, trans. Cuthbert Fursdon (Douai: 1638).

Griffin, Richard (ed.), *The Private Correspondence of Jane, Lady Cornwallis, 1613–1644* (London: 1842).

Guild, William, *Popish Glorying in Their Antiquitie Turned to Their Shame* (London: 1626).

Guild, William, *An Antidote against Poperie: Fit (God Willing) to Preserve and Arme Everie One Agaynst the Seduction Thereof. Most Necessarie For All, in This Back-Slyding Age* (Aberdeen: 1639).

H., R. (trans.), *The Misticall Crowne of the Most Glorious Virgin Marie* (Douai: 1638).

Hall, Joseph, *The Olde Religion: A Treatise Wherein Is Laid Down the True State of the Difference Betwixt the Reformed, and Romane Church* (London: 1628).

Hall, Joseph, *An Answer to Pope Urban His Inurbanity, Expressed in a Breve Sent to Louis the French King, Exasperating Him Against the Protestants in France* (London: 1629).

Halliwell, James Orchard (ed.), *The Autobiography and Correspondence of Sir Simonds D'Ewes, Bart, During the Reigns of James I and Charles I*, 2 vols (London: 1845).

Halliwell, James (ed.), *Letters of the Kings of England*, 2 vols (London: Henry Colburn, 1846).

Hausted, Peter, *The Rivall Friends* (London: 1632).

Hausted, Peter, *Ten Semons Preached Upon Severall Sundayes and Saints Dayes* (London: 1636).

Hawkins, Henry, *Partheneia Sacra: Or the Mysterious and Delicious Garden of the Sacred Parthenes; Symbolically Set Forth and Enriched with Pious Devices and Emblemes for the Entertainement of Devout Soules; Contrived Al to the Honour of the Incomparable Virgin Marie, Mother of God* (Rouen: 1633).

Henrietta Maria, *A Coppy of the Letter Sent by the Queenes Majestie Concerning the Collection of the Recusants Money For the Scottish Warre* (London: 1641).

Heylyn, Peter, *A Briefe and Moderate Answer to the Seditious and Scandalous Challenge of Henry Burton, Late of Friday-Street* (London: 1637).

Heylyn, Peter, *A Survey of the Estate of France, and of Some of the Adjoyning Ilands: Taken in the Description of the Prinicipal Cities, and Chief Provinces* (London: 1656).

Heywood, Thomas, *Porta Pietatis: Or, the Port or Harbour of Piety* (London: 1638).

Heywood, Thomas, *The Exemplary Lives and Memorable Acts of Nine the Most Worthy Women of the World, Three Jewes, Three Gentiles, Three Christians* (London: 1640).

Howard, William, *A Patterne of Christian Loyaltie: Whereby Any Prudent Man May Clearely Perceive, in What Manner the New Oath of Allegiance, and Every Clause Thereof, May in a True, and Catholike Sense, Without Danger of Perjury, Be Taken by Roman Catholikes* (London: 1634).

Howell, James, *Epistolae Ho-Elianae: Familiar Letters Domestic and Forren; Divided Into Six Sections: Partly Historicall, Politicall, Philosophicall, Upon Emergent Occasions* (London: 1645).

Ironside, Gilbert, *Seven Questions of the Sabbath Briefly Disputed, After the Manner of the Schooles* (Oxford: 1637).

Jerome, Stephen, *Ireland's Jubilee: Or Joyes Io-Paen; For Prince Charles His Welcome Home* (Dublin: 1624).

Jonson, Ben, *The Fortunate Isles and Their Union* (London: 1625).

Jonson, Ben, *Love's Triumph, through Callipolis* (London: 1630).

Kellison, Matthew, *A Treatise of the Hierarchie and Divers Order of the Church Against the Anarchie of Calvin* (Douai: 1629).

King, Henry, *A Sermon Preached at St. Pauls, March 27 1640. Being the Anniversary of His Majesties Happy Inauguration to His Crowne* (London: 1640).

Knott, Edward, *Charity Mistaken, With the Want Thereof Catholikes Are Unjustly Charged: For Affirming As They Doe With Grief That Protestancy Unrepented Destroies Salvation* (London: 1630).

Knott, Edward, *Mercy and Truth: Or Charity Maintained by Catholiques* (St Omer: 1634).

L., B., *The Answere of a Catholike Lay Gentleman to the Judgement of a Divine Upon the Letter of the Lay Catholickes to My Lord Bishop of Chalcedon*, bound with *The Attestation of the Most Excellent and Most Illustrious Lord Don Carlos Coloma, Embassadour Extraordinary for Spaine* (Brussels: 1631).

L., D., *The Scot Scouts Discoveries By Their London Intelligencer, And Presented to the Lords of the Covenant of Scotland, 1639* (London: 1642).

Laing, David (ed.), *The Letters and Journals of Robert Baillie, AM, Principal of the University of Glasgow, 1637–1662*, 3 vols (Edinburgh: 1841–2).

Laud, William, *A Speech Delivered in the Starr-Chamber On Wednesday, the XIVth of June, 1637. At the Censure of J. Bastwick, H. Burton, & W. Prinn; Concerning Pretended Innovations in the Church* (London: 1637).

Laud, William, *A Relation of the Conference between William Laud, Then, Lord Bishop of St. Davids; Now Lord Arch-Bishop of Canterbury: And Mr. Fisher the Jesuite. By the Command of King James* (London: 1639).

Laud, William, *Works*, ed. William Scott, 7 vols (Oxford: 1847).

Lechmere, Edmund, aka Stratford Edmund, *A Reflection of Certaine Authors That Are Pretended to Disavow the Churches Infallabilite in Her Generall Decrees of Faith* (Douai: 1635).

Le Moyne, Pierre, *La Gallerie des Femmes Fortes* (Paris: 1647).

Leyburn, George, *To Her Most Excellent Majestie Henrietta Maria, Queen of Great Britaign: Dr. Leyburn's Apologie* (Douai: 1660).

Lilburne, John, *A Worke of the Beast: Or a Relation of a Most Unchristian Censure, Executed Upon J. Lilburne Now Prisoner in the Fleet* (London: 1638).

Lithgow, William, *Scotland's Welcome to Her Native Sonne and Soveraigne Lord, King Charles* (Edinburgh: 1633).

Lovell, Robert, *The High Way to Honor: As It Was Delivered (For Substance) in Two Sermons At All-Hallowes, Barking* (London: 1627).

Lynde, Humphrey, *Via Devia: The By-Way: Misleading the Weake and Unstable Into Dangerous Paths of Error* (London: 1630).

Mab, Ralphe, *The Character of a Christian: As Hee Is Distinguished From Hypocrites and Heretickes* (London: 1627).

Maffei, Giovanni, *Fuga Saeculi: Or the Holy Hatred of the World*, trans. Henry Hawkins (Paris [St Omer]: 1632).

Maitland, Patrick, *King Charles His Birthright* (Edinburgh: 1633).

Mason, Henry, *The New Arte of Lying, Covered By Jesuites Under the Vaile of Equivocation Discovered and Disproved* (London: 1634).

Matthieu, Pierre, *The Historie of S. Elizabeth – Daughter of the King of Hungarie*, trans. Thomas Hawkins (Brussels: 1633).

May, Thomas, *The Tragedy of Antigone, the Theban Princesse* (London: 1631).
Mede, Joseph, *The Name Altar, or Θυσιαστηριον Anciently Given to the Holy Table* (London: 1637).
Médicis, Marie de, *A Declaration of the Queen, Mother of the Most Christian King* (London: 1639).
Middleton, Thomas, *A Game At Chaesse As It Was Acted Nine Days Together At the Globe on the Bankside* (London: 1625).
Montagu, Walter, *The Accomplished Woman* (London: 1656).
Montague, Richard, *A Gagg for the New Gospell? No. A New Gagg for an Old Goose* (London: 1624).
More, Cresacre, *The Life and Death of Sir Thomas More* (Antwerp: 1631).
Moulin, Pierre, *The Buckler of the Faith* (London: 1620, 1631).
N.,N., *Maria Triumphans; Being a Discourse, Wherin By Way of Dialogue the B. Virgin Mary Mother of God Is Defended* (St Omer: 1635).
Odell, Thomas, *A Briefe and Short Treatise called the Christians Pilgrimage to His Fatherland* (Amsterdam: 1635).
Overbury, Thomas, *Sit Thomas Overbury. His Observations in His Travailes Upon the State of the XVII Provinces as They Stood Anno Dom. 1609. The Treatie of Peace Being Then On Foote* (London: 1626).
Owen, Jane, *An Antidote Against Purgatory* (St Omer: 1634).
Owen, Lewis, *Speculum Jesuiticum* (London: 1629).
Page, William, *A Treatise or Justification of Bowing at the Name of Jesus* (Oxford: 1631).
Pagitt, Ephraim, *Christianographie: Or, the Description of the Multitude and Sundry Sorts of Christians in the World Not Subject to the Pope* (London: 1635).
Parks, William, *The Rose and the Lily* (London: 1638).
Partington, Thomas, *Worse and Worse Newes from Ireland* (London: 1641).
Perron, Jacques du, *A Letter Written from Paris by the Lord Cardinal of Peron to Monsr. Casaubon in England*, trans. Thomas Owen (St Omer: 1612).
Phillip, Robert, *The Coppy of a Letter of Father Philips, the Queenes Confessor, Which Was Thought to Be Sent Into France, to Mr Montague* (London: 1641).
Phillips, Edward, *Theatrum Poetarum: Or a Compleat Collection of the Poets, Especially the Most Eminent, of All Ages* (London: 1675).
Pocklington, John, *Sunday No Sabbath: A Sermon Preached Before the Lord Bishop of Lincolne At His Lordships Visitation At Ampthill in the County of Bedford, August 17th 1635* (London: 1636).

Powell, Robert, *The Life of Alfred, or Albred . . . Together With a Parallel of Our Soveraigne Lord King Charles* (London: 1634).
Preston, John, *The Golden Scepter Held Forth to the Humble. With the Churches Dignitie by Her Marriage and the Churches Dutie in Her Carriage. In Three Treatises* (London: 1638).
Prideaux, John, *The Patronage of Angels. A Sermon Preached at the Court* (Oxford: 1636).
Primrose, Diana, *A Chaine of Pearle: Or a Memorial of the Peerless Graces and Heroick Vertues of Queen Elizabeth* (London: 1630).
Prynne, William, *A Briefe Survay and Censure of Mr. Cozens His Couzening Devotions* (London: 1628).
Prynne, William, *The Unlovelinesse of Love-Lockes: Or a Summarie Discourse, Prooving: The Wearing and Nourishing of a Locke, Or Love-Locke, to Be Altogether Unseemely, and Unlawfull Unto Christians* (London: 1628).
Prynne, William, *Anti-Arminianisme: Or the Church of Englands Old Antithesis to New Arminianisme* (London: 1630).
Prynne, William, *The Church of England's Own Antithesis to New Arminianisme* (London: 1630).
Prynne, William, *Histriomastix: The Players Scourge or Actors Tragaedie* (London: 1633).
Prynne, William, *Certaine Quaeres Propounded to the Bowers At the Name of Jesus* (London: 1636).
Prynne, William, *A Looking Glasse For All Lordly-Prelates, Wherein They May Cleerely Behold the True Divine Originall and Laudable Pedigree, Whence They Are Descended* (London: 1636).
Prynne, William, *Newes from Ipswich* (Ipswich: 1636).
Prynne, William, *A Quench-Coale: Or, a Briefe Disquisition and Inquirie, in What Place of the Church or Chancell the Lords-Table Ought to Be Situated* (London: 1637).
Quarles, Francis, *Hadassa: Or the History of Queene Ester* (London: 1621).
Quarles, Francis, *Divine Poems: Containing The History of Jonah. Ester. Job. Sions Sonets. Elegies* (London: 1630).
Quelch, William, *Church-Customes Vindicated in Two Sermons Preached At Kingstone Upon Thames* (London: 1636).
Racan, Honorat de Bueil, Marquis de, *L'Artenice* (n.p.: E. Allde, 1626).
Read, Alexander, *A Sermon Preached April 8th 1635, At a Visitation At Brentwood in Essex* (London: 1636).
Reynolds, John, *Vox Coeli; Or Newes From Heaven of a Consultation There Held by the High and Mighty Princes, King Hen. . . . Edw. 6, Prince Henry, Queene Mary . . . Elizabeth and Anne. Wherein Spaines Ambition and Treacheries . . . Are Unmasked . . . Particularly Towards*

England, and Now Especially Under the Pretended Match of Prince Charles with the Infanta Dona Maria. Whereunto Is Annexed Two Letters Written by Qween Mary From Heaven (London: 1624).

Rhodes, John, *The Countrie Mans Comfort: Or Religious Recreations Fitte For All Well Disposed Persons* (London: 1588, 1637).

Richards, Nathanael, *The Celestiall Publican* (London: 1630).

Richards, Nathanael, *The Tragedy of Messallina, the Roman Emperesse* (London: 1640).

Richards, Nathanael, *Poems Sacred and Satyricall* (London: 1641).

Robartes, Foulke, *Gods Holy House and Service* (London: 1639).

Robertus, Prior of Shrewsbury, *The Admirable Life of Saint Wenefride, Virgin, Martyr, Abbesse*, trans. John Falconer (St Omer: 1635).

Robinson, Thomas, *The Anatomy of the English Nunnery At Lisbon* (London: 1622).

Rogers, Nehemiah, *The Wild Vine* (London: 1632).

Rous, Francis (the elder), *Testis Veritatis: The Doctrine of King James Our Late Soveraigne of Famous Memory* (London: 1626).

Rous, Francis (the elder), *The Heavenlie Acadamie* (London: 1638).

Rowland, Daniel, *An Historical and Genealogical Account of the Noble Family of Nevill, Particularly of the House of Abergavenny* (London: Samuel Bentley, 1830).

Rowley, Samuel, *The Noble Spanish Souldier* (London: 1634).

S., B., *An Excellent and Materiall Discourse: Prooving What Great Danger Will Hang Over Our Heads of England and France If It Shall Happen That Those of Germaine Which Are Our Friends Be Subdued and the King of Denmark Vanquished* (London: 1626).

S., T., *Sermons, Meditations, and Prayers Upon the Plague, 1636* (London: 1637).

Sales, Francis de, *A Treatise of the Love of God*, trans. Miles Car (Douai: 18th edition, 1630).

Sales, Francis de, *Delicious Entertainments of the Soule*, trans. Agnes More (Douai: 1632).

Sander, Nicholas, *A Treatise of the Images of Christ, and of His Saints: And That It Is Unlaufull to Breake Them, and Laufull to Honour Them* (St Omer: 1567, 1625).

Sanderson, William, *A Compleat History of the Life and Raigne of King Charles From His Cradle to His Grave* (London: 1658).

Scott, Thomas, *Vox Populi: Or Newes From Spayne* (London: 1620).

Scrope, R., and T. Monkhouse (eds), *Clarendon State Papers Collected by Edward Earl of Clarendon, Commencing From the Year 1621*, 3 vols (Oxford: 1767–1786).

Shelford, Robert, *Five Pious and Learned Discourses* (Cambridge: 1635).

Shirley, E. P., *Stemmata Shirleiana: Or the Annals of the Shirley Family, Lords of Nether Etindon, in the County of Warwick, and of Shirley in the County of Derby* (London: J. B. Nichols, 1841).
Shirley, James, *The Witty Fair One* (London: 1628).
Shirley, James, *The Wedding* (London: 1629).
Shirley, James, *The Grateful Servant* (London: 1630).
Shirley, James, *Love in a Maze* (London: 1631).
Shirley, James, *Loves Tricks: Or the School of Complement* (London: 1631).
Shirley, James, *The Witty Fair One* (London: 1633).
Shirley, James, *The Young Admirall* (London: 1637).
Shirley, James, *The Maid's Revenge* (London: 1639).
Shirley, James, *Via ad Latinam Linguam Complanata: The Way Made Plain to the Latine Tongue, the Rules Composed in English and Latine Verse for the Greater Delight and Benefit of Young Beginners* (London: 1649).
Shirley, James, *The Rudiments of Grammar: The Rules Composed in English Verse for the Greater Benefit and Delight of Young Beginners* (London: 1656).
Shorleyker, Richard, *A Schole-House for the Needle* (London: 1632).
Skinner, Robert, *A Sermon Preached Before the King at White-Hall, the Third of December* (London: 1634).
Smart, Peter, *A Sermon Preached In the Cathedrall Church of Durham. July 7 1628* (London: 1628).
Smith, Richard, *The Life of the Most Honourable and Vertuous Lady, the La. Magdalen Vicountess Montague* (St Omer: 1627).
Southwell, Robert, *An Epistle of Comfort, to the Reverend Priestes & to the Honorable, Worshipful, & Other of the Laye Sort Restrayned in Durance for the Catholicke Fayth* (Paris: 1588).
Southwell, Robert, *St. Peters Complaint and St. Mary Magdalens Funerall Teares. With Sundry Other Selected, and Devout Poems* (St Omer: 1596, 1620).
Stafford, Anthony, *The Guide of Honour: Or, the Ballance Wherin She May Weigh Her Actions* (London: 1634).
Stafford, Anthony, *The Female Glory: Or, the Life and Death of Our Blessed Lady, the Holy Virgin Mary* (London: 1635).
Stapleton, Thomas, *A Fortresse of the Faith* (St Omer: 1565, 1625).
Swan, John, *Profano-Mastix* (London: 1639).
Sweetnam, John, *S. Mary Magdalens Pilgrimage to Paradise* (St Omer: 1617, 1627).
Sydenham, Humphry, *The Athenian Babler: A Sermon Preached At St Maries in Oxforde, the 9. of July, 1626* (Oxford: 1626).

Synge, George, *A Rejoynder to the Reply Published by the Jesuits Under the Name of William Malone* (Dublin: 1632).
T., T., *The Whetstone of Reproofe* (Douai: Catuapoli, 1632).
Tabaruad, M., *Histoire de Pierre de Bérulle*, 2 vols (Paris: 1817).
Taylor, Jeremy, *A Sermon Preached in St. Maries Church in Oxford Upon the Anniversary of the Gunpowder Plot* (Oxford: 1638).
Taylor, John, *The Needles Excellency: A New Booke Wherin Are Divers Admirable Workes Wrought with the Needle* (London: 12th edition, 1640).
Taylor, John, *A Swarme of Sectaries, and Schismatiques: Wherein Is Discovered the Strange Preaching (Or Prating) of Such As Are by Their Trades, Coblers, Tinkers, Pedlars, Weavers, Sowgelders and Chymney-Sweepers* (London: 1641).
Taylor, Peter, *A Sermon Preached in St. Maries Oxford on the Anniversary of the Gunpowder Plot* (Oxford: 1638).
Taylor, Thomas, *A Mappe of Rome, Lively Exhibiting Her Mercilesse Meeknesse and Cruell Mercies to the Church of God: Preached in Five Sermons On Occasion of the Gunpowder Treason* (London: 1619, 1634).
Tell-Troath, Tom, *Tom Tell-Troath: Or a Free Discourse Touching the Manners of the Tyme* (London: 1622).
Torsellino, Orazio, *The Admirable Life of S. Francis Xavier*, trans. Thomas Fitz-Herbert (Paris [St Omer]: 1632).
Valentine, Henry, *Noahs Dove: Or a Prayer for the Peace of Jerusalem* (London: 1627).
Valentine, Henry, *Private Devotions, Digested into Six Letanies* (London: 1640).
Verheiden, J., *The History of the Modern Protestant Divines*, trans. Donald Lupton (London: 1637).
Wadding, Lucas, *The History of the Angelicall Virgin Glorious S. Clare*, trans. Sr Magdalen Augustine (Douai: 1635).
White, Francis, *A Treatise of the Sabbath-Day. Containing, a Defence of the Orthodoxall Doctrine of the Church of England, Against Sabbatarian-Novelty* (London: 1635).
Wickins, Nathaniel, *Wood Street-Compters Plea for Its Prisoners* (London: 1638).
Widdrington, Roger, aka Thomas Preston, *A Theologicall Disputation Concerning the Oath of Allegiance* (London: 1613).
Widdrington, Roger, aka Thomas Preston, *R.W.'s Last Reyoynder to Mr. Thomas Fitz-Herberts Reply Concerning the Oath of Allegiance and the Popes Power to Depose Princes* (London: 1633).
Wilson, John, *The English Martyrologe Conteyning a Summary of the Most Renowned and Illustrious Saints of the Three Kingdomes England, Ireland and Scotland* (St Omer: 1642).

Wilson, Matthew, *A Direction to be Observed by N. N. If Hee Meane to Proceede in Answering the Booke Intituled Mercy and Truth, Or Charity Maintained by Catholiks* (printed secretly in England: 1636).

Wilson, Matthew, *Christianity Maintained: Or a Discovery of Sundry Doctrines Tending to the Overthrowe of Christian Religion* (St Omer: 1638).

Wither, George, *Britain's Remembrancer* (London: 1628).

Wither, George, *A Collection of Emblemes, Ancient and Moderne* (London: 1635).

Wood, Anthony, *Athenae Oxonienses*, 4 vols (Oxford: Oxford University Press, 1813).

Yaxlee, Henry, *Morbus et Antidotus: The Disease With the Antidote. Or a Declaration of Henry Yaxlee of Bouthorpe in the Countie of Norfolk, Wherein He Sheweth How He Was a Papist and How by God's Grace He Is Now Lately Converted* (London: 1630).

Works and editions of works published after 1850

Akrigg, G. P. V. (ed.), *Letters of King James VI and I* (Berkeley: University of California Press, 1984).

Allott, Kenneth (ed.), *The Poems of William Habington* (London: University Press of Liverpool, 1948).

Armstrong, Ray (ed.), *The Poems of James Shirley* (New York: King's Crown Press, 1941).

Baker, Lily M., (ed.), *The Letters of Elizabeth Queen of Bohemia* (London: Bodley Head, 1953).

Beaude, Joseph, Michel Join-Lambert and Rémi Lescot (eds), *Pierre de Bérulle: Oeuvres Complètes*, 5 vols (Paris, Oratoire de Jésus: Les Editions du Cerf, 1996).

Brooke, G. M. S., and A. N. C. Hallen (eds), *Transcript of the Registers of the United Parishes of St. Mary Woolworth, S. Mary Woolchurch, Haw, 1531–1760* (London: 1886).

Bruce, John (ed.), *Letters and Papers of the Verney Family Down to the End of the Year 1639* (London: John Bowyer Nichols, 1853).

Carter, John, S. (ed), *The Traitor* (London: Edward Arnold, 1965).

Chalmers, Hero, Julie Sanders and Sophie Tomlinson (eds), *Three Seventeenth-Century Plays on Women and Performance* (Manchester: Manchester University Press, 2006).

Clayton, Thomas (ed.), *The Works of Sir John Suckling*, 2 vols (Oxford: Clarendon Press, 1971).

D'Avenant, William, *The Dramatic Works of Sir William D'Avenant*, 5 vols (Edinburgh: William Paterson, 1873).

D'Avenant, William, *The Works of Sir William D'avenant, First Published London 1673* (London: Benjamin Blom, 1968).

Duncan-Jones, Katherine (ed.), *Sir Philip Sidney* (Oxford: Oxford University Press, 1992).

Edwards, T. B. (ed.), 'Salamcida Spolia' within *A Book of Masques: In Honour of Allardyce Nicoll* (Cambridge: Cambridge University Press, 1967).

Flavin, Martin (ed.), *The Wedding* (New York: Garland Publishing, 1980).

Gayley, Charles Mills, *Representative English Comedies*, 4 vols (London: 1914).

Gibbs, A. M. (ed.), *William Davenant: The Shorter Poems and Songs From the Plays and Masques* (Oxford: Clarendon Press, 1972).

Gifford, William, and Anthony Dyce (eds), *The Dramatic Works and Poems of James Shirley*, 6 vols (London: J. Murray, 1883).

Green, Mary Anne Everett (ed.), *Letters of Queen Henrietta Maria, Including Her Private Correspondence With Charles I* (London: Richard Bentley, 1857).

Hicks, L. (ed.), *Letters and Memorials of Father Robert Persons, SJ* (London: John Whitehead and Son, 1942).

Howard-Hill, Thomas (ed.), *A Game at Chess* (Manchester: Manchester University Press, 1993).

Keeble, N. H. (ed.), *Memoirs of the Life of Colonel Hutchinson, With a Fragment of Autobiography* (London: J. M. Dent, 1995).

Kinsley, James (ed.), *The Poems and Fables of John Dryden* (Oxford: Oxford University Press, 1962).

Larson, Deborah Aldrich, *The Verse Miscellany of Constance Aston Fowler: A Diplomatic Edition* (Tempe, Arizona: Centre for Medieval and Renaissance Studies, 2000).

Lindley, David (ed.), *Court Masques: Jacobean and Caroline Entertainments, 1605–1640* (Oxford: Oxford University Press, 1995).

Loomie, Albert (ed.), *Ceremonies of Charles I: The Notebooks of John Finet, 1628–1641* (New York: Fordham University Press, 1987).

Montagu, Walter, *The Shepherds' Paradise*, ed. Sarah Poynting (Oxford: published for the Malone Society by Oxford University Press, 1997).

Orgel, Stephen, and Roy Strong (eds), *Inigo Jones: The Theatre of the Stuart Court*, 2 vols (Berkeley and Los Angeles: University of California Press, 1973).

Parr, Anthony (ed.), *Three Renaissance Travel Plays* (Manchester: Manchester University Press, 1999).

Poynting, Sarah, 'A Critical Edition of Walter Montague's *The Shepherds' Paradise*, Acts 1–3' (PhD Dissertation, University of Oxford, 2000).

Puttenham, George, *The Arte of English Poesie, 1589* (Menston: Scolar Press, 1968).
Raspa, Anthony (ed.), *John Donne, Devotions Upon Emergent Occasions* (Oxford: Oxford University Press, 1987).
Seddon, P. R. (ed.), *Letters of John Holles, 1587–1637*, 3 vols (Nottingham: Thoroton Society 1975).
Shakespeare, William, *Much Ado About Nothing*, ed. J. Waters-Benett (Harmondsworth: Penguin, 1969).
Shakespeare, William, *The First Part of King Henry IV*, eds Herbert Weil and Judith Weil (Cambridge: Cambridge University Press, 1997).
Shakespeare, William, *Richard II*, ed. Andrew Gurr (Cambridge: Cambridge University Press, 2000).
Simpson, Evelyn M. and George R. Potter (eds), *The Sermons of John Donne*, 10 vols (Berkeley and Los Angeles: University of California Press, 1953).
Skemp, A. R. (ed.), *The Tragedy of Messallina, the Roman Emperesse* (London: David Nutt, 1910).
Smyth, John, *The Berkeley Manuscripts: The Lives of the Berkeleys, Lords of the Honour, Castle and Manor of Berkeley In the County of Gloucester from 1066 to 1618*, 3 vols (Gloucester: John Bellows, 1883).
Spalding, Ruth (ed.), *The Diary of Bulstrode Whitelocke, 1605–1675* (Oxford: Oxford University Press, 1990).
Steible, Daniel J., 'A Critical Edition of Sir William Davenant's *The Temple of Love* and *The Platonic Lovers*' (PhD dissertation, University of Cincinnati, 1939).
Tomkins, Henry Barr (ed.), *The Manuscripts of Henry Duncan Skrine, Esq., Salvetti Correspondence*, trans. Heath Wilson (London: 1887).
Townshend, Dorothea, *Life and Letters of Mr Endymion Porter: Sometime Gentleman of the Bedchamber to King Charles the First* (London: T. F. Unwin, 1897).
Tupper, J. W. (ed.), *Love and Honour* and *The Siege of Rhodes by Sir William D'Avenant* (Boston: D.C. Heath & Co., 1909).
Yearling, E. M. *The Cardinal* (Manchester: Manchester University Press, 1986).

Secondary sources

Adams, Joseph, *Shakespearean Playhouses, a History of English Theatres From the Beginnings to the Restoration* (Boston: Houghton, Miffin Co., 1917).
Albion, Gordon, *Charles I and the Court of Rome: A Study in Seventeenth Century Diplomacy* (London: Burns, Oates and Co., 1935).

Anstruther, Godfrey, *A Hundred Homeless Years. English Dominicans, 1558–1658* (London: Blackfriars Publications, 1958).
Armstrong, Ray (ed.), *The Poems of James Shirley* (New York: King's Crown Press, 1941).
Arthur, Liz, *Embroidery at the Burrell Collection, 1600–1700* (Glasgow: Glasgow Museums, 1995).
Ashton, Robert, *The English Civil War: Conservatism and Revolution, 1603–1649* (London: Weidenfeld and Nicolson, 1978).
Atherton, Ian, and Julie Sanders (eds), *The 1630s: Interdisciplinary Essays on Culture and Politics in the Caroline Era* (Manchester: Manchester University Press, 2006).
Aubrey, John, *Brief Lives* (Harmondsworth Middlesex: Penguin Books, 2000).
Aveling, John C. H., *The Handle and the Axe, the Catholic Recusants in England From Reformation to Emancipation* (London: Blond and Briggs, 1976).
Ball, Tomas, *The Life of the Renowned Doctor Preston* (Oxford: 1885).
Barbour, Reid, *Literature and Religious Culture in Seventeenth-Century England* (Cambridge: Cambridge University Press, 2002).
Barker, Francis, Peter Hulme, Margaret Iverson and Diana Loxley (eds), *Literature, Politics and Theory* (London: New Accents, 1986).
Barnett-Smith, G., *The Gentleman's Magazine*, 246 (1880), 584–610.
Barroll, J. Leeds, *Anna of Denmark, Queen of England: A Cultural Biography* (Philadelphia: University of Pennsylvania Press, 2001).
Bas, George, 'Two Misrepresented Biographical Documents Concerning James Shirley', *RES*, 27 (1976), 304–6.
Baugh, Albert, 'Further Facts About James Shirley', *RES*, 7 (1931), 62–6.
Bawcutt, N. W., *The Control and Censorship of Caroline Drama: The Records of Sir Henry Herbert, Master of the Revels 1623–73* (Oxford: Clarendon Press, 1996).
Bentley, Gerald E., 'The Diary of a Caroline Theatregoer', *MP*, 35 (1938), 61–72.
Bentley, Gerald E., *The Jacobean and Caroline Stage*, 7 vols (Oxford: Clarendon Press, 1941–1968).
Bone, Quentin, *Henrietta Maria, Queen of the Cavaliers* (Urbana: University of Illinois Press, 1972).
Bordinat, Philip, and Sophia Blaydes, *Sir William Davenant* (Boston: Twayne Publishers, 1981).
Bossy, John, *The English Catholic Community, 1570–1850* (London: Darton, Longman and Todd, 1975).
Bouwsma, William, 'Gallicanism and the Nature of Christendome', in Anthony Molho and John Tedeschi (eds), *Renaissance Studies in Honour of Hans Baron* (Dekalb: Illinois Press, 1971), pp. 815–26.

Bowers, Fredson (ed.), *Beaumont and Fletcher Dramatic Works*, 5 vols, (Cambridge: Cambridge University Press, 1970).
Britland, Karen, 'Neoplatonic Identities: Literary Representations and the Politics of Queen Henrietta Maria's Court Circle' (PhD Dissertation, University of Leeds, 2000).
Britland, Karen, 'An Under-Stated Mother-in-Law: Marie de Médicis and the Last Caroline Court Masque', in Clare McManus (ed.), *Women and Culture at the Courts of the Stuart Queens, 1603–42* (Basingstoke: Palgrave Macmillan, 2003), pp. 204–23.
Britland, Karen, *Drama at the Courts of Queen Henrietta Maria* (Cambridge: Cambridge University Press, 2006).
Brooke, Xanthe, *The Lady Lever Art Gallery Catalogue of Embroideries* (Strow: Alan Sutton: National Museums and Galleries on Merseyside, 1992).
Burner, Sandra, *James Shirley: A Study of Literary Coteries and Patronage in Seventeenth Century England* (Lanham: University Press of America, 1988).
Butler, Martin, 'Entertaining the Palatine Princes: Plays on Foreign Affairs 1635–1637', *ELR*, 13 (1983), 319–44.
Butler, Martin, *Theatre and Crisis: 1632–1642* (Cambridge: Cambridge University Press, 1984).
Butler, Martin, 'Politics and the Masque: *Salmacida Spolia*', in Thomas Healy and Jonathan Sawday, eds, *Literature and the English Civil War* (Cambridge: Cambridge University Press, 1990), pp. 59–74.
Callaghan, Dympna, 'Shakespeare and Religion', *TP*, 15 (2001), 1–4.
Cano, David Sánchez, 'Entertainments in Madrid for the Prince of Wales: Political Functions of Festivals', in Alexander Samson (ed.), *The Spanish Match: Prince Charles's Journey to Madrid, 1623* (Aldershot: Ashgate, 2006), pp. 51–74.
Chakravorty, Swapan, *Society and Politics in the Plays of Thomas Middleton* (Oxford: Clarendon Press, 1996).
Chalmers, Hero, *Royalist Women Writers, 1650–1689* (Oxford: Clarendon Press, 2004).
Clare, Janet, *Drama of the English Republic, 1649–60* (Manchester: Manchester University Press, 2002).
Clark, Ira, *Professional Playwrights: Massinger, Ford, Shirley and Brome* (Lexington: University Press of Kentucky, 1992).
Clarke, Danielle, 'The Iconography of the Blush: Marian Literature of the 1630s', in Kate Chedgzoy, Melanie Hansen and Suzanne Trill (eds), *Voicing Women: Gender and Sexuality in Early Modern Writing* (Edinburgh: Edinburgh University Press, 1998), pp. 111–28.
Clifton, Robin, 'Popular Fear of Catholics in England during the English Revolution', *P&P*, 52 (1971), 23–55.

Coate, M., *Cornwall in the Great Civil War and Interregnum, 1642–1660* (Oxford: Clarendon Press, 1993).

Cogswell, Thomas, *The Blessed Revolution: English Politics and the Coming of War, 1621–1624* (Cambridge: Cambridge University Press, 1989).

Cohen, Sarah, *Art, Dance and the Body in French Culture of the Ancien Régime* (Cambridge: Cambridge University Press, 2000).

Collins, Howard S., *The Comedy of Sir William D'Avenant* (Paris, The Hague: Mouton, 1967).

Cust, Richard, 'Catholicism, Antiquarianism and Gentry Honour: the Writings of Sir Thomas Shirley', *Midland History*, 23 (1998), 40–70.

Cust, Richard, and Ann Hughes (eds), *Conflict in Early Stuart England: Studies in Religion and Politics 1603–1642* (Harlow: Longman Group, 1989).

Dillon, Anne, *The Construction of Martyrdom in the English Catholic Community, 1535–1603* (Aldershot: Ashgate Publishing, 2002).

Dockery, John Berchmans, *Christopher Davenport: Friar and Diplomat* (London: Burns and Oates, 1960).

Dolan, Frances, *Whores of Babylon, Catholicism, Gender and Seventeenth-Century Print Culture* (Ithaca: Cornell University Press, 1999, reprint Notre Dame, Ind.: University of Notre Dame Press, 2005).

Drury, G. T. (ed.), *The Poems of Edmund Waller* (London: 1893).

Duffin, Anne, *Faction and Faith: Politics and Religion of the Cornish Gentry Before the Civil War* (Exeter: University of Exeter Press, 1996).

Duffo, François Albert, *Henriette-Marie de France, Reine d'Angleterre, 1609–1669* (Paris: 1935).

Dures, Alan, *English Catholicism, 1558–1642: Continuity and Change* (Harlow: Longman Group, 1983).

Edmond, Mary, *Rare Sir William Davenant. Poet Laureate, Playwright, Civil War General, Restoration Theatre Manager* (Manchester: Manchester University Press, 1987).

Feil, J. P., 'James Shirley's Years of Service', *RES*, new series, 8 (1957), 413–16.

Findlay, Alison, Stephanie Hodgson-Wright and Gweno Williams (eds), *Women and Dramatic Productions, 1550–1700* (Harlow: Longman Pearson, 2000).

Firth, Katharine R., *The Apocalyptic Tradition in Reformation Britain, 1530–1645* (Oxford: Oxford University Press, 1979).

Fleay, Frederick, *A Chronicle History of the London Stage, 1559–1642* (London: Reeves and Turner, 1890).

Fletcher, Alan J., *Drama, Performance, and Polity in Pre-Cromwellian Ireland* (Toronto: University of Toronto Press, 2000).

Fletcher, J. B., 'Précieuses at the Court of Charles I', *Journal of Comparative Literature*, 1 (1903), 120–53.
Forker, Charles, 'Archbishop Laud and Shirley's *The Cardinal*', *Transactions of the Winconsin Academy of Sciences*, 47 (1958), 242–8.
Franko, Mark, *Dance As Text: Ideologies of the Baroque Body* (Cambridge: Cambridge University Press, 1993).
Frye, Susan, 'Sewing Connections: Elizabeth Tudor, Mary Stuart, Elizabeth Talbot, and Seventeenth-Century Anonymous Needleworkers', in Susan Frye and Karen Robertson (eds), *Maids and Mistresses, Cousins and Queens: Women's Alliances in Early Modern England* (Oxford: Oxford University Press, 1998), pp. 165–82.
Gaby, Rosemary, ' "Of Vagabonds and Commonwealths": *Beggars' Bush, A Jovial Crew* and *The Sisters*', *SEL*, 34 (1994), 401–24.
Gardiner, Samuel, *History of England from the Accession of James I to the Outbreak of the Civil War, 1603–1642*, 10 vols (London: Longman Green, 1883–84).
Gibbs, Anthony (ed.), *William Davenant: The Shorter Poems and Songs From the Plays and Masques* (Oxford: Clarendon Press, 1972).
Gifford, William, and Anthony Dyce (eds), *The Dramatic Works and Poems of James Shirley*, 6 vols (London: Murray, 1883).
Gillow, Joseph, *A Literary and Bibliographic History; Or Bibliographic Dictionary of English Catholics* (London: Burns and Oates, 1885–1902).
Goellner, Ellen, and Jacqueline Murphy (eds), *Bodies of the Text: Dance as Theory, Literature as Dance* (New Brunswick, NJ: Rutgers University Press, 1995).
Gough, Melinda, 'Courtly *Comediantes*: Henrietta Maria and Amateur Women's Stage Plays in France and England', in Pamela Allen Brown and Peter Parolin (eds), *Women Players in England, 1500–1660: Beyond the All-Male Stage* (Aldershot: Ashgate, 2005), pp. 193–215.
Gregory, George Mackendrick, *Two Studies in Shirley* (Durham: University of North Carolina Press, 1935).
Groves, Beatrice, *Texts and Traditions: Religion in Shakespeare, 1592–1604* (Oxford: Clarendon Press, 2007).
Guibbory, Achsah, *Ceremony and Community from Herbert to Milton: Literature, Religion and Cultural Conflict in Seventeenth-Century England* (Cambridge: Cambridge University Press, 1998).
Gurr, Andrew, *Playgoing in Shakespeare's London* (Cambridge: Cambridge University Press, 1996).
Haigh, Christopher, 'From Monopoly to Minority: Catholicism in Early Modern England', *Royal Historical Society Transactions*, 5th series, 31 (1981), 129–47.
Haigh, Christopher (ed.), *The English Reformation Revised* (Cambridge: Cambridge University Press, 1987).

Hamilton, Donna, and Richard Strier (eds), *Religion, Literature and Politics in Post-Reformation England, 1540–1688* (Cambridge: Cambridge University Press, 1996).

Hand, Sidney, *Old English Needlework of the Sixteenth and Seventeenth Centuries* (London: Sidney Hand, 1920).

Harbage, Alfred, *Sir William Davenant, Poet, Venturer, 1606–1668* (Philadelphia: University of Pennsylvania Press, 1933).

Harbage, Alfred, *Cavalier Drama: An Historical and Critical Supplement to the Study of the Elizabethan and Restoration Stage* (New York: Russell and Russell, 1935).

Havran, Martin J., *The Catholics in Caroline England* (Oxford: Oxford University Press, 1962).

Hayes, T. Wilson, 'Ben Jonson's Libertine Catholicism', in William P. Shaw (ed.), *Praise Disjoined: Changing Patterns of Salvation in Seventeenth-Century English Literature* (New York: Peter Lang, 1991).

Healy, Thomas, and Jonathan Sawday (eds), *Literature and the English Civil War* (Cambridge: Cambridge University Press, 1990).

Heinemann, Margot, *Puritanism and Theatre: Thomas Middleton and Opposition Drama Under the Early Stuarts* (Cambridge: Cambridge University Press, 1980).

Hibbard, Caroline, *Charles I and the Popish Plot* (Chapel Hill: University of North Carolina Press, 1983).

Hibbard, Caroline, 'Translating Royalty: Henrietta Maria and the Transition from Princess to Queen', *The Court Historian*, 5 (2000), 15–28.

Higham, Florence, *Catholic and Reformed. A Study of the Anglican Church, 1559–1662* (London: SPCK, 1962).

Hodson, Richard J., 'Caroline Town Comedy, 1628–1642' (PhD dissertation, University of York, 2000).

Holmes, Peter, *Resistance and Compromise: The Political Thought of the Elizabethan Catholics* (Cambridge: Cambridge University Press, 1982).

Hopkins, Lisa, *John Ford's Political Theatre* (Manchester: Manchester University Press, 1994).

Hopkins, Lisa, *The Female Hero in English Renaissance Tragedy* (Basingstoke: Palgrave, 2002).

Hopper, Andrew, ' "The Popish Army of the North": Anti-Catholicism and Parliamentarian Allegiance in Civil War Yorkshire, 1642–46', *RH*, 25 (2000), 12–28.

Huxley, Gervase, *Endymion Porter: Life of a Courtier 1587–1649* (London: Chatto and Windus, 1959).

Jameson, Fredric, 'Religion and Ideology: A Political Reading of *Paradise Lost*', in Francis Barker, Peter Hulme, Margaret Iverson and Diana Loxley (eds), *Literature, Politics and Theory* (London: New Accents, 1986), pp. 35–56.

Kirsch, Arthur C., 'A Caroline Commentary on the Drama', *MP*, 66 (1969), 256–61.

Lake, Peter, 'Constitutional Consensus and Puritan Opposition in the 1620s: Thomas Scott and the Spanish Match', *HJ*, 25 (1982), 805–25.

Lake, Peter, *Anglicans and Puritans? Presbyterianism and English Conformist Thought from Whitgift to Hooker* (London: Unwin Hyman, 1988).

Lake, Peter, 'Anti-Popery: The Structure of a Prejudice', in Richard Cust and Anne Hughes (eds), *Conflict in Early Stuart England: Studies in Religion and Politics 1603–1642* (Harlow: Longman Group, 1989), pp. 72–106.

Lake, Peter, and Michael Questier (eds), *Conformity and Orthodoxy in the English Church, c.1560–1660* (Woodbridge: Boydell Press, 2000).

Langbaine, Gerard, *An Account of the English Dramatic Poets, 1691* (Menston: Scolar Press, 1971).

Lawless, Donald, 'A Further Note on Shirley's Religion', *N&Q*, new series, 24 (1977), 543.

Leech, Clifford, *Shakespeare's Tragedies, and Other Studies in Seventeenth Century Drama* (London: Chatto and Windus, 1950).

Leith, William Forbes, *Memoirs of Scottish Catholics During the XVIIth and XVIIIth Centuries*, 2 vols (London: Longmans, Green and Co., 1909).

Lewis, Thomas Taylor, *The Letters of the Lady Brilliana Harvey, Wife of Sir Robert Harvey, of Brampton* (London: printed for the Camden Society, 1854).

Limon, Jerzy, *Dangerous Matter: English Drama and Politics in 1623–1624* (Cambridge: Cambridge University Press, 1986).

Lindley, David (ed.), *The Court Masque* (Manchester: Manchester University Press, 1984).

Lindley, Keith, 'The Lay Catholics of England in the Reign of Charles I', *JEH*, 27 (1971), 199–221.

Lockyer, Roger, *The Early Stuarts: A Political History of England, 1603–1642* (London: Longman, 1989).

Longueville, Thomas, *The Life of Sir Kenelm Digby* (London: 1896).

Lucow, Ben, *James Shirley* (Boston: Twayne Publishers, 1981).

McGrath, Juliet, 'James Shirley's Uses of Language', *SEL*, 2 (1966), 323–39.

Maclean, Ian, *Woman Triumphant: Feminism in French Literature, 1610–1652* (Oxford: Clarendon Press, 1977).

McManus, Clare, *Women on the Renaissance Stage: Anna of Denmark and Female Masquing in the Stuart Court 1590–1619* (Manchester: Manchester University Press, 2002).

Magee, Brian, *The English Recusants: A Study of the Post-Reformation Catholic Survival and the Operation of the Recusancy Laws* (London: Burns, Oates and Co., 1938).

Marchant, E., *Sir William Davenant* (Oxford: Davenant Society, 1936).

Margeson, John (ed.), *The Conspiracy and Tragedy of Charles Duke of Byron* (Manchester: Manchester University Press, 1988).

Marotti, Arthur (ed.), *Catholicism and Anti-Catholicism in Early Modern English Texts* (Basingstoke: Macmillan, 1999).

Marotti, Arthur and Cedric Brown (eds), *Texts and Cultural Change in Early Modern England* (Basingstoke: Macmillan, 1997).

Marsh, F. G. *The Godolphins* (New Milton: privately printed, 1930).

Milton, Anthony, *Catholic and Reformed: The Roman and Protestant Churches in English Protestant Thought, 1600–1640* (Cambridge: Cambridge University Press, 1995).

Morillo, Marvin, '"Frier Shirley": James Shirley and "Mercurius Britanicus"', *N&Q*, new series, 7 (1960), 338–9.

Morillo, Marvin, 'Shirley's "Preferment" and the Court of Charles I', *SEL*, 1 (1961), 101–17.

Mulryne, J. R., and M. Shewring (eds), *Theatre and Government Under the Early Stuarts* (Cambridge: Cambridge University Press, 1993).

Nason, Arthur H., *James Shirley Dramatist: A Biographical and Critical Study* (New York: Arthur H. Nason Publisher, 1915).

Nethercot, Arthur, *Sir William D'Avenant, Poet Laureate and Playwright-Manager* (Chicago: University of Chicago Press, 1938).

Orgel, Stephen, *The Jonsonian Masque* (Cambridge, Mass.: Harvard University Press, 1965).

Orgel, Stephen, *The Illusion of Power: Political Theatre in the English Renaissance* (Berkeley: University of California Press, 1975).

Orgel, Stephen, 'Plato, the Magi and Caroline Politics: A Reading of the *Temple of Love*', *Word and Image*, 4 (1998), 663–77.

Orrell, John, 'Amerigo Salvetti and the London Court Theatre, 1616–1640', *Theatre Survey*, 20 (1979), 1–26.

Parfitt, George (ed.), *Ben Jonson: The Complete Poems* (London: Penguin Books, 1996).

Parker, Rozika, *The Subversive Stitch: Embroidery and the Making of the Feminine* (London: Women's Press Ltd, 1984).

Parry, Graham, *The Golden Age Restor'd: The Culture of the Stuart Court, 1603–1642* (Manchester: Manchester University Press, 1981).

Peacock, John, 'The French Element in Inigo Jones's Masque Designs', in David Lindley (ed.), *The Court Masque* (Manchester: Manchester University Press, 1984), pp. 149–68.

Peacock, John, *The Stage Designs of Inigo Jones: The European Context* (Cambridge: Cambridge University Press, 1995).

Phelps, Wayne, H., 'The Second Night of Davenant's *Salmacida Spolia*', *N&Q*, 26 (1979), 512–13.

Poynting, Sarah, '"In the Name of All the Sisters": Henrietta Maria's Notorious Whores', in Clare McManus (ed.), *Women and Culture at the Courts of the Stuart Queens, 1603–42* (Basingstoke: Palgrave Macmillan, 2003), pp. 163–85.

Purkiss, Diane, *The English Civil War: Papists, Gentlewomen, Soldiers, and Witchfinders in the Birth of Modern Britain* (Boulder, Colo.: Basic Books, 2006).

Questier, Michael, *Conversion, Politics and Religion in England, 1580–1625* (Cambridge: Cambridge University Press, 1996).

Questier, Michael, 'Loyalty, Religion and State Power in Early Modern England: English Romanism and the Jacobean Oath of Allegiance', *HJ*, 40 (1997), 311–29.

Questier, Michael, *Catholicism, and Community in Early Modern England: Politics, Aristocratic Patronage and Religion, c.1550–1640* (Cambridge: Cambridge University Press, 2006).

Radtke, Stephen, *James Shirley: His Catholic Philosophy of Life* (Washington: Catholic University of America, 1929).

Ravelhoefer, Barbara, 'Bureaucrats and Courtly Cross-dressers in the *Shrovetide Masque* and *The Shepherds' Paradise*', *ELR*, 29 (1999), 75–96.

Ravelhofer, Barbara, *The Early Stuart Masque: Dance, Costume, and Music* (Oxford: Oxford University Press, 2006).

Richmond, Velma, *Shakespeare, Catholicism and Romance* (New York: Continuum, 2000).

Rowse, A. L., *The England of Elizabeth* (London: Macmillan, 1951).

Russell, Conrad, *The Causes of the English Civil War* (Oxford: Clarendon Press, 1990).

Samson, Alexander (ed.), *The Spanish Match: Prince Charles's Journey to Madrid, 1623* (Aldershot: Ashgate, 2006).

Sanders, Julie, *Caroline Drama: The Plays of Massinger, Ford, Shirley and Brome* (Plymouth: Northcote House Publishers, 1999).

Sanders, Julie, 'Caroline Salon Culture and Female Agency: The Countess of Carlisle, Henrietta Maria, and Public Theatre', *Theatre Journal*, 52 (2000), 449–64.

Sanders, Julie, '"Powdered with Golden Rain": The Myth of Danae in Early Modern Drama', *Early Modern Literary Studies*, 8 (2002), 1.1–23.

Sanders, Julie, 'Jonson's Caroline Coteries', in Takashi Kozuka and J. R. Mulryne (eds), *Shakespeare, Marlowe, Jonson: New Directions in Biography* (Aldershot: Ashgate, 2006), pp. 279–94.

Sargent, R., 'Theme and Structure in Middleton's *A Game at Chesse*', *MLR*, 66 (1971), 721–30.

Schwarz, Kathryn, 'Amazon Reflections in the Jacobean Queen's Masque', *SEL*, 35 (1995), 293–319.
Scott, David, *Politics and War in the Three Stuart Kingdoms, 1637–49* (Basingstoke: Palgrave Macmillan, 2004).
Sharpe, Kevin, *Remapping Early Modern England: The Culture of Seventeenth-Century England* (Cambridge: Cambridge University Press, 2000).
Shaw, William P., *Praise Disjoined: Changing Patterns of Salvation in Seventeenth-Century English Literature* (New York: Peter Lang, 1991).
Shell, Alison, *Catholicism, Controversy and the English Literary Imagination, 1588–1660* (Cambridge: Cambridge University Press, 1999).
Shell, Alison, 'Why Didn't Shakespeare Write Religious Verse?', in Takashi Kozuka and J. R. Mulryne (eds), *Shakespeare, Marlowe, Jonson: New Directions in Biography* (Aldershot: Ashgate, 2006), pp. 85–112.
Shore, Robert, '"Lawrels for the Conquered": The Dilemmas of William Davenant and Abraham Cowley in the Revolutionary Decades of the Seventeenth Century' (PhD Dissertation, University of Cambridge, 1994).
Shuger, Debora K., *Habits of Thought in the English Renaissance: Religion, Politics, and the Dominant Culture* (Toronto: University of Toronto Press, 1997).
Sitwell, Gerard, 'Leander Jones' Mission to England 1634–5', *RH*, 5 (1959), 132–82.
Smith, Charles E., *Religion Under the Barons of Baltimore* (Baltimore: E. Allen Lycett, 1899).
Smith, David L., 'Catholic, Anglican or Puritan? Edward Sackville, Fourth Earl of Dorset and the Ambiguities of Religion in Early Stuart England', *Transactions of the Royal Historical Society*, sixth series, 2 (1992), 105–24.
Smuts, R. Malcolm, 'The Puritan Followers of Henrietta Maria in the 1630s', *EHR*, 93 (1978), 26–45.
Smuts, R. Malcolm, *Court Culture and the Origins of a Royalist Tradition in Early Stuart England* (Philadelphia: University of Pennsylvania Press, 1987).
Squier, Charles, *Sir John Suckling* (Boston: Twayne Publishers, 1978).
Stafford, Helen, *James VI of England* (New York: American Historical Association, 1940).
Steggle, Matthew, *Richard Brome: Place and Politics on the Caroline Stage* (Manchester: Manchester University Press, 2004).
Stevenson, Allen, 'Shirley's Years in Ireland', *RES*, 20 (1944), 20–2.
Sturgess, Keith, *Jacobean Private Theatre* (London: Routledge and Kegan Paul, 1987).
Summerson, John, *Inigo Jones* (Harmondsworth: Penguin, 1966).

Swain, Margaret, *Figures on Fabric: Embroidery Design Sources and Their Application* (London: A. and C. Black, 1980).

Swinburne, Algernon, 'James Shirley', *The Fortnightly Review*, new series, 1 April (1890), 461–8.

Taylor, Aline M., 'James Shirley and "Mr Vincent Cane" the Franciscan', *N&Q*, new series, 7 (1960), 31–3.

Tomlinson, Sophie, '"She that Plays the King": Henrietta Maria and the Threat of the Actress', in Gordon McMullan and Jonathan Hope (eds), *The Politics of Tragicomedy: Shakespeare and After* (London: Routledge, 1992), pp. 189–207.

Tomlinson, Sophie, 'Theatrical Vibrancy on the Caroline Stage: *Tempe Restored* and *The Shepherds' Paradise*', in Clare McManus (ed.), *Women and Culture at the Courts of the Stuart Queens, 1603–42* (Basingstoke: Palgrave Macmillan, 2003), pp. 186–203.

Tomlinson, Sophie, *Women on Stage in Stuart Drama* (Cambridge: Cambridge University Press, 2005).

Traub, Valerie, 'The (In)significance of Lesbian Desire in Early Moden England', in Susan Zimmerman (ed.), *Erotic Politics: Desire on the Renaissance Stage* (New York: Routledge, 1992).

Travitsky, Betty S., '"A Pittilesse Mother"? Reports of a Seventeenth-Century English Filicide', *Mosaic: A Journal for the Interdisciplinary Study of Literature*, 27 (1994), 55–76.

Tregellas, W. H., *Cornish Worthies: Sketches of Some Eminent Cornish Men and Families*, 2 vols (London: 1884).

Tyacke, Nicholas, *Anti-Calvinists. The Rise of English Arminianism c.1590–1640* (Oxford: Clarendon Press, 1987).

Veevers, Erica, 'The Authorship of *Maria Triumphans*', *N&Q*, 34 (1987), 313–14.

Veevers, Erica, *Images of Love and Religion: Queen Henrietta Maria and Court Entertainments* (Cambridge: Cambridge University Press, 1989).

Venuti, Lawrence, *Our Halcyon Days: English Prerevolutionary Texts and Post Modern Culture* (Wisconsin: University of Wisconsin Press, 1972).

Walker, Kim, '"New Prison": Representing the Female Actor in Shirley's *The Bird in a Cage*', *ELR*, 21 (1991), 383–400.

Walsham, Alexandra, *Church Papists: Catholicism, Conformity and Confessional Polemic in Early Modern England* (Woodbridge: The Royal Historical Society, The Boydell Press, 1993).

Walsham, Alexandra, 'The Fatall Vesper: Providentialism and Anti-Popery in Late Jacobean London', *P&P*, 144 (1994), 36–87.

Walsham, Alexandra, *Providence in Early Modern England* (Oxford: Oxford University Press, 1999).

Ward, Adolphus, *A History of English Dramatic Literature to the Death of Queen Anne*, 3 vols (New York: Macmillan, 1899).
Webb, W. K. L. (SJ), 'Thomas Preston O.S.B; alias Roger Widdrigton, 1567–1640', *Biographical Studies*, 2 (1953), 216–60.
Wedgwood, C. V., *Truth and Opinion, Historical Essays* (London: Collins, 1960).
Welsford, Enid, *The Court Masque: A Study in the Relationship Between Poetry and the Revels* (Cambridge: Cambridge University Press, 1927).
Williams, Ethel, *Anne of Denmark: Wife of James VI of Scotland, James I of England* (Harlow: Longmans, 1970).
Wilson, Richard, *Secret Shakespeare: Studies in Theatre, Religion and Resistance* (Manchester: Manchester University Press, 2004).
Wiseman, Susan, *Drama and Politics in the English Civil War* (Cambridge: Cambridge University Press, 1998).
Wiseman, Susan, *Conspiracy and Virtue: Women, Writing, and Politics in Seventeenth-Century England* (Oxford: Oxford University Press, 2006).
Wolfe, Heather (ed.), *Life and Letters, Elizabeth Cary, Lady Falkland* (Cambridge: RTM, 2001).
Zimmer, Ruth, *James Shirley: A Reference Guide* (Boston, Mass.: G. K. Hall, 1980).
Zimmerman, Benedictus-Maria, *Carmel in England: A History of the English Mission of the Discalced Carmelites, 1615 to 1849* (London: Burns and Oates, 1899).
Zimmerman, Susan (ed.), *Erotic Politics: Desire on the Renaissance Stage* (New York: Routledge, 1992).

Index

Note: Literary works are listed under their author's name.

Abbot, George, Archbishop of Canterbury, 97
Abergavenny, Lord Henry, 112
Abernethie, Thomas, 184
actress, 34, 59, 65, 108, 112, 119, 123–4, 217
Adams, Thomas, 95
Ahasuerus, 2, 38–40, 115
Albion, Gordon, 142
Amazon, 10, 177, 195, 197, 202–10, 222
Anderton, Lawrence, 222
  see also Brereley, John
Andrewes, Lancelot, 53
Anna of Denmark, Queen of England,
  apostasy rumours, 19, 29
  elite performance, 34–5, 202, 217
  relations with Rome, 29
apathy, 31, 116, 163
apostasy, 3, 8–9, 19, 29, 51–3, 57–8, 92, 136–7, 140–1, 143, 154, 165
Arminian, 61, 66, 92
Armstrong, Ray, 53
Arrowsmith, Edmund, 61
Arundel, Aletheia Talbot, Countess of, 178
Arundel, Thomas Howard, Earl of, 196

Aubrey, John, 135
audience, 7, 23–4, 35–7, 50, 59, 64–5, 80–1, 105, 110, 114, 134–6, 139, 145, 147–8, 158, 175, 199–200, 217, 219

Bacon, Lady Jane, 77
del Bagno, Gianfrancesco, Cardinal, 149
Baillie, Robert, 196
Ballard, George, 186, 189
Baltimore, Sir George Calvert, Lord, 53–4
Barberini, Francesco, Cardinal, 149, 196, 207
Barnett-Smith, G., 51–2
baroque Catholicism, 110, 139, 147, 165, 181
Basil, St, 106
Bassompierre, François, Maréchal de, 61
Bath, John Granville, Earl of, 178
Batt, Anthonie, 115
Beaumont, Francis,
  Cupid's Revenge, 27–8
  see also Fletcher, John
beauty, 40, 81, 104, 108, 110–12, 117–18, 123–4, 144, 159, 161–2, 181, 192, 200
Becon, Thomas, 152

Bedell, William, 26, 73
Bedford, Thomas, 155–7
  A True and Certaine Relation to a Strange-Birth, 156
Beeston, William, 176
Belloc, Hillaire, 3
Benedictine order, 154
Berkeley, George, Lord, 103–4
Berkeley, Henry, 104
Bérulle, Pierre de, 34, 36, 59–61
  Élévation sur Sainte Madeleine, 2, 77, 81, 105–6
Bishop, William, 29
Bishops' Wars (1639–1640), 176, 194–5
Blackfriars Room incident (1623), 6, 18, 21–3
Blackfriars theatre, 134–7, 158
Blackwell, George, Archpriest, 97
Blaydes, Sophia, 189, 194
Bordinat, Philip, 189, 194
du Bosc, Jacques
  L'Honneste Femme, 159–60
Bossy, John, 5, 20, 65
Brereley, John, 105–6, 123
  see also Anderton, Lawrence
Brewer, Thomas, 19, 28, 78
Britland, Karen, 4, 33, 36, 109–10, 113, 197
Brome, Richard, 57–8, 175
Brooke, Sir Basil, 112
Brooke, Thomas, 112
Brooke, Xanthe, 39
Broughton, Richard, 124
Browne, Francis, Viscount Montagu, 178
Browning, Barbara, 33
Buckingham, George Villiers, Duke of, 1, 8, 77
Burner, Sandra, 53, 56–9
Burton, Henry, 66, 70, 78–9, 99
Burton, Robert, 103
Bushell, Edward, 56

Butler, Martin, 4, 10, 50, 135, 197, 204–9
Butterfield, Robert, 70

C., B., 91–2, 153
C., I., 73–5
C., I. B., 29
Cade, Anthony, 97
Cademon, Sir Thomas, 136
Calvert, Lady Anne, 53, 65
Calvinism, 9, 195–6
Cameron, John, 72
Camus, Jean Pierre,
  Admirable Events, 202–4, 208
Candlemas day, 59, 77
Canes, Vincent, 58
Canne, John, 186
Cano, David Sánchez, 32
Capuchin order, 2, 9, 80, 90, 92, 94, 110, 112, 115, 137–9, 141, 143, 147, 165
  see also Queen's Chapel
Car, Miles, 117
cardinal virtues, 113
Carew, Sophia, 112
  see also Neville, Sophia
Carlell, Lodowick, 135
  Arviragus, 135
  The Deserving Favourite, 62
Carleton, Sir Dudley, 106
Carmelite order, 37, 118, 221
Cartwright, William,
  The Siege, 135
Cary, Lucius, Viscount Falkland, 109
Catholic clergy, disputes between, 163
Caussin, Nicolas, 189–90
  The Holy Court, 116–17
  The Holy Court, Fourth Tome, 192–4, 209–10
Cecily, St, 149

Index

Chalcedon, Bishop of, 98, 140
Chamberlain, John, 24
Champney, Anthony, 195
Chapman, George,
  The Conspiracie and Tragedy of Charles, Duke of Byron, Marshall of France, 26
Charles I, 54, 120–1,
  Catholic hopes for conversion of, 1–2, 21, 29, 38, 139–40, 149, 157, 177
  elite performance, 35–8, 145–9, 197–210
  influence of Henrietta Maria upon, 77–9, 82, 116, 139–40, 142, 149, 161, 165, 176, 178, 186–9, 194, 210, 218
  Laudianism, 91–2, 150, 183
  marriage negotiations, 1–2, 19, 28, 161
  militant Protestants, 18–19, 26–8, 31, 41, 91
  Oath of Allegiance, 101–2, 154–5, 157, 177–8
  recusant community, 21, 29–32, 93–4, 163–4, 177–80, 195–6, 206, 222
  religious accommodation, 92, 157, 162
  Scotland, 10, 185, 194–5, 197
  Spanish Infanta, 19, 26, 161
  Vatican, 140–1, 157, 177–8
Châteauneuf, Charles, Baron de, 116
Chevalier, Jean, 137
Chevreuse, Claude de Lorraine, Duc de, 32
Chevreuse, Marie, Duchesse de, 179
choreography, 89, 147, 181
church-papist, 3, 8, 20, 24, 29, 31, 56, 70, 74–5, 92, 95, 103–4, 142, 153, 222

Civil War, 2, 5–6, 177, 196, 208, 222
Clarke, Danielle, 161
Clarke, Samuel,
  Englands Remembrancer, 22
Clotilda, Queen of France, 116–17, 223
coat of arms, 54, 56, 59
  see also escutcheon
Cohen, Sarah, 147
Colman, Walter, 58
Coloma, Carlos, 24
commercial theatre, 3–4, 10, 41, 49–50, 99, 110, 134–7, 158, 165–6, 175–7, 217, 223
Common Prayer Book, 153
Con, George, 10, 140, 142, 157, 164, 176–9, 185, 196, 207
conjoined twins, 155–7, 163
Contarini, Alvise, 77
continental theatre, 35
convents, 37, 110, 112, 191, 222
Copinger, John, 29
Correr, Angelo, 143
Cosin, John, 155
  A Collection of Private Devotions, 67–70, 150,
costume, 10, 34, 106, 135, 145, 175, 181, 197, 202
Cottingham, Francis, 92
court Catholicism, 3, 9–10, 57, 91, 106, 115, 136–7, 140–1, 145, 150, 176, 178–80, 183, 219
Courtenay, William, 155, 166
Crashaw, William, 78
Cresley, Sir George, 119
cross-dressing, 35
Curia, 140, 178, 207
  see also Vatican
Curll, Walter, 20

Cust, Richard, 56, 122
Cyprien of Gamache, 89, 106, 113, 138–41, 144, 220

Dalby, Gerald, 57
Danae, myth of, 121, 123
Daniel, Samuel,
  Vision of the Twelve Godesses, 202
Dauncey, John, 195–6, 221–2
Davenant, Sir William,
  conversion to Catholicism, 3–4, 9, 136–7
  The Fair Favourite, 10, 166, 176–7, 189–96, 208–10
  The Just Italian, 132, 134
  Love and Honour, 134, 136, 158–65, 176, 183, 189–92
  Luminalia, 176, 180–3, 219
  Madagascar, 175
  patronage of Henrietta Maria, 3–4, 6, 9–11, 124, 132–6, 158, 175–7
  The Platonic Lovers, 132
  portrait of, 133
  religious accommodation, 10, 163–6, 183, 210, 217–18
  rivalry with James Shirley, 3, 132–4
  Salmacida Spolia, 3–4, 10, 177, 195–210, 222
  The Temple of Love, 10, 134, 142–9, 159, 162, 165, 181, 197
  The Unfortunate Lovers, 135
Davenport, Christopher, 155, 164
devôt, 10, 176
D'Ewes, Sir Simonds, 17, 25
Dieussart, François, 138
Digby, Sir Kenelm, 140–1, 195
Dolan, Frances, 149
Dominican order, 102, 115
Donne, John, 28, 81

Dormer, Elizabeth, 117
Dorset, Edward, Earl of, 132
Doughty, Thomas, 154, 185
Douglas, Sir Robert, 140
Downame, George, 184
Dryden, John, 7
Dyce, Anthony, 62

Edmondes, Sir Thomas, 97
Edwards, T. B., 197
Eglesfield, Francis, 50
elite theatre, 2–3, 4, 7, 10–11, 33–7, 50, 59, 77, 108–14, 123–4, 136, 143–9, 158, 162, 175–6, 180–2, 195–210, 217–18, 222
Elizabeth I, Queen of England, 26, 106–7
Elizabeth of Bohemia, 19, 26–7, 109, 153, 199
embroidery, 7, 38–41
  see also stump-work
escutcheon, 54, 56, 59
  see also coat of arms
Esther topos, 2, 7, 10, 38–41, 79, 90, 115–16, 153, 197, 209, 217, 223

Fage, Mary, 103
Falconer, John, 118
feast days, 100
Featley, Daniel, 183
female agency, 3, 8, 63–6, 100, 104–5, 117–19, 123–4, 143–4, 158–65, 199
femininity, conceptions of, 116–18
feminocentric, 4, 51, 65, 118, 124, 217
femme forte, 159–64
Fenton House, 38, 217
Finet, Sir John, 134
First Bishops' War, 194
Fitton, Peter, 139–40, 148

Index

Fletcher, Alan, 134
Fletcher, J. B., 143
Fletcher, John,
   Cupid's Revenge (with Francis Beaumont), 27–8,
   The Faithful Shepherdess, 134
Floyd, John, 21, 41, 181, 185
Ford, John, 6
Fortune theatre, 218
Franciscan order, 9, 20, 58
Franko, Mark, 37, 199
French Catholicism, 7, 59, 65–6, 116–17, 139, 144–5, 165, 179–81, 189, 192–3
French court, 35, 63, 143, 161, 179
Fuller, Thomas, 184

Gardiner, Richard, 184
garlic, 63
Gee, John, 21, 23, 41, 64
Geoghegan, Arthur, 102, 115
Gerrard, George, 138
Gifford, William, 62
Gillow, Joseph, 51
Goad, Thomas, 22
golden rose, 105
Golding, Sir Edward, 56–7, 94
Gondi, Giovanni Battista, 35
Gorges, Sir Ferdinando, 20
Goring, George, 25
Gough, Melinda, 35
Grey, Lady Jane, 152
Griegny, Duc de, 139
Gunpowder Plot, 56, 79
Gurr, Andrew, 65

Habington, William, 57, 135
Haigh, Christopher, 5
Hall, Joseph, 70, 134
Harbage, Alfred, 95, 135
Harley, Lady Brilliana, 179, 192–3, 197

Hausted, Peter, 151
Hawkins, Henry, 72, 144
Helena, St, 29
Henri IV, King of France, 25–6, 143, 200
Henrietta Maria, Queen of England,
   Civil War, 10, 196, 221–2
   coronation, 60, 90, 113
   court of, 50, 114–15, 135–7, 150, 176, 190, 195, 206
   Esther topos, 2, 7, 79, 90, 115–16, 148, 197, 209, 217, 222–3
   fashion, 50, 62–3
   female agency, 8–9, 41, 50, 113, 123–4, 143–9, 177–8, 195–6
   influence on, and relationship with, Charles I, 77, 154, 165, 186, 200, 209–10, 218
   marriage negotiations and treaty, 1, 18, 21, 24, 30, 32, 80, 161
   motherhood, 77, 105, 149, 186, 200
   performances given by, 2, 7, 9, 18, 34–7, 41, 50–1, 59, 77, 91, 108–9, 112, 114, 142–9, 177, 180–3, 191, 197–210, 217
   portraits and likenesses of, 38, 105–7, 114, 188
   religious belief, observance and papal mission of, 1, 4, 10, 17–21, 24–5, 30–4, 41, 59–61, 66, 89–91, 105–8, 113–17, 124, 139–42, 195, 200, 206–7, 217, 221–3
   Scottish campaign, 195–7, 208–10
Henry Stuart, Prince of Wales, 25
Henry V, King of England, 25
Herbert, Sir Henry, 71

Heywood, Thomas,
  Exemplary Lives, 39–40,
  Porta Pietatis, 180
Hibbard, Caroline, 30, 36–7, 178, 196
Hilliard, Nicholas,
  Queen Elizabeth I, 106–7
Hirst, Richard, 61
Holbein, Hans the Younger,
  Noli Me Tangere, 76
Holywell, 64
honnête femme, 145, 159–64
Hopkins, Lisa, 6
Hopper, Andrew, 220
Howard, William, 98
Howell, James, 80, 132, 197
Hudson, Jeffrey, 134
Huguenot, 25, 29–30

international Catholicism, 2–5, 9–10, 66, 105, 140, 176–80, 183–4, 196, 200–2, 207, 222
Irish Catholics, 220
Ironside, Gilbert, 155
Isabella, Infanta of Spain, 19, 161

James I, King of England,
  death of, 19, 27
  dynastic ambitions of, 19–20, 23–4
  Mary Stuart, Queen of Scots, 29
  policy of pacification, 19, 202
  recusant community, 1, 20
Jameson, Fredric, 6
Jermyn, Henry, 132, 175
Jesuit order, 18, 20–2, 30, 61, 64, 67, 78, 97, 99, 101, 116, 122–3, 163, 165, 178–9, 185, 195
Jones, Inigo, 4, 10, 110–11, 142, 145–6, 177, 180–2, 197–209
Jones, Leander, 9–10, 154–5, 164

Jonson, Ben, 6, 91, 175
  Chloridia, 208
  The Fortunate Isles and Their Union, 25
  Love's Triumph, 208
  Masque of Queenes, 202

Kellison, Matthew, 82
Killigrew, Thomas, 175
Knott, Edward, 93–4

Lake, Peter, 21
Langbaine, Gerard, 7
Lashford, Sir Richard, 155
Laud, William, 20, 92, 140, 148, 150–1, 154–5, 163–5, 183
Laudianism, 5, 9–10, 20, 66, 70, 73, 91–3, 108, 118–20, 124, 137, 148–55, 176, 184–6
Lechmere, Edward, 153
Leech, Clifford, 95
Lenton, Francis, 175
Leslie, Andrew, 185
Lewis, St, 209–10
Leyburn, George, 4–5, 142, 163, 165, 223
Lilburne, John, 184
Lindley, Keith, 208
Lister, Joseph, 220
Litany of Loreto, 106, 123
Loate, Thomas, 63
Lockyer, Roger, 5
Louis XIII, King of France, 1, 30, 37
love-lock, 121
Lovell, Robert, 63
Lucow, Ben, 7, 52

Mab, Ralphe,
  The Character of a Christian, 67–70
Macbreck, James, 185, 195
Macclesfield, William, 122–3

McGrath, Juliet, 61–2
Maclean, Ian, 159
Maffei, Giovanni, 94
  Fuga Saeculi, 94
McManus, Clare, 34
map of Christianity, 152
Marchant, E. C., 143–4
Markham, Gilbert, 57
Mary I, Queen of England, 103–4
Mary, the Blessed Virgin, 36, 66, 72, 75, 105–6, 114, 123, 144, 159, 161, 177, 180–1
Mary Magdalene, St, 8, 66, 73–7, 114
Mary Stuart, Queen of Scots, 29, 36, 112
masque, 3, 9–10, 94, 119, 132, 134, 138, 143–9, 176–82, 197–210, 217, 219
Massinger, Philip, 103
  Cleander, 134
Matthew, Tobie, 112
May, Thomas, 158
Mead, Joseph, 60, 134
Meautys, Thomas, 77
Meddus, Dr, 17, 19–20, 25
Médicis, Marie de, 2, 10, 21, 37, 60, 107–8, 176, 179, 197–200, 206, 208
Middleton, Thomas,
  A Game at Chesse, 6, 18, 23–4, 27–8, 91
Mildmay, Sir Humphrey, 158
militant Catholicism, 3, 10, 26, 56, 66, 114, 122–3, 153–4, 164, 196, 200–2, 217
militant Protestants, 19, 26–7, 91, 106, 137, 149, 196
Milton, Anthony, 30–1
Milton, John,
  Paradise Lost, 36
Montagu, Walter, 140, 159
  The Shepherds' Paradise, 9, 91, 108–14, 217

Montague, Magdalen, Viscountess, 117
Montague, Richard, 20, 155
Mordechai, 40, 116, 118, 124
More, Thomas, St, 94, 100
Morillo, Marvin, 49
Muscott, G. M., 1, 3, 30, 32
Mytens, Daniel, 186
  Charles I and Henrietta Maria, 188

Nason, Arthur H., 49
neo-platonism, 132, 143–4, 158–64, 190, 194, 209
Nethercot, Arthur, 158, 189
Neville, Sir Charles, 112
  see also Earl of Westmorland
Neville, Richard, 112
Neville, Sophia, 112, 114
Newcastle, William Cavendish, Duke of, 222
Nonconformist, 11, 70, 151, 185
Northumberland, Earl of, 197

Oath of Allegiance, 97, 101–2, 154–7, 164, 177–8, 222
Odell, William, 153
Oratorians, 30, 60
Orgel, Stephen, 143
Overbury, Sir Thomas, 25–6
Ovid, 41
Owen, Jane, 121–2, 153

Page, William, 92–3
Paget, Justinian, 119
Pagitt, Ephraim,
  Christianographie, 152
Panzani, Gregorio, Cardinal, 140–2, 148, 154, 163
papal chapel, London, 178
  'Altar of Repose in George Con's Chapel, *1637*', 179
Parker, Rozika, 39

Parry, Graham, 143
pastoral, 34–5, 59, 109–10, 113–14, 134, 217–18
Peacock, John, 110, 181, 204
Pembroke, Philip Herbert, Earl of, 106
Pennant, Ed, 64
performance theory, 33, 37, 147, 199
Perron, Cardinal, 29
Persons, Robert, 181
Philip IV, King of Spain, 32
Phillip of Sanquhar, 140, 221, 223
Phillips, Edward, 49
Phoenix theatre, 99
Pocklington, John, 150
'Popish Army', 222
Porter, Endymion, 57, 136–7, 175
Porter, Olivia, 136, 141
Pory, John, 60, 90–1, 112
Poynting, Sarah, 109, 112–13
Preston, John,
  The Golden Scepter, 186–7
Preston, Thomas, 97, 102
Prideaux, John, 150
Prynne, William, 63, 67, 153
  Histriomastix, 119–21
Purbeck, Lady, 141
purgatory, 62, 64–5, 121–2, 153,
puritanism, 4, 20, 50, 70, 72, 78, 115, 120, 147–53, 164–5, 176, 184–6, 220–1
Puttenham, George, 114
Pym, John, 220–1

Quarles, Francis,
  Divine Poems, 75,
  Hadassa: Or the History of Queene Ester, 1, 116
Queen's Chapel, Somerset House, 2, 9, 89–96, 106–12, 115, 117, 137–43, 147, 180, 219–22

Quelch, William, 151
Questier, Michael, 92, 97, 102, 208

Racan, Honorat de Bueil,
  L'Artenice, 2, 7, 18, 33–8, 41, 50–1, 59, 65, 77, 108, 119, 191, 197, 217–19, 222
Ravelhoeffer, Barbara, 181
Rawlins, Thomas, 218
realpolitik, 24, 164–5
Rebecca, 39
recusancy laws, 31, 34, 61, 91, 93–4, 96–8, 101–2, 115, 121–2, 178, 180
recusant community, 1, 3, 7–8, 11, 18, 20, 24, 29, 34, 40–1, 50–1, 56, 58, 61–2, 73–5, 81–2, 93–4, 96–8, 100, 109, 113–18, 121–2, 142, 147, 165, 185, 195, 206, 208, 219, 222–3
recusant, demonised image of, 11, 21, 91, 96–105, 220–1
recusant language, 8, 50, 61–5, 81–2, 105, 122
recusant women, 40–1, 51, 53–4, 56, 65, 96, 103–4, 112, 117–18, 123–4, 180, 196
regicide, 99–100, 202
religious accommodation, between the established and Catholic Churches, 3, 9, 90, 96, 124, 136–7, 154–8, 163–5, 189, 218
Rhodes, John, 152
Richards, Nathanael,
  Messallina, 11, 218–19
Richelieu, Cardinal, 31–2, 106, 108, 116, 139, 165
romance, 109, 123, 161, 202, 218
rose imagery, 25, 105–7, 114, 183
Rosendale, Agnes, 118

Index

Rous, Francis, 70, 186, 189, 194, 221
Rudyerd, Benjamin, 34

S., T., 164
Sales, Francis de, St, 116–17, 144–5
Salvetti, Amerigo, 33, 35, 54, 61, 108
Sander, Nicholas, 31
Sanders, Julie, 4, 121, 136
Sanderson, William, 119, 149, 183
Savage, Anne, 103
scenery, 143, 145, 175, 181, 200, 204
Schreiner, Olive, 40
Schwarz, Kathryn, 202
Scottish Calvinists, 176, 195
Scottish Kirk, 10, 184
Scottish prayer book crisis, 185, 195
Scottish recusants, 185, 195
Second Bishops' War, 176
Seghers, Gerard, 75
Selby, Dame Dorothy, 40
Shakespeare, William, 6, 74
  Hamlet, 50
  Henry IV Part I, 27–8
  Much Ado About Nothing, 71–2
  Titus Andronicus, 41
Sharpe, Kevin, 6
Shelford, Robert, 20, 155
Shell, Alison, 6, 33, 74
Shirley, Anthony, 54
Shirley, Lady Dorothy, 57, 96, 104, 109, 113
Shirley, Elizabeth, 56
Shirley, Evelyn, 54
Shirley, Lady Frances, 65, 104
Shirley, Sir George, 56
Shirley, Sir Henry, 56

Shirley, James, 41, 148, 222
  allegiance, spiritual and temporal, 94–6, 98–105
  The Bird in a Cage, 9, 49–50, 91, 118–24
  The Cardinal, 148
  A Contention for Honour and Riches, 94
  conversion to Catholicism, 3, 8, 51–9
  Esther topos, 9, 76–7, 79–81, 118
  The Grateful Servant, 8, 51, 65, 79–81, 134
  Honoria and Mammon, 55
  Love in a Maze, 8, 91, 94–6, 120
  patronage of Henrietta Maria, 8, 66, 79, 104–5, 118, 123–4, 218
  portrait of, 55
  recusant language, 8, 61–6
  recusant patrons, 53–8, 94, 96, 103
  Roman Catholic community, 8–9, 50–9, 121–3, 217
  The School of Compliment, 61
  The Traitor, 8–9, 91, 96–107, 120
  The Triumph of Peace, 132
  The Wedding, 8, 51, 65–77, 81–2
  The Witty Fair One, 8, 50, 59–66, 81
  The Young Admiral, 9, 91, 98, 101–5, 118, 120
Shirley, Thomas, 56, 122–3, 196
Shorelyker, Richard, 39
shrine at Loreto, 36
Sidney, Sir Philip,
  The Defence of Poesy, 82
Skinner, Robert, 150
Smith, Richard, 38

Smuts, Malcolm, 106
Somerset House, 20, 33–4, 36–7, 89, 96, 134, 221–2
  see also Queen's Chapel
Southcott, John, 116, 157
Southwell, Robert, 31, 73–4, 82, 202
Spanish Armada, 23, 40, 196
Spanish Catholicism, 23, 25–6, 28, 32, 165, 179–80
Stafford, Anthony, 104, 150
Stockdale, Thomas, 220
Strafford, Thomas, Earl of, 57, 221
  see also Wentworth, Sir Thomas
Strode, William,
  The Passions Calm'd, 4–5, 162
stump-work, 7, 38–41, 217
  see also embroidery
Sturgess, Keith, 135
Suckling, John, 175
  Aglaura, 135
Sweetman, John, 73–5
Swinburne, Algernon, 49, 81, 95
Sydenham, Henry, 66
Synge, George, 8, 97
synthesising English and French Catholicism, 116–19, 147, 165, 181

Taylor, Aline, 58
Taylor, John, 39, 41, 220
Taylor, Joseph, 108
Taylor, Thomas, 151
temporiser, 8–9, 91–101
Tixall family of Staffordshire, 109, 113–14
Tomlinson, Sophie, 4, 62, 65, 108, 111, 119, 218
Torsellino, Orazio, 96, 104
tragicomedy, 158, 218
Tresham, William, 56

Tulipomania craze, 39
Tyburn, 59, 102

University theatre, 4–5, 162
Urban VIII, Pope, 2, 21, 30, 34, 37–8, 59, 105, 140, 157, 177–8

Valaresso, Alvise, 23
Valentine, Henry, 67
Van Dyck, Sir Anthony, 105–7, 114, 186, 188
Vatican, 140, 152, 154–5, 164, 176–9, 207
  see also Curia
Veevers, Erica, 4, 117, 143–4, 147–8, 181, 200
du Verger, S., 202
Verney, Sir Edmund, 196
Visitandine nuns, 110, 222

Wadding, Lucas, 153
Waddsworth, James, 26
Walton, Izaac, 57
Wandesford, Christopher, 8
Ward, Adolphus, 51
Ward, Samuel, 40
Ward, William, 32–3
Webster, John, 103
Wedgwood, C. V., 204
Wentworth, Sir Thomas, 7, 92
  see also Strafford, Earl of
Werburgh Street Theatre, Dublin, 134
Westmorland, Charles Neville, Earl of, 112
White, Francis, Bishop of Ely, 151
Whitehall, 10–11, 17, 27, 30, 33, 59, 92, 134, 136–8, 140, 143, 158, 166, 178, 180–1, 189, 197, 202, 218
Widdrington tracts, 97
Williams, Thomas, 163, 165
Wilson, John, 222

Wilson, Matthew, 9, 154
Winnifride, St, 64
Winter, John, 178–9, 206
Wither, George, 63, 67, 70, 78, 96, 137, 157, 166

Wood, Anthony, 51–4
Woolley, John, 31
Wright, Abraham, 49–50

Zimmer, R. K., 52